Hardeep Matharu is a journalist and editor of *Byline Times* based in south London. With a decade's worth of experience working across local, national and independent media, Hardeep learned her craft at a local newspaper, the *Epsom Guardian*, where she was awarded for her 'forward-thinking attitude' and stories on issues that were a 'perfect example of why local papers matter' by the National Council for the Training of Journalists. The London-born daughter of immigrants from Kenya and India, Hardeep completed a Law degree at Cambridge University before entering journalism, and is passionate about bringing investigatory, thought-provoking and diverse reporting to the British media.

Wokelore

Boris Johnson's Culture War and Other Stories

Byline Times

Edited by Hardeep Matharu

unbound

First published in 2022

Unbound
Level 1, Devonshire House,
One Mayfair Place, London W1J 8AJ

www.unbound.com

Two articles were originally published by *openDemocracy* and are
reproduced with kind permission: 'Why would Russia Want to Interfere
in British Politics?' by Misha Glenny and 'From 9/11 to Insurrection:
How Trump Went to War with His Country and America United to
Fight Back' by Anthony Barnett

Text design by Ellipsis, Glasgow

A CIP record for this book is available from the British Library

ISBN 978-1-80018-125-0 (paperback)
ISBN 978-1-80018-126-7 (ebook)

Printed and bound in Great Britain by Clays Ltd, Elcograf S.p.A.

For the subscribers of *Byline Times*

Contents

6 JANUARY 2021

Foreword

Musa Okwonga

In Berlin, there is a type of dry, harrowing cold that I haven't found anywhere else. If I step outside in winter and forget to put my gloves on in time, this cold slices at my hands, as if trying to strip away skin and sinew. This cold is a scalpel, and it is with this same sharpness that I try to write.

With this type of writing, my aim is to convey what I call 'moral fury': an equal mix of almost overwhelming anger and absolute precision. While some people are afraid of rage when they write, I embrace it. Both of my essays within this collection are full of it. I find that rage gives me clarity. It burns away my doubt, it carves away my hesitation.

That is not to say that I write without fear: quite the opposite. Fear is my guide. If I am worried or concerned about a social or political issue, if I am informed about it yet am scared to express a view upon it, then that is precisely the subject that I must write about. I do that because our silence is how unchecked power perseveres.

My two essays in this book were written to address two fears. The first was how white supremacy and its enablers continue to evolve. The second was how the avoidance of hard conversations with our loved ones leads directly to the resurgence of old monsters. In both cases, I tried to give the readers memorable language for what they were seeing, so that they could easily say: 'look, that is racial gatekeeping' and 'look, there are once again Nazis by the lake'.

If we give people the diagnosis for their discontent, then we bring them so much closer to a cure.

That is why I am so proud to be part of this book. Everyone in here is working with the same urgency to bring their readers closer to that cure. We will all keep writing, and I hope that our words keep slicing as faithfully as the Berlin cold.

Introduction

Hardeep Matharu

It was late 2018 when Stephen Colegrave, Peter Jukes and I first let it be known that we would be launching a newspaper. The main response was: why? Why, at a time when sales of long-established mainstream editions were declining, did we think it was time to bring a new publication to market? Our answer was as clear then as it still is now: because there is a crisis in the political and social fabric of Britain and this is connected to a crisis in its journalism.

Over a number of years, fearless and independent investigative reporting in this country has all but disappeared – and with it, that spirit of a 'heroic' press holding power to account and acting as the fourth estate. If British democracy is to survive and flourish, we need citizens who are properly informed and encouraged to think critically and openly; who believe that journalism can speak to them and is relevant to their lives.

And so *Byline Times* was born: funded by our readers, covering 'what the papers don't say', not afraid to question power, providing a platform for under-reported and diverse issues and voices, and making people think more about where we find ourselves in Britain today and why.

At its core, I believe that the newspaper's lifeblood is that it sits outside of the system. We do not attend dinner parties with media figures or politicians, rely on Government sources for stories, or look round our shoulders as to whom we might upset or the repercussions of this. Instead, we aim to shine a light on the systemic problems facing Britain, without fear or favour, and create a vehicle for change for all those who believe in the importance of truth for a healthy society.

On a personal note, it has allowed me to put into action a philosophy passed down by Stephen and Peter: don't change yourself to fit the system, change the landscape. Build your own platform. Having entered journalism after completing a Law degree – driven by my passion for inquiry and justice – I worked in local and national news reporting and then as a freelance journalist. But where was my place? Where did I feel I could make a difference and find the freedom to explore in a wider sense? For all of us – writers and readers alike – who do not feel we 'fit' or are reluctant to be placed in any one box, we aim to create a new community in *Byline Times*.

The decline of Britain's public interest journalism has been happening in plain sight for many years.

The phone-hacking scandal in 2011 laid bare the deep-rooted corruption at the heart of newspapers owned by billionaire proprietors in advancing their private interests, their power over politicians, and the methods of criminality employed to further their aims. At the same time, the information age has exploded, with a 24/7 online news cycle in which publications are incentivised to produce stories for clicks – to bring in ad revenue rather than change people's lives. In this age of bombardment, all context has been lost, while radicalisation on social media platforms spreads with alarming ease. News organisations no longer join the dots, tackle structural causes, or interrogate the systems of power on which so much of Britain is based. Compounding all of this has been the decimation of local journalism. I was proud to learn my craft at a local paper, full of talented reporters hungry for genuine scoops important to people's lives. I saw the impact repeated cuts, imposed by corporations, had on the basic work of journalism. Now, reporters sit staring at screens rather than scribbling shorthand in planning meetings or attending preliminary hearings at the magistrates' court. So many of the structural problems which can be identified at a local level everywhere are going unreported.

All of these distortions have led to, and exacerbated, our current 'post-truth' world; an age in which the primacy of individual feelings rather than a shared reality has been fostered through populism, and a 'divide and rule' politics has been weaponised through identity and 'culture wars'. We have seen where this can ultimately lead, across the Atlantic but also in Modi's India and in pockets of Europe. The emergence of 'illiberal democracy' is a shocking state of affairs which I believe should alarm us all, particularly as collective crises such as the climate emergency and the Coronavirus pandemic cannot be demarcated according to borders and nation state propaganda.

Over the past two years, through its 2,500 articles by more than 400 authors, *Byline Times* has sought to be part of the solution in whichever way, at whichever level, it can. From exposing the scandal of Government procurement around Coronavirus contracts, investigating Russian interference, leading analysis on Empire and the culture wars, and tackling the nexus between a far-right resurgence, disinformation and the vulnerability of democracy, *Byline Times* has sought to give its readers the information to think with and offer much-needed perspective.

But the investigative mission which drives us is a wider one. Investigation is not only about looking outwards at the world with a sharpened focus, but turning that focus back towards ourselves; it involves questioning and challenging ourselves to investigate what is going on within and why.

This collection speaks to that broader spirit of investigation. Taken from *Byline Times'* first two years, each of the essays in this book aims to provide a window on the world and a mirror for the reader. They raise searching questions about society, but also searching questions for ourselves.

Introduction

In our too often atomised lives, in which everything seems to move so quickly and nuance and complexity is easily lost, I hope this book will act as a space for reflection and a call to action. If we are to start to tackle some of the biggest challenges facing us, we need to first understand how we got here. I hope each one of you holding this book in your hands finds that this collection helps you to begin to do just that.

15 March 2019

A terrorist attack on two mosques by a single gunman in Christchurch, New Zealand, leaves fifty-one people dead and forty injured.

The Multi-Million-Dollar Anti-Muslim Propaganda Industry

Caroline Orr

18 MARCH 2019

The 17,000-word manifesto posted online by the gunman of the terrorist attack targeting worshippers at two mosques in Christchurch, New Zealand, makes it clear that far-right internet culture and white-supremacist propaganda played an integral role in radicalising the twenty-eight-year-old murderer.

In it, he made frequent reference to the 'white genocide' conspiracy theory, which falsely claims that white people are being replaced by non-whites through changes in birth rates, mass immigration and 'forced assimilation'. According to the Anti-Defamation League, the belief system surrounding so-called white genocide represents 'one of the most deeply held white supremacist convictions'.

The manifesto is riddled with anti-immigrant and anti-Muslim rhetoric. Throughout, the terrorist repeatedly referred to Muslims as 'invaders' who are trying to take over 'the West' and lamented the 'high fertility' rates among Muslim populations. The gunman frequently returned to the conspiratorial idea that whites are facing an existential threat due to increasing numbers of Muslims and other immigrants coming to predominantly white countries and 'destroying' the culture. The word 'destroy' appears twenty-five times in the document, while references to 'birth rate' and 'fertility' appear forty-three times, alongside forty-seven references to Western or European 'culture'.

Such extremist views are common in the modern white-supremacist movement, with the terrorist's manifesto mirroring the rhetoric found on forums and message boards such as *4chan* and *Stormfront*, as well as websites such as the *Daily Stormer*, *VDARE* and *Vanguard News Network*.

But, the gunman's Islamophobic rhetoric isn't confined to the dark corners of the web. Inciting hatred towards Muslims is part of a multi-million-dollar propaganda business funded by some of the most prominent right-wing donors and organisations in the United States – including many that have direct ties to the Donald Trump administration.

According to a June 2016 report by the Council on American-Islamic Relations and the University of California Berkeley's Center for Race & Gender, more than $200 million was pumped into the anti-Muslim propaganda industry between 2008 and 2013. That money funded the activities of several dozen groups, with the primary purpose to 'promote prejudice against, or hatred of, Islam and Muslims' and to push their Islamophobic rhetoric from the fringes into the mainstream.

They achieve that goal, in part, by working hand-in-hand with media and tech companies to disseminate their propaganda via right-wing 'scholars', media personalities, grassroots organisations and other associated entities. 'This enables them to mutually reference each other's highly inaccurate or purposefully deceptive material as facts and then subsequently disseminate it to other grassroots groups and politicians through right-wing media outlets,' the Center for American Progress explained in a 2011 report.

Among the most prominent donors backing America's anti-Muslim propaganda industry is Robert Mercer, whom the *Washington Post* named as one of the 'top 10 most influential billionaires in politics'.

Mercer – the top contributor to Trump's presidential campaign – is affiliated with a slew of right-wing organisations, but he is perhaps most notorious for launching the now-defunct, scandal-plagued data analytics firm Cambridge Analytica and funding the far-right *Breitbart News* network run by the far-right ideologue Steve Bannon.

Mercer, his daughter Rebekah, and the vehicles they use to influence policy and society, are a case study in for-profit hate, showcasing the inner workings of an anti-Muslim propaganda industry, the tentacles of which stretch from the fringes of the internet to establishment think tanks – and all the way into the White House.

Between 2014 and 2016, the Mercer Family Foundation donated $250,000 to the New York-based Gatestone Institute, an anti-Muslim think tank that warns of a looming Muslim takeover of Europe leading to a 'Great White Death'. The organisation is also notable for its close ties to the Trump administration. Rebekah Mercer sits on its board of governors, former Trump campaign chairman Steve Bannon has been a speaker at Gatestone events, and Trump's national security advisor John Bolton became the group's chairman in 2013.

In 2016, the Gatestone Institute partnered with far-right Canadian website *Rebel Media* to produce a dozen 'cross-branded videos' warning about the supposed dangers of Islam and refugees from Muslim-majority countries. The clips were posted on the Gatestone Institute's YouTube page and cross-posted on *Rebel Media*'s website between May and October 2016.

Rebel Media has produced a number of prominent anti-Muslim and anti-immigration activists – including Lauren Southern, Laura Loomer, Faith Goldy, Gavin McInnes and Stephen Yaxley-Lennon (known as 'Tommy Robinson'). These activists, along with ideologically aligned figures such as Stefan Molyneux and Milo Yiannopoulos – whose activism on behalf of neo-Nazis and white nationalists was funded by Mercer dollars – form a global network of Islamophobia spanning the UK, US, Canada, Australia and South Africa, among others.

The video series produced by *Rebel Media* and Gatestone covered topics including Sweden's migrant rape epidemic, the growing influence of Sharia law and the Islamisation of Europe – which the video claimed was a threat to 'Western values'. Other videos asked if Europe is 'doomed by migrants' and whether Europeans 'will rise to fight radical Islam and hold onto Western values'. Some pushed fear-mongering disinformation about so-called no-go zones and propaganda claiming that Islam is inherently linked to terrorism.

The New Zealand gunman referenced many of these topics in his manifesto and the underlying theme of Muslims as a threat to 'Western culture' – whiteness – featured prominently in both his videos and manifesto. Notably, the list of speakers featured in the video series includes Dutch far-right leader Geert Wilders and Daniel Pipes, president of the Middle East Forum, which has been identified as one of five key think tanks fuelling the anti-Muslim propaganda industry.

Not coincidentally, many of the videos also feature clips of news articles from *Breitbart*, the far-right platform financed by Robert Mercer – just one of many examples of how this network of Mercer-affiliated, anti-Muslim organisations and individuals uses its own propaganda across platforms to make it appear more credible and to expand its reach.

The partnership between *Rebel Media* and the Mercer-backed Gatestone Institute demonstrates how the anti-Muslim propaganda industry pushes its Islamophobic messaging from seemingly serious think tanks and other conservative organisations to far-right websites and activists, who then recycle the talking points and disseminate them to new audiences.

Prominent tech companies such as YouTube, Google and Facebook play a major role in this cycle by disseminating extremist content to specific audiences through features such as micro-targeting and algorithmically produced recommendations and suggestions.

This was the case with Secure America Now, a secretive right-wing organisation bankrolled by Robert Mercer. In 2016, it produced a series of Islamophobic propaganda videos and aired them during the final weeks of the US Presidential Election. However, most Americans never saw the fear-mongering videos – and that's no accident. Secure America Now worked closely with Facebook and Google to target the anti-Muslim ads only at voters in swing states who were deemed most likely to be receptive to the messaging, which was 'meant to stoke viewers' fears of imminent Muslim conquest'. This type of targeting falls squarely within the purview of Cambridge Analytica, the data firm funded by Robert Mercer.

Former Cambridge Analytica employee-turned-whistle-blower Chris Wylie has described how the company used Facebook data to build a system that could profile individual voters to target them with political ads. 'We exploited

Facebook to harvest millions of people's profiles,' he said. 'And built models to exploit what we knew about them and target their inner demons. That was the basis the entire company was built on.'

As journalist Carole Cadwalladr has explained in the *Observer*, adware and tracking cookies from websites such as *Breitbart* can also be used by companies such as Cambridge Analytica to track and monitor people's online activity. This data can be mined to profile people based on their internet browsing history and then, with Facebook's help, target them with ads.

'With this, a computer can ... predict and potentially control human behaviour,' Professor Jonathan Rust, director of the Psychometrics Centre at Cambridge University, told the *Guardian*. 'It's how you brainwash someone. It's incredibly dangerous. It's no exaggeration to say that minds can be changed. Behaviour can be predicted and controlled. I find it incredibly scary. I really do. Because nobody has really followed through on the possible consequences of all this.'

Those consequences are coming to light in real time and, all too often, come in the form of hate crimes and violence. It would be foolish to overlook the influence of a multi-million-dollar propaganda industry that creates the very same anti-Muslim rhetoric found in the New Zealand gunman's manifesto.

The Story of Brexit is the Story of Empire: Why Did Asian Immigrants Vote to Leave the EU?

Hardeep Matharu

8 APRIL 2019

Why, in British public life, do we almost never speak about Empire?

It was a question that struck me again recently as I was watching the news with my parents. Another day in Parliament with Theresa May embroiled in the continuing chaos around Brexit.

My parents migrated to Britain from Kenya and India more than forty years ago, so I still find it perplexing that they both voted to leave the EU in the 2016 Referendum.

Responding to their disillusionment on May's attempts to deliver Brexit, I asked them whether they would still vote in the same way again, knowing what they do about all that was to follow.

'Yes,' they both said without hesitation. 'It was still the right thing to do.'

That the Brexit vote was, in no small part, about Empire for Commonwealth immigrants, and their love-hate relationship with its legacy, has long needed discussion in British society.

Although non-white groups were generally more pro-Remain than white British people, 'ethnic minorities showed a non-negligible level of support for Leave, which was twice as high amongst Indians as amongst other minority groups', according to one report on the matter.

The relationship of Britain's longstanding immigrant communities with the Empire is a complex one. At once, British imperialism has created a patriotic allegiance in immigrants who see themselves as 'British' – more British than the British – rather than as migrants, while at the same time demanding reparation and recognition for all the damage Britain inflicted on countries such as India.

In many ways, the story of Brexit is the story of Empire. An unfinished, untold story on which the sun won't set for a very long time.

Swaraj, the first name of my father, means 'self-rule' and was a term used by Mahatma Gandhi to describe India's quest for independence from hundreds of years of British rule. My grandfather gave him the name as he was born in August 1947, the month and year India finally achieved self-governance.

Raised in Nairobi, Kenya, until he was eighteen, my dad spent two years in India, before coming to Britain in 1967 aged twenty. His family, Indian Punjabis, had originally migrated to Kenya to build the railways in the country for the British.

While recognising the violence of colonisation, my father

enjoyed growing up under British influence. 'I liked the way of life when I was in Kenya under the British rule; everything was run properly, all the laws, the administration,' he told me. 'It was a very nice place to be and that's how I've always had this loyalty to Britain and I always wanted to come to England and I wanted to be part of this country. I had no problems settling here.

'I used to read magazines like *Time* magazine, *Life* magazine, *Reader's Digest* and the old *Daily Mirror* papers, *Eagle* comics in Kenya. I learned to speak, read and write English at school because we had English teachers so I had no problem when I came over to Britain.'

What about racism? I asked him. 'Racism was something I was used to in Kenya as well,' he said. 'I knew that it existed – over there they used to call it "colour bar". There were certain hotels that were only meant for white people and there were certain parts of Nairobi where only white people could buy houses and live; Asians weren't allowed. So I knew from a very young age that this went on. There was a lot of racism [when I came to Britain], but one had to learn to live with it.'

On voting for Brexit, my father admits harbouring 'resentment' at how Britain has changed, in his eyes, for the worse – something he feels is linked to being part of the EU.

'My allegiance is to Britain. I don't see myself as part of Europe, I don't want to be,' he said. 'Europe is trying to impose its own rules, regulations and laws onto this country.

Britain should have kept on its own. We were better off that way.'

He believes that Britain was always renowned for its fairness and that it seems unfair that immigrants from Europe can come here relatively easily to work and make their lives. 'It's changed the whole culture of this country now,' he added.

The issue, however, is not that simple.

My father often speaks about how wrong it was of a morally corrupt Britain to impose its rule on countries more prosperous than itself. Both my parents made a point of telling me, when I was younger, about the Jallianwala Bagh Massacre in Amritsar in 1919, in which Colonel Reginald Dyer brutally killed hundreds of non-violent Indian protestors. Upon visiting the site of the killings last year, I was shocked by how close it was to the Golden Temple, a place of profound peace and a site considered the most sacred for Sikhs. But, paradoxically, because of this brutal history, my father feels that Britain owes a loyalty to its former colonies over Europe.

'They had a very good time in those countries and they benefited a lot from them and they built their own country as well during those years of the Empire,' he told me. 'This country was built on the Empire; they took a lot of money from India ... They should have some allegiance to those countries as well. Whereas Europe? I don't see what Europe has ever done for Britain.'

My mother Baljeet agrees. She left India for Britain aged twenty-six in 1975 to marry my father and sees herself as British, having worked hard to contribute to the country and assimilate into life here. She said she voted to leave the EU on grounds of British sovereignty because 'we should have our own laws and policies to run the country'.

We have had many a passionate discussion in which I have argued that Britain is sovereign, and that only a minority of laws emanate from the EU.

My mother also feels that Britain does not need immigration from Europe.

Speaking to other immigrants from former colonies, it is clear that – like my parents – the reasons why Asian communities voted to leave the EU are nuanced and difficult to presume.

One second-generation immigrant I spoke to said some Pakistani people campaigned for Brexit because they wanted to 'control immigration in a way that was favourable to the Indian subcontinent'.

'One of their arguments was that, if we leave, we'd be better able to accept people from the Indian subcontinent, professionals such as doctors, rather than taking them from Europe,' he said. 'There was that strand that we'd lost control of immigration, that lots of people from eastern Europe were coming over, but, therefore, people from the Indian subcontinent weren't getting a fair crack at the whip and it was that disparity. They felt the immigration system was unfair.'

While EU migrants generally benefit from freedom of movement, those from countries such as India and Pakistan are subject to visa and work restrictions – a distinction that was played on by Vote Leave's Michael Gove during the referendum campaign when he suggested that Britain's immigration system was 'racist'.

Another second-generation immigrant, whose parents also migrated to Britain from Pakistan, told me he voted for Brexit because he had concerns about the EU 'being an economic bloc to the detriment of the rest of the world'.

'I had no animosity towards the eastern Europeans because, if I was in their position, I would do the same for economic reasons and my parents did the same when they came to Britain,' he said.

But, he now believes a second referendum should be held as Brexit is 'fragmenting our society' and fuelling far-right racism against the very immigrant communities that voted to leave the EU. 'The day after I voted, there were people in white vans with Union Jacks driving around where I live and that shocked me,' he said. 'I didn't vote for nationalistic reasons so to see the way the white racist community behaved on winning the vote gave me serious concerns about the dynamic in Britain.'

For him, notions of Empire played a role in immigrants voting to leave the EU. 'People like me were born here, my parents migrated here,' he said. 'If it wasn't for the British Empire and the rule of India we wouldn't be here. My uncle fought in the Second World War in Burma and our ancestors have been entwined in the British Empire and Britain, but we have been given fewer rights in terms of migration into this country as compared to some eastern European countries who were actually fighting the British during the Second World War. So, what's that about?'

Shahmir Sanni, who was born in Pakistan, worked for BeLeave – an offshoot of the Vote Leave campaign during the EU Referendum. He turned whistleblower last year, when he exposed electoral wrongdoing at the organisation. Tasked with targeting and persuading black and ethnic minority people to vote to leave, Sanni said that many of the second-generation immigrants he spoke to in areas such as London and Birmingham were already set on voting for Brexit.

'They would say "we don't need the EU, we were born here, we were bred here, we have worked here, we don't need it, we have never associated with it so why would we focus on it?"' he told me. 'They would also say things like "it takes so long for my friends and cousins to get a visa". There was a lining of xenophobia towards eastern Europeans among Asian and Afro-Caribbean communities. There was the perception that people from Europe have got a free pass to come here.'

He believes that such communities have 'a huge feeling of being left behind'.

'In the last twenty to thirty years they've seen greater integration with Europe and not with their own communities and they have seen the benefits the Europeans have gotten, particularly in terms of immigration and free rein to go back and forth. But, then there's also a huge population of the South Asian community who have a very strong sense of patriotism, who are very proud to be living in the UK and, sure, they will criticise the British Government, but they are still very proud Britons and that's where you can have the same sort of mentality among the majority of Leave voters which is that Britain can be better on its own.'

According to Sanni, notions of the Empire and immigrants from former colonies feeling an allegiance to Britain had a huge part to play in why they voted to leave the EU. 'Previous generations weren't educated in the way that we were as young millennials who are hyper-aware of colonialism and imperialism and the effect it had on our ancestors,' he said. 'If you look at it from the frame of immigrants then who saw no opportunities back home and came here and were suddenly comfortable, and very comfortable, even if they were working class, the fact that they had a council house if they were working class was a blessing. It was huge. "The Government of this country gave me a home."'

He said his work at BeLeave was designed to play on this allegiance to the Commonwealth over Europe.

'It stirred this colonial mindset within non-EU immigrants

that the Commonwealth and Britain have so much more in common than the EU,' he said. 'So there was this false idea that we would be back with the Commonwealth again. An older generation of non-EU immigrants do feel like Britain has a solid connection with places like India; that we have a relationship and a friendship with Britain – and that stems from colonised minds.'

And why did he vote to leave the EU? 'Because I didn't like Europe as a white super-state,' he told me. 'Britain has a moral obligation to reconnect with the Commonwealth and I consider that a form of reparations. That, if we're going to have free movement, it should be between Britain and India, Pakistan and countries like Nigeria, not with the EU. I also think it's unfair that European migrants get privileges over non-EU migrants. You can argue that there are people of colour in Europe, but these countries have been desecrated by Britain and it has an obligation to cater to that.'

These will clearly be difficult conversations for some to hear.

Politicians over a number of years have made a mistake in not challenging inaccurate narratives around immigration, as well as not engaging with the views of immigrant communities long settled in Britain and their thoughts about our relationship with Europe and the rest of the world.

As the British-born child of parents who were raised in

countries of the Empire, I was taught nothing about it at school. Even when I did learn about the slave trade and Britain's Industrial Revolution, these were not set within the wider context of colonialism.

It may be an uncomfortable and challenging area of our history to probe, but not doing so ignores the effect it still has on how many feel and think about Britain today.

The longer we refuse to hold a mirror up to Britain's past, the longer we will fail to properly understand how we have arrived at the present and the consequences of this for the future.

In a post-Brexit world, this will be more vital than ever.

Nick and Me: The Great Brexit Storm Uprooting Old Friendships

Otto English

22 MAY 2019

I first met Nick in the early 1990s in a staff room in Essex.

It was the year after I had left university and, following some protracted dithering, I had found myself living with my parents and working as an English teacher at a language school on the fringes of Harlow.

The rest of the staff was made up of borderline sociopaths so, when Nick turned up one day, looking the very essence of 'normal', it was as if the cavalry had arrived. We quickly became mates as neither of us wanted to be there.

I longed to be free and had plans and ambitions. And Nick wanted to be where he had been before – for just a few months before we met, he had been a professional cricketer for Surrey. Destined to go right to the top of the game, an injury had cost him his career aged twenty-five and he was struggling to find new purpose in his life. Perhaps he had thought that becoming an English teacher would open up the chance to travel to exotic places, but, like me, he had ended up in Harlow New Town.

Nick had also found God in the wake of his accident, but he wasn't a holier-than-thou Christian. I was an avowed atheist and we had one of those great friendships where we could be completely straight with each other.

One night, the two of us tumbled out of an Essex pub and into the fields behind my parents' house. The countryside bristled with barley and we made a den in the middle of a field and smoked and drank wine I'd managed to purchase before last orders. We talked about all the stuff you talk about when you're wasted and in your twenties beneath the stars – neither of us ever forgot it.

Eventually, we escaped. Nick got a job in Spain and I moved to London.

Two or three years later, he rang and asked if he could stay with me. We had a bizarre night out in Brixton that ended with us sleeping in a car. He'd lost God and found politics. So now we could argue about that. We weren't that far apart politically, but just enough and we enjoyed arguing – it was our thing – and it sustained us over the next decade.

I got married and settled down, but it was hard for Nick. His former friends and teammates had gone on to be household names and big sporting stars and, while he never complained, it clearly gnawed at him. Of course it did – the weight of what might have been. He and his partner had a son and, when the relationship ended, he moved to Cheltenham to be closer to his boy. I'd sometimes get a call or a text or a thumbs-up on Facebook and, every now and then, we'd go for pints if he was around and laugh about that time we got drunk in a field and that other time when we slept in a car.

Then, Brexit happened.

Nick voted Remain but, having done so, believed that we should accept the result and leave. By now, he had become a psychotherapist and he talked a lot about the importance of moving on from trauma.

Thinking back, I realise now that his whole adult life after his accident had been dedicated to that aim, but instead of trying to engage with his point of view, I started to clash with him. We argued a bit on Facebook and then a lot. It was friendly at first, but then he began to post articles by *Spiked*

Online and Brendan O'Neill and I began to wonder what had happened to him. I couldn't stop myself.

If this had been in the pub we'd have been fine but, in the arena of social media, we both began to square up to each other and dig in over our respective positions. It felt nastier.

'What's happened to Nick?' like-minded friends who had seen his posts and my replies would ask. But, they might as well have asked what had happened to me.

Our relationship became frostier and sometimes I'd find myself feeling a bit sad about it and suggesting we go for a drink. 'Yes,' he'd reply, 'pint would be good next time I'm in London.'

I'm not sure if he meant it – but I certainly did. Either way, it never happened.

On Tuesday morning this week, as I sat on the District Line trundling towards Hammersmith, I discovered that Nick had died.

He had been ill for almost a year. In the past, he would have told me and I would have gone to see him but, given the state of our friendship, at the end of his life he didn't even tell me.

In the back of my head I had always imagined that we would one day sit down over a beer and thrash it out. It was not to be.

Nick was one of those people who make life worthwhile. He was funny, engaging, larger than life, thoughtful and poetic. It is rare to have a friend you can so understand and who so understands you, and now I've lost him. Brexit has cost us all so many things – and now it has cost me the chance to say sorry and goodbye to my friend.

I wonder whether, in ten years, all of us – so engaged in this mad civil war – will wonder if such things were a price worth paying.

London was Never an English City

Count of the Saxon Shore

30 MAY 2019

John Cleese's controversial tweet that 'London was not really an English city any more' has provoked much criticism, some seeing this comment as a way of stirring up emotions around the current debate on Brexit and the larger issue of immigration. But I'd say he's missing the point: London was never exclusively an English city in the first place.

I don't simply mean that it was originally an imperial metropolis – the square mile of the old city and its bridge still mark out the boundaries set by the Romans nearly 2,000 years ago. No, the relationship between London and the English has always been a complex one. As it has with every other tribe that has chosen to settle here.

When the Anglo-Saxons first established themselves in the south-east, their attitude to London was quite simple: they avoided it. The early English didn't begin as city dwellers, but the port on the Thames continued to be a vital trading centre throughout the Dark Ages.

The very first English account of London comes in Bede's *Ecclesiastical History of the English People* written in AD 731 where it's described as 'a great emporium for many nations that come to it by land and sea'. Note the crucial phrase: 'many nations'. Bede is making a clear reference to the multicultural nature of the city, more than 1,200 years ago. This is the continuity in history that is worth looking at when we start asserting what is 'English' or not.

And, when the English did start to settle here, they did it outside the square mile of the city walls. The Anglo-Saxons built *Lundenwic* in what is now Covent Garden and the Strand. *Wic* is Old English for 'town' and so the Aldwych is a reference to the Saxon 'old town'.

Alfred the Great re-founded the City of London proper as part of his defences against the Danes and this was known as *Lundenburg*, but for the next two centuries, possession of it was contested by the Vikings and the English. By the turn of the first millennium, the political centre of England remained in Winchester.

In 1042, Edward the Confessor built the new power base of Westminster, in the neighbourhood but quite geographically distinct from the City. And it was here that Harold II, the last Anglo-Saxon king of England, was crowned.

After 1066, it started to become a major urban centre once more, with great architectural projects such as the Tower of London. Built by Normans, from France. It became our capital and home to a series of royal houses, none of which were actually 'English' in the narrow sense of the term.

In adversity, London thrived on diversity. Conditions were so bad by the 18th Century that the death rate was greater than the birth rate and, without immigration, the city would have shrunk rather than expanded.

So this 'great emporium for many nations that come to it' is as English as it is international: it belongs to everybody and everybody who lives here belongs – as Londoners.

Pessimism is for Lightweights: No Room for Fear

Salena Godden

8 AUGUST 2019

'There is no time for despair, no place for self-pity, no need for silence, no room for fear. We speak, we write, we do language.' —Toni Morrison

Iconic and prolific, the Pulitzer and Nobel Prize-winning author Toni Morrison has passed away aged eighty-eight.

Now, in the future when they ask me 'where were you when you heard Toni Morrison died?', I will say how I was sitting at my kitchen table holding a crucifixion figurine in my hand. It was a plastic and tacky thing I'd just found in a market stall, all cheap and gaudy with pink plastic flowers at the feet of Christ. I was trying to remove the plastic Jesus from the cross, so I could swap the Jesus figure to a She-Ra superhero doll on her period. I won't forget I was doing that at that moment.

When I heard Toni Morrison died, I was immersed in making a new piece of art for an upcoming exhibition and replacing Jesus on the cross with a bleeding woman. The synchronicity and symbolism of that moment isn't lost on me. I feel like I'm running out of saviours, losing alive and living superheroes.

For those not familiar with Morrison's work, I'd recommend *The Bluest Eye*, *Beloved* or *Sula* as great books to start with. *The Bluest Eye* is my favourite as I read it at a time when I was vulnerable. Sometimes books find you when you need them. This book affected me most profoundly as a brown girl born with light eyes. It gave me insight; it was the first book that had me examine my relationship with shade, with self-loathing and self-doubt, and belonging in the state of unbelonging. The weight I have carried of feeling I'm not enough and that I'll never be enough, black enough or white enough, or just enough-enough.

'You wanna fly, you got to give up the thing that weighs
you down.'   —Toni Morrison

Toni Morrison was significant and vital for over five decades.
Black women were at the centre of her work and, as an editor,
she elevated and encouraged new work and new black writers.

She was more than a deft writer, a successful and well-loved
author. She was a lighthouse in the stormy weather of rising
division, inequality and racism. She sang loud to drown out
the deafening silence of others. She was a symbol of courage.

And, for me, it was as if by magic that Toni Morrison's work
appeared. It came from some glamorous desk in far-away
America and somehow reached me. I loved my local library; I
went there to discover others' stories and to find myself in
books. But I couldn't find a story of a UK childhood like mine,
in the 1970s and '80s, and being the only brown girl in the
school and living on Thatcher's breadline. And so I began to
write *Springfield Road*. That childhood memoir took around a
decade to write and fight to get into print. I took Toni's most
famous quote quite to heart. 'If there is a book that you want
to read, but it hasn't been written yet, you must be the one to
write it.'

As an avid reader, I needed there to be Toni Morrison; a
someone to look up to, a someone to try to be as strong as. I
needed her shining there, unapologetically, just as I also
always needed Maya Angelou and Nina Simone and Aretha

Franklin and all the other working-class black women who came up through poverty and rose to use their craft and artistry as a passport to some freedom.

'The function, the very serious function of racism is distraction. It keeps you from doing your work. It keeps you explaining, over and over again, your reason for being.'   —Toni Morrison

Thank you for all the work you did, Toni Morrison. Thank you for speaking up and speaking out. Thank you for blazing a trail and smashing through. Thank you for showing us the path, thank you for making our stories heard and making us feel that our stories were worthy of being printed. Thank you for empowering brown girls like me with wild and unruly hair, wild and unruly passion, and wild and unruly mouths to use that wild and unruly fury and not get distracted.

The 2020s already mirror the 1920s in so many terrifying ways, politically and economically, and so the roaring we do must be loud, resilient and resistant. And now, more than ever, we must not get distracted from the work needed to lift each other, to help others to help others, to seek heroes in the everyday, discover the undiscovered, make space and room for the indie and the underground, the others and the outsiders, the counterculture. Rise and raise up the work of black women, the visibility of the working class and marginalised.

'Tell us what the world has been to you in the dark places and in the light. Don't tell us what to believe, what to fear. Show us belief's wide skirt and the stitch that unravels fear's caul.'   —Toni Morrison

After you've visited the work of Toni Morrison, I'll leave you with this recommended reading list of a handful of the UK's powerful female writers, alive and living authors and poets from across the diaspora; please raise each other up, make some space, make some noise, buy some books, listen to the work of these women: Reni Eddo-Lodge, Irenosen Okojie, Candice Carty-Williams, Mona Arshi, Patience Agbabi, Jackie Kay, Victoria Adukwei Bulley, Catherine Johnson, Hannah Lee, Vanessa Kisuule, Theresa Lola, Dorothea Smartt, Zena Edwards, Ysra Daley-Ward, Selina Nwulu, Chimene Suleyman, Malorie Blackman, Vera Chok, Coco Khan, Imtiaz Dharker, Kat François, Malika Booker, Kit de Waal, Bernadine Evaristo, Hannah Pool, Diana Evans, Patrice Lawrence, Sabrina Mahfouz, Lisa Luxx, Zadie Smith, Hafsah Aneela Bashir, 4 Brown Girls Who Write, Deanna Rodger, Warsan Shire, Jane Yeh, Elizabeth Uviebinené and Yomi Adegoke.

Please read and share and remember the golden rule: every good book leads to another good book, as every author leaves a trail of breadcrumbs that take you to the work of the author they read and every act of kindness and courage can only lead to encouraging others and more acts of kindness and courage and more resistance and hope.

'There is no time for despair, no place for self-pity, no need for silence, no room for fear.'   —Toni Morrison

Rest in power!

History's Rhyme: Henry VIII, Thomas Cromwell, Johnson and Cummings

Arthur Snell

3 SEPTEMBER 2019

Britain loves a historical analogy.

For Brexiters, this is usually a comic-book version of the Second World War with EU politicians – many of whose parents suffered German occupation – offensively cast as Nazis.

They seem so gripped by this historical delusion that one is left suspecting that some of them believe themselves to be veterans of that conflict. 'I was in the army, I wasn't trained to lose,' the former Territorial Army officer and Conservative MP

Mark Francois explained, neglecting to mention that he had never seen active service.

The point about historical analogies is that they are always contested: the same events can be endlessly reinterpreted. Brexit is 'Parliament versus the Crown'; the 'sober hard-working Roundheads against the profligate, aristocratic Cavaliers'. Or is it the other way around? A narrow band of Puritan zealots determined to protect England from pernicious continental influences such as Catholicism?

How about England's break with the Roman Catholic Church?*

At the outset, the English king and his advisors thought that they could easily get what they wanted from the Church – a supra-national authority that was political, economic and cultural. The King sent his secretary to Pope Clement VII to demand a divorce, but the English had fatally misread continental politics.

Catherine's nephew was Emperor Charles V, the most powerful man in the world, who held Rome and the Pope in his power. There was no way that this deal was going to be 'one of the easiest in human history', to quote Conservative MP Liam Fox.

---

* As is well known, this separation was largely driven by King Henry VIII's desperation to divorce his first wife, Catherine of Aragon, to enable him to marry Anne Boleyn, whom he hoped would bear him a son. With his numerous wives and an indeterminate number of children – not to mention his physical bulk and occasional charm – Henry VIII seems a very good historical rhyme for Boris Johnson.

Contrary to what Michael Gove might have said, Henry did not hold all the cards.

So his advisors went for the 'no deal' option – they decided that they would take back control of England's sovereignty from a 'foreign' Church, proclaiming in the key withdrawal Act of Parliament in 1532 that 'England is an Empire, and so hath been accepted in the world, governed by one Supreme Head and King'.*

The concept of national sovereignty would have been confusing to a 16th Century Englishman, but then our departure from the EU won't stop us from being subject to the European Court of Human Rights or the requirement to wage war in defence of other members of NATO, so it remains confusing to the present day.

Just as Conservative prime ministers plan to use Brexit to return a huge array of powers directly to the executive, bypassing Parliament entirely (the 'Henry VIII powers'), Henry's break with Rome increased his power and his wealth. Over a five-year period, hundreds of monasteries were dissolved and the Crown's wealth transformed. At a time when one in fifty adult men were monks, this also represented a transformation of England's social structure.

As the 1530s progressed, the King tended towards tyranny and a key figure in this was Thomas Cromwell.

---

* Henry's talk of empire was disingenuous – a convenient argument to justify a power grab by the English monarch. And he didn't stop with the divorce.

If the unfaithful, vain and voracious Henry makes a good comparator for Boris Johnson, then Thomas Cromwell's present-day analogue would have to be Dominic Cummings.

Cromwell was utterly ruthless, highly intelligent and totally dedicated to remaking England.

Henry was a lifelong Catholic and his break with Rome was merely the necessary expedient to enable his divorce. But Cromwell was the true believer, placing a Bible in English in every church and promoting Protestant reformers such as Hugh Latimer. He was also prepared to play by different rules, and his lack of respect for traditional authority, including great aristocrats and churchmen, left him with many enemies.

Cromwell insisted on absolute loyalty to Henry, introducing a new Treasons Act in 1534 that made it a capital crime even to 'imagine ... any bodily harm' to the King. It was this Act that allowed Cromwell to make the case against Anne Boleyn once he felt that she was an obstacle to his plans, leading to her beheading in May 1536.

In the end, Cromwell overreached. Henry came to regret the execution of Boleyn and decided he didn't like Anne of Cleves, whom Cromwell had lined up as a match for the King after the death of his third wife, Jane Seymour.

In 1539, Cromwell implemented a Statute of Proclamations, allowing the King to rule by decree. Cromwell's opponents coalesced around the argument that he had hijacked Henry's power. Having made so many enemies, Cromwell fell swiftly and was beheaded on the day that Henry married his fifth wife, Catherine Howard.

Like any historical analogy, there are limitations to all this. The EU promotes peace and liberalism across the continent – not something the 16th Century Catholic Church can credibly claim. But, history helps us to recognise the difference between belief and bluster, principle and power. We would do well to keep studying it.

10 September 2019

The UK Parliament is prorogued by Queen
Elizabeth II on the advice of Prime Minister Boris
Johnson, in a move which was later ruled unlawful
by the Supreme Court.

A Hard Border in Ireland Threatens a Return to a Murderous Bigotry

Frank McGuinness

16 SEPTEMBER 2019

I was born in Buncrana, an Irish town beside the border. Reared in its shadow, our big Northern Irish city, Derry, was fourteen miles away.

It stood divided, Catholic and Protestant, within itself, and we in Donegal were divided from it by a small stretch of land of no more than fifty yards. Two rather wretched customs houses were manned by bored men in uniforms of not too impressive regalia, trying to do their job of stopping butter and cheese, clothes and curtain fabrics passing illegally between the United Kingdom of Great Britain and Northern Ireland and the Free State of Eire.

One defender of the economic realm was possessed by a particular mania to stop chicken being unlawfully consumed. An eminently, respectably dressed woman put a stop to his gallop when he challenged the contents of her sandwich, she loudly impersonating a clucking hen, the whole bus joining in, the lady having patiently explained to no avail that it was the remains of her lunch brought home from work.

This was the type of daily idiocy travellers faced in those dark days, which are now threatening to return to torment us.

Clever ways can be radically devised to defy red tape and restrictions on free movement. But I do hope that we will not, on either side, resort to the tactics that left one of those wretched customs houses standing for years as a ruin – bombed to oblivion – and then its ghostly shell dismantled again and again; an act of hatred perpetuated by those who considered it to be a valid target for demolition purposes long after it served no practical function in the partition of the island.

I never ceased to register a slight spasm of fear passing it on the road, a ghostly reminder that war stirred always in the hinterland, threatening to erupt and do what all wars do – change our lives for the worse.

The long fight to stop these conditions prevailing in Ireland North and South now meet their sternest challenge in the contemptuous madness shown by those mismanaging Brexit. They believe most profoundly in borders, in division, in *their* country and *my* country, at each other's throats, wangling, dealing, corrupting all goodwill that had managed to secure something more than a semblance of a truce to end the sickening conflict that disfigured relations between us for too long.

*

I was born in 1953, grew up shaped by The Troubles, and the one consequence of that historical reality is that I know men and women of violence when I see them.

Boris Johnson, Jacob Rees-Mogg, Dominic Cummings, Michael Gove and their allies in all parts of the UK conform to the cruelty that arrogance always embodies.

Bring back the border, you bring back bloodshed. On their heads and on our heads be it.

They will feel that as profoundly as they ignored it, before and during the accursed referendum. The signs of a return to murderous bigotry are there, and have been there, for the past three years for all to see. And I cannot say how much I hope I am wrong. For this time no security blanket will save us.

The Hollow Heart of the British Constitution

Anthony Barnett
18 SEPTEMBER 2019

What is the role of the Queen?

Many, perhaps most, think that the Queen has amazing political judgement. Some may even think that this is what has held the country together for more than sixty years. But, in reality, the crisis over the prorogation of Parliament demonstrates that the Queen has no political judgement whatsoever – good or bad. She is a nothingness, the hollow heart of the unwritten British constitution.

The more the constitution is now debated in the way all constitutions should be – as something vital, consequential and therefore relevant to the way we live – the clearer this becomes. As it does so, the monarchy becomes increasingly redundant. For, surely, not even the most admiring wish to be ruled by a useless crown.

The justification of deference for the monarchy is that one feels enhanced by the special enchantment of royal meaning and can share in its aura. If this drains away and the monarchy becomes irrelevant, allegiance to it becomes more shameful than enriching. Who would pledge one's loyalty to a cipher?

The monarch's nothingness is drawing the entire political system into the void that Elizabeth II has so meticulously and understandably defined as her role. To understand why this is happening with respect to the prorogation case before the Supreme Court, it is necessary to grasp the nature of its quandary.

The court's decision hinges on how it perceives the blazing deception of Prime Minister Boris Johnson, who is claiming that his unprecedented closing down of Parliament had nothing to do with Brexit and was merely normal.

It is striking that no one, apart from Johnson himself at his most feeble, is making any effort to pretend that the Government's description of its motives is true. No member of the Government has been willing to swear an affidavit or appear in court for cross-examination about its decision-making. Indeed, in his memorandum to the Supreme Court, Johnson in effect concedes this and merely states: 'The courts have no jurisdiction to enforce political conventions ... because those matters are determined within the political world.' In other words, he can do what he likes and break conventions at will for they are not legally binding or, to use the technical term, justiciable.

This puts the Supreme Court in a bind. The Prime Minister has acted in a despotic fashion by proroguing Parliament, the country's sovereign body and home of what passes for our democracy. If the court concludes that this is unlawful, it shatters the separation of the judiciary from the executive that is the hallmark of the British constitution. But, if it agrees that the Prime Minister can breach any convention he wishes because that's politics and nothing to do with them, it endorses the destruction of the informal checks and balances on which the constitution rests. Either way points to a constitutional revolution.

What does this have to do with the Queen? Quite a lot.

In a narrow sense, she was correct. She wielded her authority to prorogue Parliament on the advice of her Prime

Minister, given to her in her Privy Council. This advice was transmitted to her by Jacob Rees-Mogg, the leader of the House of Commons, who wrote in the *Spectator* about the advantages of prorogation for Brexit.

The rules of the Privy Council are written in obscure language, in the oath its councillors take, but are basically clear. Everything said in Council is secret. What anyone says in the presence of the monarch cannot be revealed. But, the councillors are obliged to be truthful with the Queen – it is not just what they say which has to be true, it has to be the whole truth for they must 'faithfully and truly declare' their 'mind and opinion'.

Clearly, neither Rees-Mogg nor, through him, the Prime Minister did so. The monarch was misled as to her Government's true reasons for closing Parliament and Rees-Mogg breached his ancient pledge of faithfulness in doing so. The Queen should have replied: 'Mr Rees-Mogg, as a Privy Councillor, you may kiss my royal arse, but you are forbidden to pull my royal leg.' She did not do so because she followed a lifetime practice of never doing anything that might be deemed political.

Had she been a president or sworn to uphold a documented constitution, it would have been her duty to expose Johnson's request for what it was. But Elizabeth II has survived a lifetime on the throne by never appearing to be an agent. She preserved the regime through unprecedented change by floating.

Her reward for being true to this extraordinary abnegation was having to give the go-ahead to the toxic cynicism of Johnson and his Svengali, Dominic Cummings.

The greatest distinction of her realm – that she has always been 'above' politics – has led to her historic humiliation.

I believed that Brexit was always like a supernova, a great flash of democratic energy that would collapse into a dark hole. What I hadn't foreseen was the part that would be played in this by the absent centre that is the British monarchy.

Thanks to its passivity, the singular majesty that has endowed the United Kingdom with continuity could not withstand Johnson's brutal carelessness with its vital conventions. Elizabeth II and the constitution enter their final reckoning.

Europe's Forgotten War: A Hospital on the Edge of Civilisation

Iain Overton

23 SEPTEMBER 2019

Abandoned hospitals are, like former asylums and empty prisons, places that unnerve. Leprous walls, where wallpaper peels off like a diseased skin. Dark corridors that lead to locked doors, silent as a morgue. Empty chairs waiting for patients who will never come. The stuff of nightmares.

In Avdiivka hospital's abandoned wing, though, this nightmare is born from a living one.

In the spring of 2014, this hospital was caught in a whirlwind of violence. What first began as a dispute over a trade agreement transmuted into what became the bloodiest conflict Europe had seen since the former Yugoslavia was engulfed in war in the early 1990s.

Russian troops, and those they supported, launched a major assault across this region, after annexing the Crimea. The eye of that bloody storm was to become the eastern Ukrainian city of Donetsk. Avdiivka lies 20km from that city centre, and just 6km from the regional airport.

Separatists in Donetsk and nearby Luhansk declared independence after unrecognised referendums and, as fighting intensified, the numbers of civilians harmed began to rise significantly.

Avdiivka hospital found itself overrun with casualties – more than 500 civilians wounded, many by shrapnel from explosive weapons. At least fifty-four more locals were killed. It was to see the war unfold terrible chapter by terrible chapter.

Water and electricity were cut off. Eight missile strikes hit the medical centre; two doctors were killed and one nurse badly wounded. Patients died on operating tables with the sound of mortar-fire creeping inwards. Mothers gave birth in crowded corridors. Medical supplies ran dangerously short, and all but the most urgent of medical procedures were abandoned.

Throughout those dark months, the staff worked tirelessly. Three-day shifts became commonplace, doctors taking brief naps where they could, sleeping upright wrapped in borrowed blankets. It was still April, the cruellest month, and the winter winds had not lessened. With no heating, the staff would crowd around coal and wood burners, urging their frozen fingers back to life so that they could operate on the incoming wounded.

The war changed everything.

Today, swathes of the hospital lie unused. Meanwhile, the lands that surround the hospital are filled with late summer wheat that undulates in an eastern wind; beneath those golden waves, landmines lie. The doctors call them the 'forbidden fields', and the legacy that explosive violence has visited on this medical centre seeps into everything.

This war has done as much as diseases can ever do. It has contaminated all that it touched, including the people and places that survived.

Dr Vitaliy Danylovych Sytnik has a nervous tic. He rolls his wedding ring in his fingers when he speaks, but his voice resonates with the authority that comes with his position: the deputy director of the hospital. A specialist in systemic diseases, he oversees the care for patients for a region that now covers 34,000 citizens in the local city, and some 15,000 in the regions surrounding.

He has spent the past twenty-five years working in this hospital – half his life – and the staff are, to him, like family. He was here when the news on their television screens turned, terribly, into reality, and the first patients began pouring into the emergency clinics. They bore injuries that a civilian centre rarely saw. Bullet wounds in the arms of children. Shrapnel embedded in the heads of pensioners. Flesh ripped apart by a storm of steel. For every death, ten more people were wounded.

Without urgent medical intervention, he estimates that at least 50% of patients would have died. And the same percentage needed blood transfusions too – a sudden descent into conflict surgery for him and his team.

'We did what we had to do,' he says, his glasses perched upon his forehead, under his cropped, greying hair. 'We were covered in blood, but we went into autopilot.' The conditions worsened and soon they were doing surgery by candlelight, shadows cast against the operating theatre's walls. 'While the hospital had enough medicines in reserve, what we lacked most was manpower,' he says. 'Before the war, we had eighty doctors, now we have just forty. We had 450 workers in total – now just 190.'

This drop in his workforce came alongside a sharp increase

in patients demanding care. In addition, the establishment of an artificial border between Avdiivka and Donetsk, where the main regional hospital stood, meant they had to take on an added burden. At the same time, damage to the hospital meant that they were forced to shut down crucial departments. In turn, the infectious diseases, paediatric and neonatal clinics closed.

'We just lost specialists,' Dr Sytnik says. 'First a cardiologist, then an endocrinologist, then more.' Now, they have to refer patients to clinics 40 or 50km away. Even their ambulance crews struggle to find staff. There is also a crucial shortage of family doctors and the few specialist clinics they can operate are overrun.

For those with lifelong disabilities caused by explosive weapons, this lack of specialist care can be devastating. The hospital has no rehabilitation centre and even lacks an operating lift. Incredibly, its x-ray department is up four flights of stairs. Patients have to be carried up the broken steps by relatives, cradled in blankets. One doctor later complained of having hurt his back carrying an injured patient up those flights.

Dr Sytnik points through a dirty window over to the abandoned wing of his hospital. It could once accommodate 220 patient beds, he says. Now it's down to 150. Some rooms have eight beds in a space designed for four.

Below us, the sound of drilling can be heard. They are renovating an entire floor, he explains, funded by the local

Avdeyevskiy Coke Plant, which produces 18% of Ukraine's coal coke output. The repairs are much needed, judging by the chipped floors and peeling wallpaper of the doctor's office, but they are expensive – costing as much as 7 million Ukrainian hryvnia or some $300,000, a fortune in a place where some junior doctors get paid just $120 a month. The hospital is in dire need of an upgrade, but any repairs are costs that come on top of a budget already stretched thin by the war.

With the poor conditions and overwork, his job seems Sisyphean. 'Doctors who have left ring us up and call us crazy,' he says. 'The levels of work, the conditions, the lack of specialists, all fall on our shoulders. One doctor does the job of two here.'

He claims tens of thousands of doctors have left Ukraine in the past five years, with as many as 16,000 in 2019 alone. It is hard to confirm this, but it is easy to see how an attractive job in Poland or further afield attracts. His secretary earns just $130 a month and has to ask her mother to help support her and her child.

When asked if he feels supported by the Ukrainian Government, Dr Sytnik goes quiet. He cannot leave a city where six generations of his family once lived, where his pregnant daughter is expecting her first baby, where he has to take out a loan to afford the renovation for the newborn's room in a shared flat. If you ask him how this war has impacted him personally, he shrugs. 'What can you do?' he asks. He knows what a psychiatrist will say: go away, go to the seaside, go camping. But he has no money to do this and, besides, he has to spend his weekends repairing his parents' house which has been destroyed by the fighting.

And with that, this softly spoken man, in his canvas shoes and plaid shirt, rises to go. He has a clinic. Heart attacks are on the increase, he says, along with mental health issues, suicide attempts, depression and physical disorders related to poor psychological health. The list goes on. His work is never done.

'We will survive,' he says, and extends his hand. This is what war does: it reduces everything to a simple binary. Survive or die.

The three male doctors gather in their faded common room. A dusty games console sits to one side. One of them, Alexandrz, is in his late forties. The other two – Orlov and Arkatov – are in their sixties. The youngest doctor in this hospital is forty-two. The younger doctors left long ago, before the roots that tie a person to a place grew too deep.

The sound of patients comes from outside. Opposite is a room garishly covered in flock wallpaper where nine beds are squeezed in. Two patients lie inert, facing the wall, curled up in sickness. But others have their families there, and bread is being shared, slices of meat offered up, cheese laid upon thick black bread. Spirits are raised where they can be.

The three doctors speak above the noise. They talk to each

other in the way that soldiers do. One begins a sentence, the other finishes it. The oldest seems frail, even beyond his sixty-eight years.

'We have two psychologists,' he jokes, 'three stars and five stars.' He is referring to brands of cognac in the region. The others do not laugh.

The lack of electricity was one of the hardest things about the war, they say. They froze. They had to operate without x-rays. One man with a subclavian arterial rupture died under their knives as they just didn't have enough blood in the bank for that one. Then there were the children who were brought in with head traumas. That was the hardest of all.

They lacked supplies. Basic pain relief, antibiotics, dressings all ran perilously short and, while they were able to treat everyone, they had to make hard decisions as to how much treatment they could give. They became experts at triage – who needed help and who did not. Without assistance from aid groups – the Red Cross, Médecins Sans Frontières, Première Urgence Internationale – they do not know what they would have done, they say. Dozens of medical items around the hospital are labelled as gifts from the Germans, the Czechs, the French and the Swiss.

'What doesn't kill you makes you stronger,' the anaesthesiologist says, as the older surgeon trembles. 'You know the US have "Vietnam Syndrome"?' he continues. 'And in Chechnya, they have the "Chechen Syndrome"? Well, here you have the

"Donbas Syndrome",' he says, referring to the region of eastern Ukraine and south-western Russia. You see it, he explains, 'in the mass of internally displaced people, in the inhibited economy, in the reduced quality of life, in the people whose paths in life have been disrupted so deeply'.

A list of the things that have been lost begins. Access to transport, access to study, access to entertainment, the theatre, cinema. They have seen a rise in alcoholism. A rise in drunk drivers. Traffic accidents have spiked in a population for whom death's presence became all too familiar. Data, too, has been a victim of the conflict. During the fighting, the internet was down, computers not working. Much evidence recording the harm of the conflict was lost in the chaos.

What they do know is that, today, they have seen a spike in tuberculosis – caused by the fact that many were forced to shelter in damp cellars for months at a time, herded together under the threat of shellfire. The exodus of the young to Kiev and abroad has also brought a shortage of young medical personnel. Underpinning everything is the shadow of the war, leaving them perplexed and filled with sorrow.

'How is it,' the anaesthesiologist says, 'that here, in the middle of Europe, in the 21st Century, you have such a war? Such things you cannot understand.' And he looks down at the pockmarked floor, where a broken tile reveals a square of crumbling concrete, and no one answers. 'We are living in a strange reality,' he continues. 'A lost time. A lost dimension. We live on the edge of civilisation.'

The hospital bears scars, just like its patients. Outside, a group of medics huddle, dragging at contraband cigarettes. Dying from lung cancer is the last of their concerns. They stand next to a man slumped to one side. On his bandaged hand can be traced a line of blood, from a finger lost in an industrial accident.

Beside him is a man from UNFPA, the United Nations sexual and reproductive health agency. Yes, there has been a rise in HIV rates here, says the official, pulling at a cigarette. Where there are more men than women, he says, referring to the massive influx of soldiers, you'll get that. It is not just the HIV virus that is spreading. A shortage of medicines to combat the spread of sexually transmitted diseases; a lack of funding for condom disbursement; a rise in risky behaviour among young people – all of these have led to a spike in sexual diseases such as chlamydia, gonorrhoea and hepatitis C.

What starts as explosive violence has transmuted into other healthcare impacts, transforming into deep, private tragedies. Ill health stalks bomb craters.

'Some tests you have to pay for personally too,' the man says, and because of this, all too often a disease goes undiagnosed. It then spreads through a community unchecked, transmitted by people for whom intimacy might offer the kindest relief from the trauma of war.

The radiologist, Marina, dreams of army tanks. 'They are not nightmares,' she says, but it is hard to see how a line of attacking soldiers can be anything but.

She sits alone in a building abandoned by everyone. The only operating part of the hospital in this building is the one she oversees – the x-ray department. There, she records every visit from every patient in neat blue lines in her neat blue folder. Three days ago, there were fifty-three x-rays taken. Yesterday, thirty-seven. Today, fifty.

She will input them into the computer later. When the war took away the electricity, she says, it seemed that a written record was the best thing to have. In the meantime, she sits alone, four floors up, waiting for her patients to come. When you ask her what she would like most, she replies: 'Another Marina. To keep me company.'

Dr Tatiana Teplyakova points to a hole in the desk. 'Shrapnel,' she says. She points to a hole above the door, and another above a lintel, and says the same.

A burst of shellfire pierced her laboratory, shattering glass and plaster. Luckily, it was deep into a night shift and no one was hurt, but these are pockmarks that haven't been fixed. Perhaps they are there as a reminder.

That attack led to her having to shut down one of her test-ing laboratories: the bacterial infectious disease unit. The vials of disease that she, as head of Avdiivka's testing laboratory, once stored there could easily have been weaponised. Besides, if a shell had wiped out that centre ... Today she makes do with what she has. She urgently needs modern testing devices, but the budgets have already been depleted, and the war has delayed countless upgrades.

'Stagnated,' she pronounces – a statement that shows her love of getting to the heart of the matter. It's a skill she devel-oped during the conflict. She used to have thirty people work-ing for her in the testing facilities, now they have just six, and they have to cater for the military wounded too. Hers is a burden that is unrelenting.

During the height of the conflict, when the power was cut, they really struggled. Even when the generator was in use, they only had time to recharge their cell phones and do some urgent testing. Complex tests became a rarity and, instead, their focus was on emergency analysis – white blood cell counts became the mainstay. All they had left was glucose tests and urine analysis.

Even running water they could do without. They took it from the pond, filtered it, boiled it, filtered it again and then used that to wash their implements. But without electric-ity, testing devices, communications, email, data – all was impossible. She wonders what western Europe would do if it ever had such a descent into the pre-modern.

Complex tests have to be sent 70km away. Once, she could send samples to the laboratories of Donetsk. No longer. This means she can no longer test for drug-resistant MRSA. Luckily, basic sputum tests mean that tuberculosis can be identified. But the rest? She shrugs. 'We do what we can,' she repeats.

And here, in this hospital on the edge of civilisation, it seems that is all they can do.

Europe's Forgotten War: 'Who Can I be Angry With? Who is Going to Compensate Me? What are They Going to Compensate Me For?'

Iain Overton

25 SEPTEMBER 2019

It is hard to find the home of Eugeniy Dubitsky. As you drive along roads pockmarked by potholes in Mariinka, eastern Ukraine, you pass just some of the 1,000 apartment buildings and 12,000 private houses that have been damaged or destroyed here during the war.

Half of them reportedly still remain unrepaired, and boarded-up windows in some blocks take up the best part of the building. Signs for the numbers of houses and street names are all but absent.

It was not just the buildings that were impacted. About 2 million people live along this, the Government-controlled side of the frontline in the Donetsk region. Some 13,000 people have been killed here, a quarter of them civilians, and as many as 30,000 wounded in the war that has plagued this region since it broke out in April 2014.

But, one of them, Eugeniy, a heavily wounded fifty-one-year-old, has been unable to flee the region. He still lives here, close to the war's jagged edge.

His mother, Elena Ivanouha Dubitskaya, is his only carer and she directs me through the tumble-down garden out to the small cottage where her son now spends his days. She is spritely for her eighty-one years, but perhaps she has no choice but to be. Her son relies on her for everything.

Eugeniy is in the living room, perched against a pillow to help relieve pressure sores. His legs are thin under loose track-suit bottoms and he trembles with neurological damage. A picture behind him shows him in healthier days – he used to be a special forces soldier in the Soviet Union Army. Then he worked for a gas utility service and, latterly, as a coal miner. That was before everything changed on 9 June 2017.

On that evening, as he was preparing to take his wife out to a comedy night and was watching television in his kitchen, an explosive shell shattered the window and his life with it. The blast knocked him down onto the floor, along with his wife, who had just left the shower in a bathrobe and towel. Blood poured out of both of them. He grabbed more towels and stemmed the flow, but it was clear the damage was extensive. Shrapnel had pierced his left thigh and gone right through his legs. His calf was in shreds. His wife was lying with both hips punctured, screaming in pain.

Eugeniy describes these events in a slow, faltering way. The shell's impact robbed him of his voice for a while and, even now, his words are broken, like those of a stroke victim.

'Ambulances refused to come help,' he says. 'It was only when my mother came that soldiers got us and carried us out into the street.' It took hours for them to be seen by a doctor. By then, they were clinging to life.

It was not the first time that violence had descended. Their house had been hit twice before. Neighbours had been killed. One old-age centre had been hit, harming seven pensioners inside. But, he said, he had nowhere else to go. His mother had been, until recently, looking after his seventy-eight-year-old father, who had been living paralysed for eighteen years with a stroke. They had thought about leaving for family in Kharkiv, but then . . . he lets the words trail out.

He had three operations and spent two months in hospital.

The International Committee of the Red Cross gave him medicine and pain relief and his mother brought him his meals. His wife lay nearby, in intensive care, for weeks. Now, she lives two hours away, looked after by her daughter from another relationship. They have only seen each other once since the incident.

Today, he needs help to go to the toilet, to dress, to cook. He has gone out only twice in the last year, once to get teeth pulled by a dentist. Two friends come from time to time to visit. The rest of the time, he sits on his couch, smoking cigarettes, doing word puzzles and watching Russian state television.

His legs shake as he talks, and he holds a floral handkerchief to his mouth to catch the saliva that spills from trembling lips. His mother looks on. It is not the first person that she has had to care for, she explains. Her own mother had a stroke at eighty-two and lived for five more years, immobilised. Then, her husband had his stroke. And now her son has this. Behind her, a picture of a saint peers through a veil of lace curtain.

Despite the suffering, though, they do not complain. They have received no funds from the Government to help with their new situation. They have had no visits from physiotherapists and no mental health counselling either. But this does not seem to upset them.

'What can you say?' he says. 'Who can I be angry with? Who is going to compensate me? What are they going to compensate me for, even?'

There is a fortitude to him and his mother that is striking. They do not dwell on the pain of the present, nor on the possible challenges of the future. When I point out that his mother is already old and may not be able to look after him for much longer, he does not say anything. She speaks out. 'A mother will never leave her child alone,' she says. And that is all that is said on the matter.

Their world is very small, yet they get by. The war has ripped into their lives, but they still live the best they can. And with that, he hauls himself from his bed and, taking painful steps using a stroller, walks through the small bungalow out into the morning sunshine.

He sits down in an electric wheelchair that lacks a working battery, and pulls out another cigarette, and smiles a thin smile.

The Dangers of Priti Patel's Racial Gatekeeping

Musa Okwonga

3 OCTOBER 2019

'This daughter of immigrants needs no lectures from the north London, metropolitan, liberal elite,' said the Home Secretary as she addressed the Conservative Party Conference.

A gleeful smile played across her face as she continued, stating her pledge to 'end the free movement of people once and for all'.

Priti Patel's remarks were greeted, one suspects, with much of the reaction that she desired: applause from her audience and condemnation from those appalled by the joy she seemed to take in the removal of their EU citizenship. Her words had two interesting elements.

Firstly, there is the phrase 'north London, metropolitan liberal elite'. This is a use of language which has been identified by leading commentators as having anti-Semitic connotations. Even if this wording was merely reckless or negligent, it is unacceptable in any political climate, particularly this one. There are far smarter ways to critique Jeremy Corbyn and Diane Abbott, who we could charitably assume were her intended targets, than reaching immediately for age-old racist tropes.

Secondly, there is the implication that as the 'daughter of immigrants' she will somehow not act against the rights and interests of immigrants, even as she seeks to usher in an era where freedom of movement will end. This implication is what we might call an act of racial gatekeeping.

Racial gatekeeping, put simply, is the assertion that the political figure in question could not possibly be criticised for regressive policies against a particular racially marginalised group, because they themselves are members of that group.

After all, how could a proud daughter of immigrants introduce laws so severe that they might have prevented her own parents from entering the country?

The racial gatekeeper is a crucial role because it allows a group of white people with racially regressive views to say 'look at us, we have found a non-white person who agrees with us, our policies therefore do not have racially regressive effects'. It is a flimsy intellectual premise – after all, our recent politics continues to remind us that gay people can support homophobic policies, and groups of women can support misogynistic politicians. But, the premise is not there to provide debate-winning logic. It is there to provide a sense of emotional validation for their audiences. Priti Patel knows this and that is probably a key reason why she was smiling when she gave her speech.

Racial gatekeepers are an interesting contradiction: they pride themselves on their rebellious streak, defying what people expect them to think; yet the positions which they take rigidly reinforce the racial status quo.

In the US, Candace Owens has urged black voters to abandon the Democratic Party and throw their electoral weight behind Donald Trump, arguing that the Democrats are not entitled to the black vote. That is of course entirely true, yet Owens has gone a step further – disregarding the testimony of a renowned academic that white nationalism is a grave problem in America. She has most recently been welcomed by

Marion Maréchal-Le Pen, a French politician with presidential ambitions. In an era where the far-right has seen startling electoral gains across the world, these supposed contrarians on the subject of race have rarely been so utterly conventional.

Racial gatekeepers are not mere careerists; these are political positions that they honestly hold. Neither are they self-loathing or ashamed of who they are – if anything, they are supremely proud of themselves, a defiant minority. They typically tend to believe that the problem of racism is exaggerated by the left, whom they see as all too ready to complain. In the case of James Cleverly, co-chairman of the Conservative Party, they have downplayed the use of blackface by their colleagues.

For them, society seems to be a sort of assault course, and those who rise do so by right – that with the sufficient amount of intelligence and diligence they can conquer all. If Patel can work her way up the political ladder, then why can't others who look just like her?

Their tragedy, though, is that they have fallen for the myth of meritocracy. At times, they have apparently told themselves that if they embody the most hardline aspects of their political parties – normally involving what they would call 'hard questions' about law and order, race and immigration – they will be embraced by their peers. And so, as recently as 2011, Patel voiced her support for capital punishment, a view from which she has since retreated. Last spring, Conservative MP Kwasi

Kwarteng mounted a defence of the Government's policy on Windrush that was striking for its lack of empathy.

Last winter, then Home Secretary Sajid Javid, keen to emphasise what he saw as a key racial element to paedophile rings, tweeted about 'sick Asian paedophiles'. By contrast, Javid has been curiously silent on the subject of paedophilia in English football, a case which broke earlier that year and the numbers for which are astonishing in their scale – 300 suspects identified, 849 victims and 340 clubs named. There were no tweets from Javid about 'sick white paedophiles', even though the overwhelming number of coaches and therefore abusers are likely to have been white. There were no public questions from Javid about what cultural reasons in the white community might have led these men to abuse boys, leading to, in the words of FA chairman Greg Clarke, 'the biggest crisis in the history of the sport'. It is interesting to see where and how Javid chooses to talk about race, and where and how he chooses not to.

Despite these exhaustive efforts, though, several of them may privately wonder if these lonely roads – roads which they assuredly chose – will ever end in the warm embraces which they seem to seek.

Javid, despite having shown his 'tough on refugee' credentials by returning early from a family holiday to patrol the English Channel, found himself inexplicably shunned by Donald Trump when the President visited the UK. Cleverly, despite routinely showing his party extraordinary loyalty, was not rewarded with the same support when he ran for its leadership, dropping out of the race only a few days after announcing his candidacy.

Meanwhile, Patel's ascent continues. On the same day that she made her speech about ending freedom of movement, in order to enable the arrival of the world's finest scientists, a story broke about how her Home Office had denied access to the family of one of those scientists. It was grimly fitting: a preview of Patel's world where the rhetoric will be brutal, the policies more brutal still.

It is unclear where Patel's journey will end. All that appears clear is that, before she is done, the happiness of many more people will be mere collateral damage for her ambition.

The Perversion of 'Press Freedom': Words Without Consequences

Brian Cathcart

1 NOVEMBER 2019

Rod Liddle, the associate editor of the *Spectator* magazine, which is edited by Fraser Nelson and published by BBC political interviewer Andrew Neil, published an article this month containing the following paragraph: 'My own choice of election date would be a day when universities are closed and Muslims are forbidden to do anything on pain of hell, or something. There must be one day like that in the Muslim calendar, surely? That would deliver at least 40 seats to the Tories, I reckon.'

What sort of person writes those words? For a start, obviously, someone who holds Muslims in contempt; who despises 4.4% of the UK population because of their religion and their ethnic heritage. For no other reason, he wishes to see them excluded from the franchise.

It hardly needs to be said, because no effort is being made to conceal it: he is a racist and those who collaborated in publishing these words are complicit in his racism. But there is more, for this is incitement to hatred: it encourages the idea that Muslims are contemptible, are pariahs and sub-human, and in doing so it feeds and legitimises racial hatred.

Those responsible for publishing Liddle's words in the *Spectator* know all about rising hate crime in this country. They know that every day in our streets, workplaces, trains and buses Muslims are subjected to racist abuse. They know they frequently suffer physical violence at the hands of the haters.

Anyone with an ounce of humanity would hesitate before taking any action likely to contribute to that suffering, such as expressing a view that might legitimise or inflame the feelings of those who inflict it. Such hesitation, such reflection is a basic element of civilised behaviour. In contrast, anyone who takes such an action casually and flippantly, and who does so more than once, is complicit in hate crime. And so are the people who facilitate their actions. That is where Liddle, Nelson and Neil now stand.

We know their defences: 'It was only a joke.' No it wasn't. 'Islam is a religion not a race, so this can't be racism.' First, such a claim is so ludicrously disingenuous only a fool would give it credit. And second, on its own terms, the paragraph is explicitly abusive of Muslims, not of Islam, and it is also explicitly ignorant of Islam.

Then there is the argument that it is Liddle's opinion and he is entitled to express it and that any attempt to prevent him expressing it is an attack on freedom of expression and on the freedom of the press. This is a grotesque perversion of what freedom and rights are really about. It is like saying: 'I have a sacred right to throw stones. Throwing stones is an expression of freedom, so nothing should stop me throwing stones. And I have no responsibility whatever for where the stones fall or for the damage they may cause.'

Liddle, Nelson and Neil pervert freedom of expression to diminish the rights of others. As they know, Muslims suffer a loss of rights because of this kind of hate speech. They are less able to live fulfilled lives, their freedom to worship is inhibited, their employment opportunities are restricted, their freedom of movement is curtailed, their physical safety is impaired.

In other words, the stones that Liddle throws hit people. He is a hate preacher, a radicaliser of youth, a siren voice calling out to bigots and thugs across the country and telling them it's okay to despise and vilify Muslims because they don't belong in our democracy and they should not enjoy the rights of white people. In invoking freedom of speech to defend such conduct, the *Spectator* appeals not to a reality in terms of human rights, but to a myth, and one that has been elegantly deconstructed by Nesrine Malik: 'The purpose of the myth is not to secure freedom of speech – that is, the right to express one's opinions without censorship, restraint or legal penalty. The purpose is to secure the licence to speak with impunity; not freedom of expression, but rather freedom from the consequences of that expression.'

They throw stones and they demand – in the name of press freedom – that we ignore the consequences of their stone-throwing. It goes without saying that they would never tolerate such treatment if it were meted out to them.

It is flagrant racism, but it is by no means a first for the *Spectator*. Don't look to the press 'regulator' IPSO to do anything about it because, by not taking group-based complaints, it is a facilitator of hate speech. And don't expect the BBC to ask its star political presenter Andrew Neil to account for his complicity in racism because it just won't. Neil and company do this stuff because they know they will get away with it; that is the world they have engineered.

13 December 2019

A general election in the UK results in a landslide majority of eighty seats for the Conservative Party led by Boris Johnson, while the Labour Party led by Jeremy Corbyn sinks to the lowest number and proportion of seats since 1935. Six weeks later, the UK officially leaves the European Union.

This is My England, and Yours –
Reclaiming Englishness

Peter Jukes

18 DECEMBER 2019

A photo passed to me by my mother was taken soon after the last war in the Suffolk garden of my adopted grandfather, Sidney Cox, a retired solicitor. Next to him in the scene is a Jewish refugee from Germany he housed for the duration of the war (I wish I could find her name). Next to her is my mother, Jean Cox, born of an Armenian asylum seeker and a Welsh mother, whom Sidney had adopted when she was six weeks old in 1926. Next to my mother is my dad, John Jukes, who had just joined the Royal Artillery.

This is my England and a part of yours too – so different from the English Defence League versions of bigotry or the white Etonian dream of exclusion and superiority.

Sidney, who died soon after this picture was taken, not only took in war-time refugees and adopted a daughter of a refugee, he was an early supporter of the Beveridge reforms for social welfare. The son of Birmingham grocers, he worked to pay to put his younger brother Clarence through college. Clarence did extremely well. He became speaker of the Oxford Union and a Liberal Party candidate during the 1910 General Election, during which he shared the hustings with none other than Winston Churchill.

Both brothers fought in the First World War; Sidney on the Western Front where he was at the cataclysmic Battle of the Somme (my mother said he refused to ever talk about it); Clarence joined the Suffolk Regiment and by 1917 he was attached as a pilot to the newly formed Royal Flying Corps. As the Ottoman Empire crumbled, and General Allenby sent his armies to take Jerusalem, my great-uncle was shot down over the ancient contested city. He died of his wounds weeks later and is now buried in Egypt.

While my adopted great-uncle's remains lie buried in the Saharan sands, my biological relatives were suffering from the first great genocide of the 20th Century in the deserts north of Jerusalem – an apocalypse which created the legal framework which was used to prosecute the Nazis at the Nuremberg Trials. More than a million Armenians were slaughtered by the Ottoman Turks in 1917, many of them led into the Syrian desert, not so far from where my great-uncle Clarence was shot down, and left to starve. That genocide was an inspiration to Hitler when planning to massacre the Poles. 'Who remembers the Armenians?' he said, dismissively.

All we know about my mother's biological father is that he was a violinist who fled from Armenia via Paris, and then met up with a smart Welsh woman in London who had matriculated (not usual in those days) from grammar school. When my mother finally decided to try to find out who they were many years later, she discovered the church adoption records had been destroyed in the Blitz.

Britain's imperial connections have always made England, and particularly London, one of the most diverse places in the world. The Empire was built on African slaves, Irish navvies, Malaysian sailors, Indian indentured labour, Sikh soldiers. By the time my mother was born, London had more Scottish inhabitants than Edinburgh, more Irish people than Dublin, and more Jews than the whole of Palestine. Much of this was economic, but Britain was also famed for its lack of secret police and tolerance of free speech, which encouraged Voltaire, Zola, Marx and Freud to seek asylum on our shores.

So much of our recent 'Airfix patriotism' omits the reality of loss and suffering. And all those expressions of Empire 2.0 – the white 'Anglosphere' aspirations of extreme Brexiters and the opaquely funded think tanks which want to recreate an offshore archipelago of deregulated dark money – miss the obligations that came with it.

One of the other key identifiers for Englishness is class and its confused permutations along economic, regional and cultural lines. As George Bernard Shaw once said, 'It is impossible for an Englishman to open his mouth without making some other Englishman hate or despise him.'

With seven out of the last ten Conservative prime ministers having been educated at one school – Eton – anyone would be forgiven for thinking that England was still stuck in a feudal state of serfs and liege lords. But England's post-war mobility, thanks to the Attlee Government, defined the 1950s and '60s. That mobility cuts two ways.

For my mother, it was mainly downward. She was sent to a fee-paying boarding school during the war and then made it to Royal Holloway College to study Chemistry. But all her six children went to state school: only three went to college, and she lived in humble and often impoverished circumstances. A lot of this was down to my dad, who at first blush looks like the epitome of upward mobility. Though he left school at fourteen, he was bright and was fast-tracked into the army officer class and taught Russian ('because they are the next enemy', he was told). He was a classic *Room at the Top* figure of 1960s mobility, training himself through night-school diplomas into the management class – however, this didn't last long.

He had met my mother at a dance in Royal Holloway College and it was passion at first sight. But he was unreliable and disappeared for months on end. By the time her father had died in 1949, my mother discovered she was pregnant and my dad disappeared again. It turned out that he had been sectioned with acute manic depression, as it was then known, at the British Army psychiatric hospital at Netley (where the famous Scottish psychiatrist R. D. Laing first practised). He was discharged from the army on medical grounds.

He married my mother and had another son. But soon my father was in prison – a two-year sentence for embezzlement which the judge made particularly harsh because my father had been an officer. Alone with two young kids, my mother had to commute right across London from Ilford to Teddington where she worked as a chemist at the Admiralty Research Laboratory.

None of her next three children were planned. I was number four, born during a brief period in the early 1960s when my dad was doing well as a management consultant. After my younger sister was born, her fifth child, my mother was sterilised. But, as soon as she returned to work, having trained as a social worker, she had another child: only this time fostered and then adopted.

Despite what Enoch Powell was claiming during his infamous speech in 1968 about Britain 'foaming with blood', England was integrating in many personal and unpredictable ways.

My kid brother Steven was handed over to Islington social services by his Scottish mother partly, it seems, because he was visibly of Afro-Caribbean origin – his father was Bajan and from Barbados.

My mother met Steven while she was training as a social worker and, in 1970, he came to live with us as a foster child. We all adored him immediately: he was funny, bright and we loved running our hands through his curly black hair. He changed his surname to Jukes and my mother adopted him, just as she had been adopted.

That, to me, with my half-Armenian mother and half-Bajan brother, was the key thing about the wider civil Englishness that is so opposed to the Powellite version: you can adopt it. Civic nationalism is not, nor ever should it be, a matter of blood or filiation, but freedom and affiliation.

In that way, I think of my mother and brother as quintessentially English, even if some English people often didn't think we were.

With her deep olive skin, black eyes and black hair (until it went white because of us!) my mother always told us it was a good thing that Hitler didn't win the war or she wouldn't have survived. My dad had blond hair and blue eyes. Taking more after my mother, I was dark enough to be mistaken for an Indian prince at primary school and, at a church choir, was mocked as 'Jewboy Jukes' (my mother told me to remind them that Jesus was Jewish). 'Spic' and 'dago' were the other common insults, but nothing compared to the litany of names my kid brother suffered – 'n***er', 'c**n', 's*mbo', 'jungle bunny' always seemed to run together. (It should be noted, though, that, for all the abuse, many English people treated our differences with

76

fascination and a slight amount of jealousy.)

The sense of racial vulnerability was not helped by the sudden onset of downward economic mobility as the post-war boom came to an end. Whether it was his own mania, or being conned by the various Scientology groups he had joined since the early 1960s, my dad went bankrupt – not once but twice – in the early 1970s.

By 1974, we were technically homeless and my kid brother was in danger of being returned to a children's home. Fortunately, my mother had just got a job as a psychiatric social worker. She separated from my father and the remaining family went to live in a tiny, pebble-dashed council house in a large, grim (now demolished) mental hospital miles from anywhere. I was going off the rails, even at fourteen, drinking, smoking, spending many nights out and getting endless detentions at school.

While my closest friend at the time ended up in prison, my destiny was different – partly due to the kindness of strangers and support from educational grants (which the 'culturally' middle class know how to access). With help from my oldest brother, my mother had, by the time I survived to sixth form, scraped together the deposit for a small end-of-terrace house. As always, even with a tiny garden, my mother managed to transform it with herbs, flowers and shrubs into a typical English garden. I still shared a bedroom with my kid brother, but I was now only minutes away from school. I got a scholarship to

Cambridge University, developed a posher accent and, for all intents and purposes, was identified by my Scottish friends as essentially 'English' – though I am loath to admit it and prefer to call myself an Armenian Welsh Londoner.

For years, I abandoned the notion of Englishness because of its ethnic and exclusive overtones. Now it's time to claim it back.

My personal history is not special. Go back a generation or two with most people in Britain and you'll find a family member with just as epic a story of migration and class displacement, resettlement and assimilation.

But, in terms of the current debate about 'white communities' or 'northern working-class men' and the struggle to find an English identity now that Scotland and Northern Ireland are moving away, let's not forget this quintessential thing about England: it is not an ethnicity, it is a culture – an incredibly wide and varied culture.

Its symbolic figure is Shakespeare, a channel beyond all others for a plurality of voices, an outward-looking fascination with other cultures and countries, who is – in the words of Jorge Luis Borges – 'everyone and no one'.

Everyone and no one. That could apply 400 years later to those sons of Irish immigrants in Liverpool – John Lennon and Paul McCartney – who learned to play Deep South rhythm and blues in Hamburg clubs and created that globally identified motley English tone you can also hear in David Bowie and Stormzy.

In all her varied migrant genes and imperial influences, my mother – who was born in the same year as the Queen – was quintessentially English. For her, 'manners' meant kindness to strangers and avoiding arrogance, and her favourite phrase to me if I achieved any success was 'well done, but don't get big-headed'.

Her influences were very English, from the liberal Anglicanism of *Honest to God*, to Vaughan Williams and 'The Lark Ascending', which reminded her of her Suffolk childhood. Her favourite film was *A Matter of Life and Death*, produced by Michael Powell and Emeric Pressburger (another immigrant!). Her accent sounded just like Jill Archer from the inveterate Radio 4 soap, and the sound of the *Archer's Omnibus Edition* heralded every Sunday, along with the pressure cooker hissing, the windows misted with condensation and food that tasted like boiled fog.

This is our England and ask anyone you know and they'll have a material link beyond this country because of our island status, at the centre of so many historic migrations since the Ice Age. The most English people I know can trace their lineage back to – wait for it – the Normans, who were of course originally Vikings.

This settled/settler Englishness is not the same as being a 'citizen of nowhere', as Theresa May called it, even if its manners and ethics treat others as citizens, wherever they come from in the world.

My mother, unlike the trite generalisations of academics of those who live 'somewhere' and metropolitan elites who live 'anywhere', was deeply rooted in time and place. The class mobility, regional migration and ethnic diversity in her background is ingrained in our national imperial story, like layers of geological strata, as soon as you look beyond the pale white cliffs of focus groups and political slogans.

Let us finally put paid to that narrow and untenable ethnic Englishness that has emerged from the wreckage of Brexit and rescue that other civic and civil England which welcomes strangers and has always accommodated difference.

Now is the Time to Uphold Metropolitan Values

Bonnie Greer

23 DECEMBER 2019

One of the things that has always fascinated me is how little the UK seems to care about its cities. Not that its cities are neglected or powerless. It is just that the country does not really seem to like them – not in the way that Americans like cities, or the French.

In Britain, the city seems to have a slightly sinister, foreign air; an ambiance of treachery and dishonesty. You move out of the city, not to one. Agatha Christie, that master of the prejudices of the English, places her detective Hercule Poirot in the centre of London. Whenever he goes to a village or a small town, he is treated with suspicion.

Once, during my time with an arts organisation based in Yorkshire, I spent some time in what could be called a 'pretty English village', with its carefully preserved streets and houses, tiny and authentic and pristine. It did not seem to matter to the present-day inhabitants of this village that these houses had once been cottages back in the 19th Century – hell holes where people were crammed like animals as they lived and died over a spinning loom; or that the well, now close to a fashionable restaurant, once carried disease and death. There is a heritage train close to the outskirts of the village, a slow-moving thing that chugs through the hills and through the vales. It even has steam. The city close to it, one of the great cities of the world, is referred to like some den of evil lurking in Another Place.

The election of a Conservative-majority Government under the slogan 'Get Brexit Done' hastens the divide between the city and those outside. The Tories are launching their latest attempt at division as a battle between the city and 'everywhere else'. This is because the city is a place where a dangerous cabal live known as 'the elite', who control everybody and everything. The 'real people' live outside of it. This idea could accelerate as the next five years crawl on, with the very reality of the metropolis – its complexity, multiculturalism, uncertainty and the fact of strangers – deemed somehow un-British.

This projection is positioned, for instance, on the royal family, those silent movie actors the nation apparently uses as exemplars of its dreams and hopes. There is a narrative around the Cambridges and the Sussexes which highlights this divide between the city and the village. Prince Harry, with his multicultural family, is seen as suspect, rogue, strange. That he and his wife and son reside in the grounds of the massive Windsor Castle, away from the public gaze, deep in a kind of countryside does not take away the point. The Duke and Duchess of Sussex are actually urban, international, multicultural. Therefore, in time, they will be rendered as 'bad'.

In contrast, the Duke and Duchess of Cambridge exemplify the village, the small town, the countryside. This is despite the fact that they mainly reside in Kensington Palace, a compound a few feet from a major road in Notting Hill. But they look and feel like the village. Catherine makes tree houses and William has pet names for the kids.

Now, more than ever, is the time to uphold the metropolitan values of live and let live; of embracing the world. The city does not 'take back control'; it relinquishes it.

In stating that an 'urban elite' runs the country, Boris Johnson – a product of the very elite he rails against – does not encourage unity, but sows discord.

I choose to live in the West End of London. I was born in a

big city and moved to another big city and I suspect that I will die in a big city. Let me state for the record that it is not nice to be awakened at four in the morning by 'I Will Survive' blasting out of a rickshaw. But I prefer that to the sound of a fox rattling around my bin.

Cities encourage, cities generate the thing that takes our species forward; that develops our brains: emergence – by the constant encountering of the new and the strange, which allows our brains to grow and change.

It is not that living in a village or a small town makes a person less clever. Rather, that the city and its collisions add another dimension to our humanness. One which is vital for the 21st Century – a century in which, soon enough, we will have to begin out-thinking machines in order to retain what it is that makes us human.

Omnicide: The Gravest of All Crimes

Danielle Celermajer

7 JANUARY 2020

As the full extent of the devastation of the Holocaust became apparent, a Polish Jew whose entire family had been killed,

Raphael Lemkin, came to realise that there was no word for the distinctive crime that had been committed: the murder of a people.

His life's work became finding a word to name the crime and then convincing the world to use it and condemn it: genocide.

Today, not only has genocide become a dreadful part of our lexicon, we recognise it as perhaps the gravest of all crimes.

During these first days of the third decade of the 21st Century, as we watch humans, animals, trees, insects, fungi, ecosystems, forests, rivers (and on and on) being killed, we find ourselves without a word to name what is happening.

In recent years, environmentalists have coined the term ecocide, the killing of ecosystems, but this is something more. This is the killing of everything: omnicide.

Some will object, no doubt, that the fires unfolding in Australia do not count as a 'cide' – a murder or killing – because it is a natural phenomenon, albeit an unspeakably regrettable one. Where is the murderous intent? It is difficult to locate, admittedly, but a new crime also requires a new understanding of culpability. Indeed, one of the most serious problems with the laws against genocide is that they were written in a way that requires that the specific intent to destroy a people can be shown to have existed. Even where it did exist, such intent most often remains hidden in people's dark hearts.

This time, though, we need to go much further. We need to understand that the responsibility for omnicide is various and layered. The role that those responsible play this time is almost always less direct, but its effect no less devastating. We are unlikely to identify anyone actively scheming the death of the 500 million wild animals believed to have died in the first month of this summer's Australian bushfires.

We can, however, identify the political representatives who refused to meet with fire chiefs who had tried to warn of, and act to mitigate, the impending disaster. The same political representatives who approved, and continue to approve, new coal mines in the face of scientific consensus on the effect that continuing to burn fossil fuels will have on the climate in general, and drought and temperatures in particular. The same political representatives who approve water being diverted to support resource extraction, when living beings are dying for want of water and our landscapes are drying to the point of conflagration.

We can identify the media owners who sponsor mass denial of the scientific evidence of the effects of a fossil-fuel-addicted economy on the climate. The same media owners who deploy the tools of mass manipulation to stoke fear, seed confusion, breed ignorance, and then provoke hostile divisions within communities.

We can identify the financial institutions that continue to invest in, and thereby prop up, toxic industries and that support the media owners to protect themselves from accumulating stranded assets. We can identify the investors who use their financial and social capital to support politicians who will protect their financial interests.

We can identify a corporate culture and a legal system – populated by lawyers, management consultants and financial analysts – that incentivise or even require companies to maximise short-term shareholder profit and externalise costs to the future and the planet.

And then we can identify parties closer to home.

Business owners and investors whose profits depend on systems of extraction and resource exploitation. Consumers addicted to lifestyles based on resource extraction and the exploitation of the natural world. Citizens who prioritise narrow, short-term interests over the sustainability of the planet and who lack the courage or fortitude to undertake the social and economic transformations required to give our children and the more-than-human world a future. People who do not bother to take the time or to make the effort to develop well-informed opinions, but would rather run to the comfort of the truisms of their tribe.

We can also identify the humans and human cultures that have told themselves that they are superior to, and thus have the right to dominate and exploit, other animals and the natural world. That they are the ones who get to flourish and that everything else that is here is here for our use. That other beings are seen not as life but resources.

None of those mentioned in this list developed a specific intent to kill everything. But all of us have created, and are creating, the conditions in which omnicide has become inevitable.

When I was growing up, my parents used to play a Bob Dylan song called 'Who Killed Davey Moore?' about a boxer who died in the ring when he was just thirty years old. Each verse begins with some party – the coach, the crowd, the manager, the gambling man, the boxing writer, the other fighter – answering the title's question: 'Who killed Davey Moore?' They each respond with 'not I' and then explain that they were just doing what it is that they do: going to the fight, writing about the fight, throwing the punches and so on. And, of course, they each told the truth.

We too are just doing what it is that we do: ensuring that the largest political donors support our political campaigns, maximising profits, ensuring a high share price, living a comfortable lifestyle, avoiding change, and lazily buying back into the conceit that we humans are special.

But, sometimes, just doing what it is that we do is sufficient to kill – not just Davey Moore, but everything. Omnicide is the gravest of all crimes. And, as with all crimes, those responsible must be held accountable.

How Apple is Aiding China's Repression

Stephen Delahunty

23 JANUARY 2020

In 2018, Apple CEO Tim Cook gave a speech in which he railed against the 'data industrial complex' and chastised companies such as Google and Facebook for weaponising user data.

'This is surveillance,' he said. 'This should make us very uncomfortable. It should unsettle us.'

In reality, the tech boss seems at ease with forgoing those virtues as the company's recent actions in China demonstrate: Apple's care for privacy, security and human rights appears to have a limit.

Apple's business relies on China. Its iPhones and other products are largely manufactured and assembled there and it is considered a key growth market.

Its stock reached an all-time high last month, with Chinese Government data showing a spike in iPhone sales. In the last quarter, the company reported $9 billion worth of revenue in China. Assuming Apple pulls in around $10 billion for the current quarter, that would amount to around $43 billion of revenue from China for the 2019 financial year.

China, Hong Kong and Taiwan together constitute Apple's

second largest market after the US. While Cook was having breakfast with President Donald Trump at Davos last month, pro-democracy protestors were clashing with police in Hong Kong, where Apple has been caught between its stated values and lucrative business interests.

Last month, the US company published its latest biannual transparency report, detailing government and private party requests for the period 1 January to 30 June 2019. It showed that Beijing – which is seeking to exert draconian control over Hong Kong, despite its agreement that the latter should retain its autonomy – made more than 15,000 data user requests and asked for 196 apps to be removed from the App store. Apple complied with 194 of the demands on the basis of 'alleged/ suspected violations of local law'. In addition, the company accepted ninety-four take-down requests for 'platform policy violations' from Chinese authorities, claiming that 'the vast majority relate to illegal gambling'. In October 2019, Apple removed HKmap.live from its App store, which was being used by pro-democracy protestors in Hong Kong to track police activity.

'We're experiencing human rights violations in both the digital and physical space,' said Andy Li, a rights activist in Hong Kong. 'It's notable that China is asking the company to take down apps that aid pro-democracy movements. China subsumes human rights freedoms to economic development. When you look at Chinese development projects around the world, they go ahead on the condition that those countries turn a blind eye to what's happening in China.'

Apple maintains that it removed HKmap.live not because of pressure from China, but because it posed a safety risk.

In Tibet, China's system of control has seen many arrested and accused of 'crimes' such as flying the Tibetan flag, showing support for the Dalai Lama, speaking in support of their culture and language, or contacting the outside world via social media.

After the passing of the new US cyber security laws in 2018, Apple announced that it was moving its iCloud data centre for Chinese users into a new local data centre in China in partnership with the state-owned company Guizhou-Cloud Big Data (GCBD).

'If you understand and agree, Apple and GCBD have the right to access your data stored on its servers,' said Lobsang Gyatso, the digital security programme director at the Tibet Action Institute. 'We found around twenty-nine Tibetan apps which are blocked on the Chinese App store and, when we contacted a developer, he had no idea this was happening. This lack of transparency and how Apple uses local laws as an excuse is a worrisome trend for me.'

Karen Reilly, a community director at GreatFire.org – an organisation that monitors internet censorship in China – said that the website *Applecensorship.com* was created because 'it compares the availability of apps by country' and 'this information was not readily available before'.

'This censorship continues, even when someone leaves China,' she added. 'App store censorship is particularly troubling because it expands the reach of censors past the Great Firewall.'

Last August, iPhone vulnerabilities were revealed that compromised a person's phone if they visited certain websites and it was reported that the exploits were used to target China's minority Uyghur Muslim population – more than a million of whom have been thrown into camps in the western Xinjiang province. When Apple finally published a statement addressing the vulnerabilities, it acknowledged that Uyghur Muslims had been the intended target.

IBM has helped design China's surveillance regime through the use of smart cities, which has essentially automated racism.

'In East Turkistan, the Chinese Government has established a tight network of police checkpoints and CCTV cameras, including "three-dimensional portrait and integrated data doors", which scan the faces of individuals and read information from their electronic devices,' Zumretay Arkin, a Uyghur human rights advocate from the World Uyghur Congress, said. 'Since 2018, mainland Chinese provinces and regions have been investing in facial recognition systems for public surveillance which are claimed to be able to identify "Uyghur attributes".'

In addition, Apple's 'safe browsing' feature is a Safari web browser tool that warns people when they may be visiting malicious sites. In China, it relies on a database compiled by Tencent, a Chinese internet company with ties to the Government.

Apple has argued that its presence in China 'helps promote greater openness and facilitates the free flow of ideas and information'. However, Sondhya Gupta, a campaigner with corporate watchdog SumOfUs, said that Apple has twisted itself into a knot of hypocrisy.

'Corporations and governments alike have long argued that it's by trading with repressive regimes we can challenge them on human rights and improve the lives of people living under their rule,' she said. 'But it's clear that this is far from reality. The Chinese Government seems to have been emboldened, not chastened, by Apple's willingness to do business with it.'

The Idea of Europe: Peter and Markie's Loon-Clad '70s Euro-Rampage

Peter Jukes

31 JANUARY 2020

It was 1977. We were sixteen. Two schoolboys from a provincial town. But Britain had just voted 'Remain' in the first Brexit referendum. We had exams coming up and a long summer holiday ahead. And we were both obsessed by the Idea of Europe.

Personally, I blame Ernest Hemingway. If we hadn't just read *For Whom the Bell Tolls*, Markie and I would never have planned to hitchhike all the way to Spain, where we expected to find some life-and-death battle between right and wrong, and some gamine-haired girl for whom we'd make the earth move.

We'd sit on Markie's veranda (his was a working-class family living in a detached middle-class house, while I was from a middle-class family living in a working-class terrace), smoking Gitanes cigarettes, strumming Am G F E on our Spanish guitars, before dancing around the electric fire with its fake-flame effect, imagining the real fires and shadows of flamenco.

The Italian film director Franco Zeffirelli is also to blame. *Romeo and Juliet* was our set text for exams that year, and we'd gone to the local cinema on a school trip to see Zeffirelli's new version. So did the girls from the high school next door. While they guffawed and squawked at the actors' codpieces, most of the grammar schoolboys were misty-eyed and mournful. Soppy romantics, Markie and I would finish our exams, and then on to Verona to fight for our lives like Mercutio in some hot, dusty Italian square.

Forty years ago, Britain still had a manufacturing industry, and our London overspill town was ringed by light industrial estates. Markie got work in his dad's aerial factory, bending bits of aluminium, plastic and wires together, while I got a summer job at a turned-parts factory where my dad was employed as a lathe operator after his multiple bankruptcies. They paid 50p an hour. After six weeks, we'd have enough to get across the Channel, and then flamenco and Juliet awaited.

But then along came Günter Grass to ruin it all. I was in the town-centre bookshop, warily looking for something to read. Back in those days, you couldn't even open a book without being forced to pay for it. A social-worker friend of my mother's appeared who pointed out a paperback with a golden cover. She knew I'd just finished the whole of Tolkien's *The Lord of the Rings* and told me that this was the closest she'd come to reading anything so fantastical.

I bought it: *The Tin Drum*. It should have come with a health warning. Günter Grass's war-time classic was like a bad trip on cannabis resin – and I'd had a few of those. It started in Gdańsk on the eve of the German invasion of Poland with a dead horse's head wriggling full of eels – and went downhill from there. I used to try to read it while cutting metal strips in the turned-parts factory. I would look up from my book at the strange beauty of the light bouncing off steel rods from the grimy skylights of the factory. And regularly explode the circular blade in a spatter of coolant fluid and sharp metal.

After six or seven lost blades, the foreman was furious. He

called me a 'f**king student' and explained how he'd gone to school with no shoes. My dad kept quiet at his lathe, with his usual Buddha-like detachment. He'd risen up to being a management consultant and, after a series of disasters, was back on the factory floor.

The workers, wearing overalls and eating fish and chips in the canteen, were completely separated from the management, who arrived in flash Rovers, wore pastel shirts, braces and ties, and were served by waitresses in their own restaurant. I didn't know how my dad coped with the snootiness and segregation, having once promoted Scandinavian theories of small egalitarian work teams as a consultant. But he smiled enigmatically still turning the lathe and said, 'Happiness can come from making a perfect cup of tea.' This was my dad: a walking, talking copy of *Zen and the Art of Motorcycle Maintenance*. If I couldn't read my book, I'd learn his way of alleviating the tedium.

They moved me on from breaking circular saws to polishing steel tubing. Every few hundred or so I'd select one or two for special treatment, filing carefully so every edge was smooth to the touch, and burnishing them so lovingly they shone like moonlight. Then I'd sneak them home. This was my revenge on class-ridden 1970s British industry. They'd make perfect slides for an American-style guitar. But, when I gave one to Markie, he pointed out that the steel was heavy for his finger, and made a wrenching sound on nylon strings like an exploding saw.

The tubes rusted unused in my bedroom. We had more important things to plan. Markie had nearly finished *The Tin Drum* and was trying to teach me swear words in German, Hungarian and Serbo-Croat. We agreed not to take our guitars because of the extra clutter. Rather than busking our way to Spain, we'd do some grape-picking near the Spanish border to top up the £120 we'd both saved. (Because of exchange controls, anything over £100 had to be stamped on the back of our passports.) I told my mother we'd be gone for about six weeks and we booked our ferry tickets. Nothing would stop us now. We were making the crossing to that vast unexplored place: the Continent.

On the platform for the night ferry at Victoria station, I first saw her. It was just like Dylan's song 'One More Cup of Coffee'. Her skin was white, her hair was black and her eyes like two diamonds in the sky. But she wasn't Mexican or Spanish. She was from north London. Her mum had spotted us waiting for the train and, since we were about her age, asked us if we could look after her daughter for the crossing. Clara. Her name was Clara. And her heart was like an ocean, mysterious and deep.

Unfortunately, Clara – whose diamond eyes were rimmed by thick glasses – didn't quite see things that way. We arrived that morning shattered at the Gare du Nord in Paris and helped her negotiate the metro to the Gare Montparnasse which would take her away to where she was staying for a summer exchange. She gave me a brochure of where she was staying – some enormous chateau near Angoulême. I promised to write and come and find her in the dark forests of Aquitaine. And then she was gone. To the valley below.

As we took the metro as far south as we could, the main thing that told us we were in Europe were the exotic overtones of digested garlic from sewers and fresh bread from shops. If not quite the Idea of Europe, this was the Smell of it. No matter: soon we'd be in Spain surrounded by the scent of orange groves. But first, we'd have to inhale petrol and diesel fumes as we pitched up on a main road heading south and put our thumbs out.

Then it started to rain.

I learned later that Paris is one of the rainiest cities in Europe, worse than London, and we weren't prepared. Markie had a relatively cool-for-the-'70s cagoule. All I had was a thick bright yellow fisherman's cape that smelt of an inflatable kids' swimming pool someone had packed away without cleaning many summers ago. The only way to wear it was to pull it over my rucksack – a grey canvas lump my oldest brother had first used in the 1950s – until I looked, in Markie's words, like some huge drowned bee.

The sight of a sixteen-year-old with his thumb out accompanied by a huge drowned bee didn't help with the lifts. It took hours to get the first ride. And every lift was just for a few miles. By the time evening came, we were dumped on the out-skirts of some outlandish suburban development near Corbeil-Essones called Évry. If this was Europe, Évry was more like some dystopia from a 1970s science-fiction novella – half-completed tower blocks surrounded by diggers and mounds of mud.

After hours walking around the modernist nightmare, we managed to find some shops open in a nearby village and bought what we thought was roast chicken from a local store (spoiler alert – it wasn't chicken!). As night fell, we bumped into some equally lost Spanish hitchhiker, and all decided to camp in a local field. It wasn't till morning that we discovered the field was actually a rubbish dump. The Spaniard only had a one-man tent and, out of sulkiness or chivalry (I can't remember which), I'd given up my place in it for Markie. Instead, I climbed up a tree and tied my belt to the trunk to stop me falling (I must have seen this in some film).

Though I barely slept, lashed semi-upright, I had a better night than Markie. He'd slept head-to-toe with the Spaniard without appreciating that the tent was pitched downhill. With his head sliding out of the tent, he became an irresistible lure for slugs. From time to time, I heard screams in the night when Markie would lash out with the scout knife he'd borrowed from our friend Paul Lennon to fight off the attack of killer slugs.

We started to hitchhike again. It started to rain again. And there were no cars here. Only one every half hour. Two years of unprecedented summer heatwaves stuck in the dull English provinces, baking in its multi-storey car parks and municipal tennis courts, and now what? The wettest summer in western Europe for years. We stood on the bleak hard shoulder and shivered. By now something very Günter Grass was obsessing me: a strange, herbal, meaty smell emanating from my sleeping bag, the bottom of my rucksack, my underarms. What was it?

Then the first car for an hour – a beaten-up Deux Chevaux – suddenly put on its brake lights and reversed. Where did we want to go? the two young men inside asked. 'Le Sud,' we said, tentatively. They laughed. They were going all the way to Provence. Well, it wasn't quite Spain, but it was our first proper lift for any distance. We were on our way.

The heavy clouds began to break up as the two students drove us south and over the Massif Central. They picked up another hitchhiker – a girl, the first girl I'd talked to since Clara. I thought of her thinking about me somewhere in the wilds of Aquitaine. Some runny cheese was handed out with fresh crusty bread. This Europe was cool – they had a guitar and smoked Gaulois and played political ballads on their tape machine. We started singing along. '*Monsieur, Le President, il faut t'ecrit une lettre*'. It was like being driven back into the 1960s, that decade our older brothers enjoyed but we'd only experienced like some bad Monday morning hangover.

Some twelve hours later, once we'd said goodbye to our radical friends at a service station somewhere near Avignon, we hitched another ride south. The driver and his passenger were turning off at a place called Sète, many miles short of the Spanish border. It was well past midnight as he dumped us on the verge of the autoroute and we looked for a place to sleep in an adjacent field: a rocky, rutted hillside, with lines of gnarled vines. The grapes were small, hard and inedible. But we ate them anyway. We'd made it to the South! It wasn't raining and below the Mediterranean was glistening in the moonlight. Instead of the meaty herbal smell in my sleeping bag, I could smell rosemary and pine . . .

Markie told me to shut up. He couldn't smell anything, or at least anything new. For some reason, the roadside car fumes or the sleeplessness, his sense of smell had seized up and the runny Camembert we ate with the students had lodged permanently in his nose. He'd tried everything – coffee, chocolate, cheap red wine and now these bitter unripe grapes. 'I can't smell anything any more, Pete!' he said. 'All I can smell is that cheese!'

Many years later, Markie discovered he had an extreme lactose intolerance and that polyps had formed in his nostrils. I thought it was just a Günter Grass moment and fell fast asleep almost immediately. But, invaded by a universe of Camembert, Markie didn't sleep at all and the next thing I knew he was shaking me: 'Pete. Get up. Someone is coming.'

A serene blue sky and bright sun. The blue Mediterranean coast below. Then a shout, a whistle and a clink of iron. I sat up to see a tough, swarthy-looking farmer bringing his horse and a plough towards us. In a second or two he would see us. What was the punishment for trespassing down here? What if we got done for scrumping his grapes? Moments later, the peasant and his horse must have seen something extraordinary: two pale, unwashed teenagers running down his vineyard towards the motorway and the sea.

We kept on running, right over the junction towards the coast. I wanted to stop and start hitching to Spain, but Markie had had enough by now. A second night in a row out in the open, a third night in a row he hadn't slept; the Smell of Europe was invading him. He needed a bed, a youth hostel, a roof over his head, and now my rucksack was broken.

So, we kept on going on the road till we hit the sea.

The *auberge de jeunesse* in Sète was run by a surly *chef d'auberge* who was so big and moustachioed we thought he looked like Obelix from the *Asterix* cartoons. We saw everything in clichés. Down in the quayside, as a sailmaker carefully stitched the straps on my mildewed rucksack back together (his nose wrinkling and the strange meaty smell persisting inside), we felt like we were in a Van Gogh painting: people sipping coffee and Pernod over bright tablecloths, azure boat hulls, white seagulls, cypress trees like dark flames on the hills.

At that time, Britain had no café culture, and unlike today, it was rare to see outdoor seating. But it wasn't just the cultural differences that made us feel we were finally in Europe, but the affluence compared to '70s Britain.

Our army surplus gear, scrawny white bodies, empty pockets that could only afford rations of sardines and cheese, all exposed just how poor England was in comparison with Europe. This was most acute and embarrassing on the town's small beach. There all the teenagers were tanned and toned and wearing sunglasses – the men in bright Speedo swimming trunks, the women in tiny chic bikinis, often with the top half removed. We tried not to look at the topless bathers. They certainly wouldn't look at us. Without sun cream, we slowly fried in the sun, turning into what the French call *crevettes* – prawns.

Famished and dehydrated, we lashed out on our first cooked meal for four days – steak frites in the harbour. Though the meat was gristly, and by 'chips' they mean 'crisps', at least the wine was cheap. And we drank a lot. Glowing with heat and alcohol, we'd then go down to the shore and sit on the rocks gazing at the waves. We seemed to have spent several days just watching waves, mesmerised.

If the French wouldn't talk to us, our fellow travellers would. At the youth hostel on a small hill overlooking the town, we shared a dorm with two young Germans. Wolfgang was our typical image of a Teuton: athletic, healthy and tall, topped with blond curly hair. His friend Roman was more wolfish: gaunt with biker-style greasy hair, drooping moustache. Markie spoke a bit of German, but typically they spoke excellent English. When not watching the waves, we'd while away the hot afternoons with them, drinking more cheap red wine, and practising knife-throwing against a pine tree.

And that's how the fight about the knife began.

One of our throws had missed the tree and skidded along the grass to where some other hosteller was sitting. He was in no danger but must have snitched on us to the *chef d'auberge*. Obelix strode up and, before we could say anything, took Markie's scout knife from where he'd deftly lodged it in the pine bark. We followed Obelix back to his office, remonstrating in broken French. Silent and unimpressed, he put the knife in one of the drawers of his desk and muttered some unknown dismissive argot before going back about his business.

Markie was not having this. The injustice was unbelievable. Firstly, this wasn't Markie's knife but Paul Lennon's. Secondly, he needed the knife to cut bread, spread runny cheese, open sardine cans and fend off marauding slugs. Markie was always less rule-bound and conventional than me, and before I could stop him, he had darted into Obelix's office and retrieved the scout knife from the drawer. We both ran back to our dorm to hide the knife, nervously laughing, and explained to Roman and Wolfgang our great escape.

That was tempting fate. Soon Obelix was back in the dorm,

bigger than ever, demanding to know which *voleur* had taken the knife. According to Markie, what happened next was my fault as I started protesting unnecessarily and incriminating myself. In my more heroic recollection, the *chef d'auberge* started jabbing his finger at me, accusingly. '*J'ai pas prit le couteau*,' I said righteously. He didn't like that. Before I could protest again, a sharp right hook had knocked me straight to the floor.

Everyone else froze. Obelix looked down, curious, obviously wondering what I'd do next. I was stunned but I didn't have the knife. I hadn't taken it. I wasn't a *voleur*. I scrambled up, my jaw hurting, but, mustering my last bit of dignity, I yelled, '*J'ai pas prit le couteau!*'

I remember his look. It was the same look my dad gave me earlier that year when he forcibly tried to make me sit down at a Sunday dinner. The strength of my resistance surprised him. I was skinny but nearly six feet tall. He could easily beat me. But was it worth the trouble? Obelix obviously had the same thought. He told us both to pack our things and be out first thing tomorrow.

When he left, we all rejoiced. Markie had kept his knife and – just as I'd dreamed watching *Romeo and Juliet* – I'd kept some dignity in a fight to the death. We got drunk with Roman and Wolfgang. Not surprisingly, given the cheap wine and adrenaline, all four of us ended up talking about being on different sides in two world wars. In a different generation, we would have been mortal enemies – instead we were comrades in arms against the oppression of the youth hostel commissar. The night ended in tears and hugs and we collapsed on our bunks, the alcohol anaesthetising my sore jaw. We shared addresses with the Germans for letter-writing, and the next day left for Spain.

Hitching in Europe then was a numbers game. Most drivers sped past without looking, and most of those who did then looked away quickly. It was only once in a while – probably one in every twenty – that the red brake lights would light up and we'd be on our way. But we didn't get back to the autoroute till evening and, under the signposts south for Narbonne and Barcelone (French spelling), we'd barely had half a dozen cars in a couple of hours.

Then a van passed, erratically stopping and starting with a grating of gears, with two men in the front seats, apparently arguing. At the bottom of the slip road, just before they hit the motorway, the van's brake lights came on and they started reversing. Our luck was up. We ran towards the van only to find two men inside still arguing, looking at a book. We waved through the window at them, our thumbs up.

The passenger wound down the window and pointed to a beaten-up road atlas of Europe. I'm still convinced to this day he was holding it upside down. Markie worked out they had taken the wrong turn. We pointed to the other side of the motorway. The men nodded and gestured for us to get in the back. We threw our rucksacks in the empty van and they carried on reversing up the slip road to the junction.

They didn't understand a word of English so Markie was trying his impressive array of languages to explain we were heading to Spain. We were across the junction when we finally understood where they were going. Switzerland. Markie and I looked at each other.

What the hell? Somewhere is better than nowhere. Neither of us had ever been. Okay. Switzerland.

As they sped north, past the vineyard where we'd slept, we settled on our rucksacks in the back of the van. From Switzerland we could go across the Alps to Italy. So Hemingway would have to be put on hold, but Zeffirelli – here we come . . .

Next thing we knew our rucksacks were flying around the back of the van and we were slithering across the ribbed metal floor. They'd missed another turning. When this kept on happening we began to realise that they couldn't actually read the motorway signs. We tried to help with navigation, but despite my 'O' Level Spanish, Markie's German and our joint French, the driver and his passenger spoke a language which had no recognisable features. Markie noticed they pronounced 'Deutsch' as 'Detch'.

To fill the silence, they started playing music on an old four-track cassette machine which sounded like the Smurfs. I joked that maybe they were Smurfs – full size for sure, and without the blue skin or white hats. Markie worked out that they came from a part of Switzerland where they spoke Romansh. This was the only romance we were going to get that night.

In the small hours they dropped us off on the outskirts of Lausanne where – of course – it was raining again. Before long, we were picked up by a well-off young guy with a top-of-the-range Citroën who offered to take us to the youth hostel, though at that hour he doubted it was open. Compared to hurtling around the van, this was the plushest ride we'd ever had, accompanied by a cool jazz soundtrack on his stereo – but it made us even more reluctant to return to the cold wet Lausanne night. When he did, he was right. The place was shut and we wandered around the heavily defended building looking for a way in.

A young Italian guy inside heard us and opened a window. In my memory, it was a high window and I helped Markie clamber in, but without someone to boost me up, I couldn't follow. In Markie's recollection, the window was easy to get into, but I just backed off because I was afraid of breaking the rules. (To which my reply is: after the knife-stealing incident, who could blame me?) Either way, in a haughty sulk, I said I'd sleep in the local railway station and find him the next morning.

Battling the rain with my fisherman's cape, I found Lausanne's main train station was still open and tried to settle down on the plastic chairs in the waiting room. But the fluorescent lights were flickering and grim, and then I noticed someone was staring at me.

At first glance, he looked like a middle-aged businessman on an important trip, albeit at four o'clock in the morning. But his eyes were gaunt and staring, and he was picking cigar butts off the floor and smoking them. I closed my eyes and tried to ignore him. Next thing I knew, a whiff of stale cigar and he was standing over me.

Close up, the businessman's brown suit was stained and dusty, as if he'd put it on a year ago and never changed. He stank of stale cigars. Though he was trim and his hair still dark, his skin was stretched taut and translucent around his hollow red eyes as if formed out of tobacco and ash. He stared at me for ages. I wondered where I'd packed my knife. Then he started talking to me in French. I thought of getting out of the waiting room, but where else was there to go? I can't remember if I said anything, but he quickly worked out I was a traveller. '*Ah, jeune homme,*' he laughed '*tu veux voyager. Tu veux voir le monde. Mais il y a rien à voir.*' He kept on like this all night.

'So you want to travel, to see the world . . . but you'll learn . . . there's nothing to see,' mocked the Man in the Brown Suit. This was worse than a physical assault. His voice was seeping into my head, trying to ruin my dreams of travel and romance. He was like a character from an Albert Camus novel, full of alienation and despair. Instead of the epic Idea of Europe, he infected me with the Boredom of Europe, its ennui, lack of identity, uniformity: a vast waiting room of plastic seats and fluorescent lights that stretched across the Continent to eternity, with nothing to look forward to.

Lausanne and Switzerland came to represent the worst of Europe, a place of cloud and rain and houses as firmly shut as bank vaults. The clouds broke long enough so we could see the Alps and take a rowing boat out onto Lac Leman. But, with a punitive exchange rate, the Swiss Franc only seemed to welcome reclusive movie stars or international financiers. I managed to spend a whole day's allowance on just one biscuit each in a pâtisserie, and it was so aniseed flavoured it made me gag. We got out of Lausanne as quick as we could, up the mountains to a town called Martigny where the *auberge de jeunesse* was modern, colourful and buried deep underground. We spent a night in the best equipped of all youth hostels of the trip. Apparently, it also doubled up as a nuclear bunker.

Next morning, a nice elderly couple took us all the way up to the Grand St Bernard Pass where we posed for photos, shivering in front of the snow. With fresh provisions and some carafes of cheap red wine we'd bought at a shack, we started to walk down the mountain towards Italy. A tractor stopped to give us a lift. We sat on the back of his trailer and, for the next hour or so, were rattled so hard that the liquid sprung from its loose corked bottles and sprayed us both with a covering of red wine.

Dumped on a lane on the edge of a forest, we couldn't tell if we were in Italy yet. The trees were deciduous and the air so cool we could have been back in Buckinghamshire. Then a guy on a scooter stopped and told us we were about twenty miles short of the town of Aosta. We checked it on the map. He offered to take one of us there on the back of his moped. Again, out of nobility, fear or sulkiness, who knows which, I let Markie take the ride to where he'd meet me at a service station. And then he was gone.

For the first time in many days, I was on my own. What was I doing here? What happened to making the earth move for that gamine Spanish resistance fighter? When would our adventures really begin? And would Markie wait for me? What if we lost each other?

I got a lift pretty quickly; in fact I overtook Markie on the scooter, and was waiting for him at the service station. The next ride took us all the way to Milan. The car was actually a taxi, but the cab driver was off work and had picked up a young communist woman and they spent the whole journey arguing about politics, each trying to co-opt us to their side.

Milan embodied the contradiction of all our travelling. Classy, expensive and unaffordable in the centre; grim and industrial on its outskirts. We spent most of the time cadging lifts on the ring roads, so we decided to cut our losses and take a train to Rome. On the train, we met two young French-speaking travellers, Denis and Pierre, who seemed – like us – to spend most of their money on cheap wine. We had a hard time understanding their thick accents until they explained they were French Canadians, Québécois. They were a bit shady, and liked the fact we both had knives. But they seemed to be on a mission to see the Pope: they kept talking about the 'Vatch-ca' in their twangy dialect.

Once again, the *auberge de jeunesse* in Rome was full to capacity, so the four of us had to sleep out on the hills where hundreds of other young travellers were sleeping rough. When it rained, we headed down to a nearby petrol station for cover until we realised it was a notorious pick-up spot for prostitutes in miniskirts and high heels. They didn't look at us ragged English boys, but more than once we were propositioned by men looking for rent boys.

At the Castel San Pietro, we met a young American backpacker who soon joined all four of us on our tours and she took a shine to Markie. In the Coliseum, which at the time was surrounded by a fast impenetrable ring of traffic, she apparently asked him to go down to the catacombs with her – but he resisted. Young Italian men would make disgusting squelching sounds with their tongues as she walked past with us. They seemed obsessed with sex and appeared to have scrubbed their jeans around their crotches so that walking in the Roman streets all you could see were bobbing pale blue codpieces.

Denis and Pierre managed to drag us along with them to the 'Vatch-ca' but all I can remember is the dome of St Peter's – how vast it was and how it barely seemed to move as we walked under it. We couldn't be bothered to queue for hours for the Sistine Chapel and instead bought more cheap wine.

Pointless sightseeing. Cheap wine. Cheap cigarettes. Tinned sardines. Cheese. Bread. The travelling was taking its toll. One evening, as the setting sun flared red on the immense white marble wedding cake of the Vittoriano monument, I burst into tears. Markie and the Québécois were mystified. I tried to explain – the kitsch beauty, the red sun. It was fascism, I explained. I was feeling the terrible glory and horror of fascism. They had no idea what I was talking about, and to be honest, neither did I. But I felt much better once the tears had expressed the overload of alcohol in my system. But time was running out. We needed to move on.

We said goodbye to Pierre and Denis and caught a train over the Apennines one dawn, heading to the Adriatic coast. At Bari and Brindisi there were no youth hostels, but at least it seemed warm, so we slept under the fishing boats, waking up every morning soaked by sea mist. Both of us began to develop wracking coughs.

As we continued north along the east coast, I was feeling more and more unwell but then a woman actually stopped to give us a lift. A lone woman? This was a first. It was only when she stopped to fill her Fiat with petrol that we understood why she'd stopped for two British teenagers. She must have been six foot six tall, and towered over both of us. She offered to take us all the way to Venice, but we were determined to see Verona where Mercutio expired. With my smattering of Spanish I could just understand her and she laughed when I said, '*Bologna basta*.'

Back to the ring roads and the gritty reality of city peripheries. We were constantly dropped off in the concrete jungle of slip roads and flyovers. On one occasion, the Italian police stopped and fined us for trying to hitchhike on the autostrada. But, unless we wanted to walk miles alongside dangerous traffic, we had little choice. Somewhere near the outskirts of Padua, we bedded down for the night in an irrigation ditch around some peach trees. But the place was infested with rats and, as they swam and jumped around us, we sat up all night, back to back, knives at the ready.

We never did make it to Verona, but instead took a lift to Venice where nemesis awaited. Once again, the youth hostel on the island of Giudecca was full, so we decided to sleep on the pavements outside. Every dawn, to accompany the glory of the sun glinting over the towers, domes and spires of Venice, a stray dog would try to burrow into our sleeping bags. I don't know what he was looking for. And he was well advised to steer clear of my sleeping bag. After the strange herbal smell from northern France, it was now dominated by something more noxious. On top of the sea-mist cough, my guts were finally rebelling from the diet of tinned sardines and wine.

We were just getting off a *vaporetto* from the Grand Canal when I realised I couldn't find them – my few remaining traveller's cheques. Incredibly, we'd been able to survive for over three weeks on only £60 each, but the last £60 had gone missing. Markie was exasperated. I was always losing things or being careless about my belongings. For the first time we argued and I told him to go ahead without me. I'd find the missing traveller's cheques; I'd go to the police, get the money back and meet him in Yugoslavia – the next phase of our trip. He resisted, but I pushed and pushed, my self-immolating pride getting the better of me. I insisted on walking him to the bus station and said I'd see him in Zadar.

And then I was alone in the big city and very sorry for myself. In the Piazza San Marco none of the drinks or food were in my price range. The waiters looked at me with disdain and sniffed (as well they would do). I was living off one tin of sardines for a whole day. What was I going to do? I reported the missing cheques to the police, but no one had handed them in. They suggested I should go to the British consulate for help, and I did, telling my story to a sympathetic secretary who immediately got me an aspirin and ushered me in to see the main consul. Bald, dapper, with a trimmed moustache and an unflappable upper-class accent, he asked me what had happened and then for my home phone number. Before I could stop him, he had called my mother (my younger sister answered the phone first) and told her to wire a bank £60 to buy a train ticket so I could go home immediately: I was only sixteen and obviously unwell.

This was not what I wanted. This wasn't the adventure I'd

planned. All those weeks saving up. All those poems, books, movies, dreams. But I was also secretly relieved. The idea of sleeping in my own bed in the room I shared with my kid brother seemed much better than tramping around these alien streets, treated like a beggar.

When I got back to the youth hostel, Markie was waiting for me. He said he couldn't bear to leave without me and would wait in Venice till I got my money back. Then I had to break my bad news. The look on Markie's face was painful. I had not only let down my own dreams, but his too. He couldn't abandon me, and now I was abandoning him. Markie resolved to continue and we had an awkward parting as I headed for the night train back to Paris.

I spent a delirious night on the train there, retching on sardines as dawn broke over the Jura Mountains. I was completely depleted. As I arrived at the Gare du Nord with my broken rucksack, my filthy clothes, all I could think about was how to explain this to my friends and family. What happened to that great narrative we'd both planned?

And then I saw her, screwing up her eyes, looking up to the train departure timetable. It was Clara! So maybe there was a point to this journey after all. Finally the story had come full circle. I told Clara the whole saga as we took the train to Calais and boarded the night ferry. She was sympathetic. I told her more of my dreams and hopes as we sat on the deck and watched the White Cliffs of Dover looming in the dark. And, on the train back to Victoria station, I tried to embrace her. She wasn't that sympathetic and pushed me away.

Back home, I slept for three days and was diagnosed with gastroenteritis. Markie took a week to hitch back home through Austria and Germany, where – on his own – he was regularly picked up by men whose intents were not innocent, and one evening had to barricade himself in a room and get out Paul Lennon's knife to defend himself from their predatory advances. (At least I hadn't been thumped by Obelix in vain.) So neither of us found romance on our adventure, in fact the opposite. But someone did find my traveller's cheques. About a year later, they were sent back via the Venice police and I could refund my mum.

It took many more years to work out the mystery of the meaty herbal smell of French chicken-that-wasn't-chicken. On an exchange trip to the US, I made the mistake of going out hunting in a Utah orchard, where they said the local buck rabbits were pests and they mesmerised them in the bright lights of a truck before shooting them with shotguns. I wish I hadn't gone. I'm still haunted by the robotic dance of a buck rabbit stricken with lead pellets and the wheezing sound it made when it died. But, when my host began to skin and gut the rabbit, the hot innards slithered out with that unmistakable smell that had penetrated my sleeping bag and rucksack in France. He explained that the rabbits sometimes fed on clover, and gave the meat this weird flavour that made the meat almost inedible.

*

Over the past four decades, Markie and I have been back to the places we visited many times. He went to live in Greece for a while. I part-owned a small gîte for a while not far away from the vineyard where we first saw the Mediterranean sun. We made it to Spain on later trips, and have been to Paris, Rome, Venice (though not Lausanne). But, if truth be told, none of these journeys ever had quite the crazy savour of our hitch-hiking adventures in 1977. We were looking for adventure and thought we'd failed to find it. But we were in it all the time. Like Britain in the European Union, we didn't know what great times we had until they were over.

Though, at the end of 2020, Britain has finally divorced itself from the EU, the Idea of Europe still hovers over my head, like golden apples on a branch I cannot reach. And the microbes are still there. The flora and fauna of that trip have now invaded my memories, my guts and my skin just as – for nearly half a century – French cheeses, Italian cappuccini, Danish flooring, Swedish furniture, Spanish banks, Polski skleps, German domestic goods, have invaded and changed our country for good. Whatever tariffs or border checks they have imposed, those continental microorganisms have become a nourishing and intrinsic part of us. And no Brexit bleach or xenophobic anti-bacterial agent can ever replace them.

Sometimes, though, I do wonder if that Man in the Brown Suit in Lausanne train station had a point, and if Europe's mystery and diversity has gone and turned into some endless waiting room or city ring road with nothing left to look forward to. Since we landed on the moon, and discovered our nearest neighbouring satellite is just a ball of monochrome dust, it's easy to lose the sense of adventure.

But then I think back to those two scrawny boys and their trip to nowhere and I realise there's so much left to explore, whatever the blandishments of ideologues or the blandness of trade deals. Those passionate fantasies and disenchantments still live on in the hearts of schoolboys and schoolgirls here, and perhaps with more intensity than ever. The future will still belong to those in Europe who have learned to live together with such dreams. And without such dreams.

'This Happens to Other People and then You Realise Other People are You'

Hardeep Matharu

5 FEBRUARY 2020

Jack Merritt was a twenty-five-year-old Cambridge University graduate passionate about society giving people a second chance when he was killed by a convicted terrorist who was attending an event organised by Learning Together – a programme in which criminal justice students help rehabilitate prisoners – at Fishmongers' Hall in central London in 2019.

Jack, who had degrees in Law and Criminology and was passionate about prison reform, worked for Learning Together and had met Usman Khan through the scheme. He had collected him from the train station on the day of the attack.

Having been released from prison, on supervision, in December 2018, after serving half of his sentence for terrorism offences, Khan killed Jack and his colleague Saskia Jones as the Learning Together event was underway, before running onto London Bridge in a fake suicide vest and being shot dead by police at the scene. In the days afterwards, the murders – which occurred during the 2019 General Election campaign – were used by the Conservatives to push the party's 'tough on crime' agenda. It was a message reinforced by sensationalist headlines in the right-wing press, which spoke of 'The Angels Stolen by Pure Evil'.

Infuriated, Jack's father David Merritt took to social media. 'Don't use my son's death and his and his colleague's photos to promote your vile propaganda,' he wrote. 'Jack stood against everything you stand for – hatred, division, ignorance.'

Three months on, David is glad he spoke out as he knew what Jack's response would have been. 'I just thought "I'm not going to have this",' he says. 'I'm not going to have the narrative being set as let's be "tough on crime". It was such a crude response. There was no nuance in it, it was all about "we've got an opportunity here" – that's what Boris Johnson saw, an opportunity to score some points, and he did. Actually, it all turned out really well because it worked – it helped to shape that narrative. As far as I can tell, there's not really been much in the way of anti-Muslim sentiment on the back of this and that's really good. I am really pleased about that ... [because] all these things, when politicians make these sorts of comments, have real world consequences – people get punched in the street, have their hijabs ripped off, are spat at and abused.'

Following Jack's murder, the Government announced plans for 'tougher sentences, an end to early release and a major review of the management of convicted terrorists' – something David says he disagrees with as it will result in people spending longer in overcrowded prisons with little to do and being further radicalised. 'It's classic,' he adds. 'The terrorists say the Government is repressive, they commit a terrorist attack, the Government clamps down and they say "there you go".'

Jack Merritt left Cambridge University with the aim of becoming a barrister, but his time at Learning Together, which he had worked on as part of his criminology master's degree there, 'really sparked his imagination'.

'He would say "we're doing this course in prison where we learn with prisoners" and we said "okay, that's interesting, sounds a bit dangerous" and he said "no it's not",' David says. 'He used to come home and be absolutely exhausted and he'd say "it's such an oppressive atmosphere in prison, I can't imagine what it would be like to be in there all the time". He was a very strong believer in rehabilitation and in people's capacity to turn their back on the things they'd been involved with in the past and become better. He saw them as people and he got to hear about how they got to be there and what sort of lives they had led. He was very empathetic.'

David says he would have many debates with his son about criminal justice issues in which Jack would 'argue the prisoner's side' and make the case for evidence-based policy. The family had 'no idea that Jack would have been in danger' on the day he died and they were in disbelief when they heard he had been killed.

'When you hear the words you think "I can't believe this, it's not happening",' David says. '"How did we come to be here? This doesn't happen to us, this happens to other people." And then you realise that other people are you.'

The family has received many tributes to Jack, including a number from the prisoners he worked with.

'Jack Merritt and the Learning Together team have given me hope,' one letter said. 'They give me my self-esteem back. Hopefully one day soon I will go back into the world a more open-minded, educated person full of confidence.' Another read: 'Jack brought hope to us here, that someone out there was working tirelessly to bring programmes and learning opportunities to those who it would really benefit.' One prisoner praised him for seeing 'the person behind the prisoner without judgement', while another said Jack 'encouraged us to be the better versions of ourselves' in a 'place where people don't really believe in you'.

'When someone connects with you on a human level and shows interest in you as a person, regardless of your crime, this increases your self-worth, a vital ingredient for building hope,' another prisoner wrote. 'And where hope resides, so does the ability to envisage a better life beyond prison.'

David says that the family is not in dialogue with anyone in Government about Jack's murder because 'how would it benefit them? I would just tell them that everything they're doing is wrong.' 'At no point did we ever receive any contact, other than the offer of a conversation with Priti Patel. We received no letter, no email, no contact whatsoever from Boris Johnson or anyone else in Government,' he adds. The family did not want to speak to the Home Secretary because 'she's so reactionary and right-wing and comes across as a very un-empathetic person'.

How has the family coped with such dignity and strength?

'I don't know, if I'm honest,' he says. 'I've never been in this situation before obviously and you don't know how you're going to react. We were lucky in that we've got lots of very, very good friends, and Jack's friends are an absolutely amazing group of young people and his colleagues as well have been incredibly supportive despite being in trauma themselves. They were there on the day, they were in mortal danger and some of them saw things that you should never see. They just kind of closed around us.'

David Merritt hopes his son's murder will make people think more deeply about the issues he gave his life for. 'I would like people to think more about how the criminal justice system works and what it's for, about public safety because there are around about sixty prisoners who will never be released, everybody else will be released,' he says. 'So the focus of the whole system should be on public safety and rehabilitation to stop people from reoffending and causing more harm and that's in all of our interests, isn't it? So if there's a bit of nuance to be had it's that and accepting that people can be helped to reform and that should be the focus of the system, and it's a hard sell as people have very negative perceptions of people who are in that situation.'

The Day I Discovered My Ancestor was a Slave Owner

Stephen Colegrave

11 FEBRUARY 2020

My family is proud of its history.

As a child, my two maiden great-aunts mixed up the centuries as they told stories of generations of family history in the fading glory of their dilapidated farmhouse, with photographs and painted miniatures of self-important ancestors. Bent nearly double with arthritis of indeterminate age, Aunt Rosalind, the indoor great-aunt, looked after a motley crew of elderly gentlemen boarders; and Aunt Muriel, the outside great-aunt, expertly kept a small herd of cows, sheep and hens.

They never had much money. They sold eggs from the door and the elderly boarders gave them their pensions, but their family history gave them a place in society and a special status – at least in their own eyes. My aunts were formidable. They were presented to court as debutantes and were tutored by a governess in the 1890s, never going to school. Early in the Second World War, they decided it was too dangerous for my father to go to school so they home-tutored him with old primers – so well that he became a straight-A student and later easily achieved a PhD.

The house was filled with family treasures such as the cannonball that an ancestor brought back from the Battle of Naseby in the Civil War. The most treasured items were from our most famous ancestor, General Tryon, who fought with General Wolfe at Quebec and was the Colonial General of North Carolina and then New York. We had his gold hunter watch, his uniform, a dress his wife had been presented to court in, portraits and a bust. I found a silver dollar that was crudely created over a Spanish piece of eight of pirate fame in his uniform pocket and my aunt let me keep it. Throughout my childhood, it was my most precious possession and it is still in my desk drawer at home.

It wasn't until recently that I decided to look into General Tryon's history.

My aunts are long dead and, since then, I have married Hilary and have three grown-up kids – Lucy, Rupert and Oliver. I am very proud that my wife is black and my children have a mixed heritage. Part of that heritage likely includes slavery as Hilary's family originally comes from Jamaica.

In researching General Tryon, I wanted to find out how much my family benefited from slavery as it never featured in the family stories from my childhood. This was also prompted by my son who sent me University College London's online resource on the Legacies of British Slave-ownership.

Some quick research revealed that hundreds of seemingly innocuous stately homes were built on the back of slaves, with the Government providing compensation for slave owners when slavery was abolished. Some establishments are still owned by descendants of the original families that were involved in the slave trade.

I vaguely remembered that the grandly named Tryon Palace in North Carolina – which was completed in 1770 for my ancestor William Tryon – was always trying to buy our Tryon treasures for its museum. My father always threatened to sell them bits and pieces of nondescript rubbish from attics that had the right date, but I don't know if he ever did. This was my starting point. If my ancestor owned slaves, it would have been when he was the Colonial General of North Carolina from 1765 to 1771 (before he became the Colonial General of New York until the rebels finally ousted him in 1780). It would have been in the American South, where slavery was embedded in all aspects of the economy and society, where I would find any evidence.

But the more I found out about him, the more I wished I wasn't descended from him.

William Tryon was a soldier who had, very practically, married an heiress, Margaret Wake, who provided him with a huge dowry of £300,000 – well in excess of £15 million today.

In the War for Independence in New York, Tryon was terribly ruthless and his conduct was savage and brutal. The historian Thomas B. Allen writes that 'Tryon's desolation warfare shocked many British officers and outraged patriots'. He goes on to describe this horror: 'It appears that no less than 23 [rapes] were committed in one neighbourhood in New Jersey; some of them on married women in the presence of their hapless husbands'. This is corroborated by other accounts of Tryon's behaviour in other military campaigns.

What about slavery? I couldn't find any estates in Carolina that he owned, so there were no large plantations. He was a soldier rather than a landowner, albeit a ruthless one.

I focused my research on his household servants to see if any of them were slaves. While I could find details of his New

York servants and the servants he brought to North Carolina in 1764, the details of his household in Carolina were not so easy to find.

But there were some. In the museum at Tryon Palace, there is a reference to him owning a man named Surry and purchasing a man named Tom, as well as paying taxes on eight black males in Brunswick County. Indeed, Surry was advertised in the *North Carolina Gazette* on 25 July 1777 as 'formerly the Property of Governor Tryon and now belongs to the Estate of Isaac Edwards, deceased'. Edwards was Tryon's private secretary so, like any other possession, Surry had been passed on or sold at a knock-down price to Edwards when Tryon was promoted to New York and then sold along with the rest of his property when he died.

Of course, it wasn't just the direct ownership of slaves that benefited my ancestors. Tryon lived in splendour in Tryon Palace in North Carolina, which he had persuaded the state to spend £10,000 building (in excess of its original generous budget of £5,000). This money was paid for by taxes, some directly paid for owning slaves, and earnings from the cotton plantations run on slavery.

When Tryon Palace was rebuilt in the 1950s using the original architectural plans, it quickly became a tourist attraction, hence the appeals to my family for our artefacts. In 1991, its curator Hilarie M. Hicks decided to tackle the history of slavery and Tryon head-on. She researched Surry and created a drama around him, *Away to Alamance*, giving Surry a voice. The character of Surry told visitors about the horrors of slavery but in a very personal manner that brought it to life in a far more powerful way.

The guilt I now feel is significant and the coin in my drawer has lost its lustre. All I want to do is sell it and give the money to charity. I wish now that I could go back to my childhood and point out to my great-aunts what sort of a man Tryon really was. I certainly want my existing family to know.

I can never appreciate or imagine the pain, degradation and suffering that slaves in North Carolina went through, but now I know that this wasn't something done by other people: it was done by my ancestor and it is all much closer to home than any of us think.

Eugenics and the Intellectuals

Stephen Unwin

17 FEBRUARY 2020

Why do the apparently intelligent and well-educated hold the unintelligent or the disabled in contempt? As the father of a young man with severe learning disabilities, it is a question I confront regularly.

It was the distinguished English scientist Francis Galton who, fascinated by his uncle Charles Darwin's *On the Origin of Species*, asked, 'Could not the race of men be similarly improved? Could not the undesirables be got rid of and the desirables multiplied?' In 1883, he coined the term 'eugenics' and set out to improve the human race by 'better breeding'. His supporters soon linked such 'undesirables' to a range of social problems and called for Government action to improve 'biological quality'.

In 1907, Galton co-founded the Eugenics Society and a senior doctor soon recommended the compulsory sterilisation of the 'feeble-minded', describing them as 'social rubbish' who should be 'swept up and garnered and utilised as far as possible'. Darwin's own son presided over the first eugenics conference in 1912 and lobbied the Government to establish squads of scientists, with the power of arrest, who would travel around the country identifying the 'unfit' and segregate those so classified in special colonies or have them sterilised.

Political supporters included the socialist firebrand Will Crooks, who described 'mentally defective children' as 'absolutely useless', comparing them to 'human vermin' who do 'absolutely nothing, except polluting and corrupting everything they touch'. Meanwhile, Julian Huxley asked plaintively, 'What are we going to do? Every defective is an extra body for the nation to feed and clothe but produces little or nothing in return.'

A bill for the compulsory sterilisation of certain categories of 'mental patient' was proposed, with the Labour MP Archibald Church wanting to stop the reproduction of those 'who are in every way a burden to their parents, a misery to themselves and in my opinion a menace to the social life of the community'. Soon, a government committee recommended legislation to ensure the 'voluntary' sterilisation of 'mentally defective women' – a move welcomed by the *Manchester Guardian* but, thankfully, never passed into law.

Confronted by a 'long line of imbeciles', Virginia Woolf insisted that they should 'certainly be killed' and the birth control champions Margaret Sanger and Marie Stopes were both confirmed eugenicists – championing not just contraception but, as Sanger put it, sterilisation for 'that grade of population whose progeny is already tainted, or whose inheritance is such that objectionable traits may be transmitted to offspring'.

Some of British socialism's most celebrated names agreed, including the founders of the Fabian Society, Sidney and Beatrice Webb, along with Harold Laski, later chairman of the Labour Party, who predicted that the time was coming 'when society will look upon the production of a weakling as a crime against itself'.

These views were echoed by John Maynard Keynes and, in 1931, the *New Statesman* asserted that 'the legitimate claims of eugenics are not inherently incompatible with the outlook of the collectivist movement'. Bertrand Russell proposed colour-coded 'procreation tickets' to prevent the elite's gene pool being diluted by inferior stock, while George Bernard Shaw insisted that 'the only fundamental and possible socialism is the socialisation of the selective breeding of man', suggesting that defectives could be dealt with in a 'lethal chamber'.

Using the same haunting phrase, D. H. Lawrence declared: 'If I had my way, I would build a lethal chamber as big as the Crystal Palace, with a military band playing softly, and a Cinematograph working brightly; then I'd go out into the back streets and the main streets and bring them all in, the sick, the halt and the maimed: I would lead them gently, and they would smile me a weary thanks; and the brass band would softly bubble out the "Hallelujah Chorus".'

He could have been describing a suburban English Treblinka.

It took Nazi Germany, and the murder of 250,000 people deemed to be living 'lives unworthy of life', to put these fantasies into action. But, the unhappy truth is that, even after the Second World War, the eugenics agenda in Britain was still current.

On the day in 1943 when his famous report was being debated, William Beveridge, the creator of the welfare state, slipped out of the gallery of the House of Commons to reassure a meeting of the Eugenics Society of his continued support. In 1952, the eminent British neurologist A. F. Tredgold concluded that 'many of the defectives are utterly helpless, repulsive in appearance and revolting in their manners. Their existence is a perpetual source of sorrow and unhappiness to their parents, in my opinion it would be an economical and humane procedure were their very existence to be painlessly terminated.'

The Nazis had been defeated but, for a moment, it seemed possible that one of their most repulsive policies might survive.

Such views are rare today, but a double standard is still in evidence in the way that abusive language is used, with racist and sexist terms being strictly taboo, but their learning disabled equivalents – 'idiot', 'cretin', 'imbecile', 'retarded' – are all too common, even in supposedly progressive circles.

Representations in drama and art are infrequent and often misguided, emphasising individual tragedy, not the broader social experience. And scholarship is hardly exempt, with the moral philosopher Peter Singer dismissing our protection of the profoundly disabled on the grounds of 'speciesism' – declaring that their intellectual capacity is less than many animals. One of his followers even wrote an article entitled 'Do the Mentally Retarded Have a Right to be Eaten?', which he insisted was a philosophical exploration, intended to 'raise the issue of rights for the retarded in its hardest context', adding sternly that 'too much well-meaning sentimentality is allowed to pass for thought in the discussion of the retarded, and I want to shock my way through this'.

And Richard Dawkins, in response to an enquiry from a woman about what to do if she discovered that she was pregnant with a foetus with Down's Syndrome, replied, 'Abort it and try again. It would be immoral to bring it into the world if you have the choice.' He denied that he is a 'eugenicist', but it is hard to understand what he means by the word 'immoral' in such a context. What, of course, Dawkins forgets is that eugenics has been tried and failed abysmally: despite the Nazi programme of murder and sterilisation, Germany's population of disabled people is entirely in line with other countries. It takes an intellectual to come up with such poisonous guff.

Protecting the rights and opportunities of the learning disabled is hard enough; what's striking is the way that so many otherwise clever people fail to get it.

From Sunderland to the Bullingdon Club: Englishness Unravelled

John Mitchinson

26 FEBRUARY 2020

'The suet puddings and the red pillarboxes have entered into your soul. Good or evil, it is yours, you belong to it, and this side the grave you will never get away from the marks that it has given you.'

George Orwell wrote these lines in the middle of the Blitz, at a point where the future of England looked as bleak and threatened as it has ever done. "The Lion and the Unicorn", the long essay they are taken from, is his not altogether successful attempt to reconcile his left-leaning self with his patriotism, his hopes of 'bringing the real England to the surface'. With the hindsight of history, we can see he scores a creditable six out of ten in predicting how the war and post-war reconstruction would turn out. Democracy did triumph, industries were nationalised, the health service was created, but the idle rich were not turfed out of their mansions, private education and the institutionalised inequality it entailed were not abolished.

But it isn't the predictions that draw me to this essay, eighty years later. It's the suet puddings and the red pillarboxes: Orwell's attempt to pin down a national culture that was worth fighting for.

It wasn't easy then; it isn't any easier now, in the ominous calm that has followed our departure from the European Union. Given the choice, like many of us who have benefited from closer ties with Europe without really admiring the political institution of the EU, I would have preferred the status quo.

Being forced to contemplate your identity is always painful because it requires you to pay attention to the extremes. With 'Englishness' this means acknowledging, on one hand, the

Faragiste bigotry and reckless hatred of outsiders that nationalism so often brings in its wake; while at the other end of the room listening to the unconvincing mantra that there are as many different Englands as there are people who live here. Both are delusional.

This is why the term 'British' has proved so useful. Despite the obvious irony that it was invented in 1707 as a brand devoted to the imperial and economic exploitation of much of the rest of the planet, it is still easier for people of different ethnicities to call themselves 'British' rather than 'English'.

But not to face up to Englishness feels like a cop-out. To pretend that we come from nowhere, that we appear as ready-formed citizens of a political construct like 'Britain' is dishonest and psychologically hazardous. Self-knowledge comes from examining what has formed us, however painful.

To do this we need to drop the idea that 'English' implies a specific ethnicity. It doesn't and never has done; it is a culture that has been fed by many different peoples and languages, in various degrees of willingness. To hide from that fact is to insult all those people who have chosen to make this country their home. Anyone who does and considers themselves English is English as far as I'm concerned. It's how we each get to that point that interests me: what feeds our individual sense of English identity. And, instead of avoiding that history, we should roll up our sleeves and start digging.

In her exhilarating and mind-clearing book *Insurgent Empire*, the historian Priyamvada Gopal provides a bold recalibration of Britain's imperial past showing that colonisation was resisted in a well-organised and politically articulate way in almost every country where it was imposed. She also reveals how these resistance movements had a galvanic effect on radical movements such as the Chartists back in England. 'We need,' she writes, 'a more demanding relationship to history than is offered by prevalent island stories', one that 'cautions against levelling and self-serving assumptions about the past in order that we might engage in a more demanding way with the present'.

This more demanding relationship is required every bit as much (maybe even more) in rural England as it is in the more culturally diverse communities that make up our cities.

I have lived in an English village – there is no such thing as a 'British' village – for the past twenty-three years. And not just any village. Great Tew is at the extreme edge of picturesque, almost oppressive in its thatched comeliness and about as challenging to received notions of Englishness as a Boden catalogue. But dig a little deeper and you find a rich history of entrepreneurialism and exploitation.

An important Saxon village with a church by the time of the Domesday Book (itself an unmatched record of theft and appropriation), it was likely built on an older settlement – there's evidence of occupation going back 7,000 years. By the early 17th Century, it had fallen into the hands of Laurence

Tanfield, Chief Baron of the Exchequer, the most powerful and influential lawyer in the land. In Tew, he soon acquired a reputation as a tyrant, enclosing the best fields of the common land for his own sheep, digging up ancient boundary stones, refusing the villagers access to the timber they needed to repair their homes and imposing savage fines on them for trespass. At the church, he stripped lead from the chancel to make his own pipes and guttering, refused to pay the manorial dues, prevented villagers from using his straw to kneel on and knocked down the churchyard wall so his cattle could graze among the gravestones. This went on for ten years until a group of 'poor oppressed inhabitants of Great Tew' petitioned Parliament in 1624. The Baron was unrepentant; his wife, Elizabeth, went even further. 'The villagers of Great Tew,' she declared, 'were more worthy to be ground to powder than to have any favour showed them' and she promised to play the 'very devil with them'. Both Lord and Lady Tanfield are reputed to haunt the village still.

A happier time ensued when the estate passed to Lucius Cary, their grandson, the Viscount Falkland (the village pub, the Falkland Arms, is named after him). He was Charles I's Secretary of State and ran an open house, gathering a collection of writers and philosophers around him, including Ben Jonson, the poet Abraham Cowley, the historian Lord Clarendon and the philosopher Thomas Hobbes. They formed a royalist think tank known as the Great Tew Circle, and tried, in vain, to persuade Charles to avoid his war with Parliament.

By the mid-18th Century, Tew had passed into the hands of George Stratton, a member of the East India Company, who bought the estate (and a seat in Parliament) with money he had made in India. In the early 19th Century, Stratton's son blew what remained of his father's fortune on a failed model farm in the village and was forced to sell to Matthew Robinson Boulton, son of Matthew Boulton of Soho Foundry, who, with James Watt, was the great architect of the Industrial Revolution. By the late 20th Century, Great Tew had fallen into serious disrepair and passed out of the Boulton family's hands. Under the entrepreneurial vision of its current owners, Tew is now restored to its former glory, home to Soho Farmhouse and the Beckhams and frequently written up as 'England's hippest village'.

So much for the quiet seclusion of rural life. Looked at properly, Great Tew teaches salutary truths about the English countryside. Over the centuries, from the Conquest through the Civil War and the Industrial Revolution to the Instagram-fuelled celebrity economy of today, this tiny backwater has witnessed huge tidal surges of investment sluice through it as one rich man's vision has replaced another's. Our village looks pretty because it was designed to look pretty 200 years ago – authenticity is relative. And Tew isn't unique in this: every view, every landscape in England is more or less the product of human agency and investment, much of it made from exploiting poorer, less powerful people, first of all on their doorstep and then in colonies far from home. There is no escape from the cruelty of history in England, no wilderness to hide in.

Great Tew had fascinated me long before I knew anything of its past. What took me there as a ten-year-old was a map – the 1968 Ordnance Survey one-inch-to-the-mile map of Banbury, sheet 145, with a bright pink cover. And, although the Ordnance Survey, like so many apparently anodyne British institutions dedicated to taxonomy, was set up to map the Highlands in the aftermath of the Jacobite Rebellion in order to track down and arrest its leaders, that particular map transformed my childhood. Footpaths, copses, caves, streams, culverts, tumuli, deserted villages all appeared in the fields near our house on the edge of town. I'd plot journeys, threading landmarks together, learning their names, and spent hours with my brother and friends walking or cycling to find them. That map taught me more about history than any textbook – it made me see the landscape, not as something 'owned' and static but as a living palimpsest where the past was still present, where time was not linear but three-dimensional.

It was the map that led us to Tew. In 1972, Great Tew was listed in Pevsner's *Buildings of England* (another taxonomic marvel) as 'unforgettable' but the rows of semi-derelict cottages were 'one of the most depressing sights in the whole county'. It was exactly that sense of buildings sinking back into the earth that my brother and I loved – that and the pub with old agricultural workers sitting outside speaking in Oxfordshire accents so broad you could sharpen a scythe on them.

It wasn't like any other village we'd visited and I quickly became obsessed with it. Who knows precisely why? In a eulogy on the garden city of Letchworth, the writer and filmmaker Jonathan Meades – a notable stormtrooper in the war against the sentimental and the picturesque – confessed similar puzzlement: 'We do not select the places which move us and to which we long to return . . . places choose us: we have no more control than we do in matters of love.'

So it has proved, and in the decades that followed, I returned as often as I could. And now it is my home; birthplace of three of my children; the prism through which I try to make sense of who I am.

It is not, however, where I'm from.

When people ask that, I always say, somewhat uncomfortably, the north-east. Uncomfortably, because I don't sound like I'm from there – we moved to Banbury in Oxfordshire when I was eight – but also because it is the area of England that has become most closely associated with a regressive, bigoted, anti-European strain of Englishness. The first result in the 2016 EU Referendum was the 61% in favour of Leave in Sunderland – a totemic moment in which even the most ardent Remainers knew their cause was lost.

My grandparents' two-bedroom council house was in Sunderland and that house was the only constant in my life until my grandmother died in 2001. It was they who connected me to the rich web of stories and places which would form my map of belonging, my origin myth.

I don't know how they would have voted had they lived to see the referendum – but I do know they would have resented the way the north-east is now talked about as a region of fools, of turkeys voting for Christmas. They were proud of their region and their town to an almost ridiculous level. I still have my grandfather's Sunderland memorial tankard. As well as local landmarks – Roker Pier, Penshaw Monument, Fulwell Mill – it has an engraving of a tram with the line underneath it: 'Remember the Trams'. No question mark; just a statement, maybe even an imperative. 'Do not forget this now outmoded form of transport!' It is touching that someone at some point signed this off as a key sentiment, one worthy of preserving in pewter.

Civic pride shading into sentimentality about the past is very typical of the north-east. But there is a dark obverse to this absurdity. This is the region that produced the coal and ships that built an empire. It made England and many individuals rich, but it never made itself wealthy. And now those industries have gone – a disappearance that has happened entirely within my lifetime.

As I get older, I find myself drawn back northwards. Not necessarily as a place to live but as a place that fires my imagination.

As a small child I would stand on the edge of Roker Pier and dream of the fjords just over the horizon (in fact, it's a flat Danish sandbank) and the terror my forebears must have felt when Viking ships appeared on the horizon. It is a landscape as rugged and empty and unforgiving as rural Oxfordshire is lush and fecund. And I miss the fierce wit and energy of the people.

I spent most of my childhood holidays with my grandparents, and my grandfather, in particular, was the grown-up who had the most time for me. He listened to my stories and taught me basic life skills I have never forgotten: how to fold my clothes and polish my shoes, how to get the timing right for jokes and combination punches (he was Sunderland amateur welterweight boxing champion in the early 1930s), how to do sums in my head and proper press-ups. His humour was bone dry, he disliked authority, he worked hard as a motor mechanic on the railways in one place for most of his working life. He suffered ill health from his early fifties onwards: stomach ulcers, debilitating arthritis, heart disease; he never complained. He was a deeply committed Christian, ill-served by the Church he was devoted to. He was a trade unionist and staunch Labour Party supporter. He had little time for most priests and politicians. He was kind to the point of sainthood, hobbling around the estate to visit those older and less fortunate than himself until weeks before he died. He didn't live to see New Labour elected but he would not have liked Tony Blair; he didn't much like Harold Wilson and loathed

Churchill. Admiring Nye Bevan was as close as he got to expressing support for a political leader.

He remains the person I miss most; the one I still most want to impress. He embodied a kind of Englishness that I try to measure my own by: a combination of kindness, restraint, scepticism and wit.

In early 1976, we emigrated to New Zealand. The experience of living in another country served to hone my sense of Englishness in ways I couldn't have anticipated. Everything from the texture of the grass to the smell of the earth after rain was different. I was bullied mercilessly at school for my accent and pale skin but, in spite of this, grew to love my new home – not least because it taught me a whole new way to look at the connection between culture, language and landscape. The revival of the Māori language and the restoration of tribal lands teach many lessons for those of us concerned with the grotesque systems of land use and ownership in this country. As the years passed, my memories of England – my grand-parents, the wild moors, the green Tew meadows – passed into a kind of internal mythological space. They were eventually to resurface in my decision to apply to study English at Oxford.

I arrived at Oxford without a past or a context. Because I'd done a year at Auckland University, I was regarded as an Antipodean with an English accent. Also, I lived in a flat outside college with my New Zealand girlfriend (later wife), who worked as a waitress in what was then Oxford's busiest restaurant, Brown's. Armed with this floating identity, my northern past and comprehensive schooling were not obvious. I was a little older than my fellow students and, with friends in the town, was known for organising good (i.e. wild) parties. All these elements contributed to the defining moment of my time there.

Somehow, I found myself elected to the infamous Bullingdon Club – surely the only state-school-educated candidate ever to have been so embarrassed. I should have rejected it with contempt but I was curious, maybe even flattered. I attended two dinners and a breakfast, witnessed some low-level vandalism, but mostly recall it being as dull as drunken, boorish behaviour is anywhere. Our current prime minister was a fellow member, and rather a tame one – he egged on his more unhinged friends, but was careful not to be caught out himself (no surprises there). For all the tedious public-school boasting about being 'wild' and 'above the law', I'd seen worse after rugby matches in New Zealand or in Sunderland pubs, the only difference being that the drinking was brisker, the banter much crisper and the trouble sorted out by the police rather than large wads of cash left on the table.

I might have written my Bullingdon experience off as mere youthful misjudgement, had it not been for an incident that took place after the end of term. My girlfriend and I were having supper in a subterranean branch of Davy's Wine Bar in central Oxford, a place noted for serving port in copper jugs. We were joined by a Bullingdon member whom I barely knew. He had the usual languid, superior air and ordered a jug of port. When it arrived he disappeared, came back with the full jug and told our waitress that the port was 'off'. She returned to our table pale-faced and said we were the most disgusting people she'd ever met. He had replaced the port in the jug with his own piss. I can still feel the intensity of the shame. In that moment, I realised what I'd aligned myself with. This was not my tribe; these were not my people. That grotesque combination of arrogance and stupidity, that lack of concern for the consequences of one's actions upon others, now looks like a dumb show for the Eton-dominated political landscape we are presently condemned to live through. I left that restaurant and never looked back but the shame still burns. The healing stubbornly refuses to begin.

'In England,' writes Orwell, 'patriotism takes different forms in different classes, but it runs like a connecting thread through nearly all of them. Only the Europeanised intelligentsia are really immune to it.'

There's probably too much of the Europeanised intellectual in me to commend an updated version of Orwell's English patriotism as the solution to our current divisions. If we are honest, we know defining a culture is impossible but describing it is not – as long as you recognise that this will always be work in progress. Culture isn't a 'thing', it's a process and English culture is changing whether we like it or not.

The suet pudding has morphed into a vegan sausage roll;

the red pillarbox, a smartphone. And the past isn't over, any more than the future is certain. The more we study the past – like a map – the less linear it seems. For all the texts, tweets, Facebook posts, selfies, likes and dislikes we bank up, we remain the products of culture, of the twin forces of language and memory. That is where we start and where we will end.

In the months before my grandfather died, I took to sitting with him for long stretches of silence. After a while, he would sigh and turn to me, his eyes bright with surprise. 'You never think this is how you'll end up, son,' he would say. Not regretful or sad, but full of wonder and mystery.

I doubt a week has passed since, when I don't remember him saying that and the look on his face as he did.

'Hybrid Warfare': The Kremlin's Disinformation Techniques

Zarina Zabrisky

4 MARCH 2020

The Kremlin's disinformation playbook for waging its self-declared 'global information war' was originally developed by Soviet military strategists.

During the Cold War, they conducted more than 10,000 disinformation operations – among them, the dissemination of conspiracy theories about FBI and CIA involvement in the assassination of President John F. Kennedy and the US Government inventing AIDS. At the height of the Cold War, up to 15,000 KGB officers are said to have worked on psychological and disinformation warfare, which they learned in a special 'active measures' course created by the then KGB head Yuri Andropov.

Russia's disinformation campaigns have evolved with the times. They now include spreading disinformation through international news agencies, television channels and online news; and have become increasingly sophisticated – moving on from outright falsehoods to more subtle forms of audience manipulation.

The main goal is to weaken the Western democratic system from within. According to experts, Russia has been trying to destabilise Europe through disinformation since 2015. However, it was the aftermath of the 2016 US Presidential Election that attracted international attention to the issue as US intelligence agencies called out Russia's propagation of false news and inflammatory media stories meant to sway the vote in Donald Trump's favour.

But how can Russia's modern 'hybrid warfare' be recognised? Here are its key elements.

1. *Pushing Kremlin Narratives*

The Kremlin aims to create the sense of a new 'post-Western world order', in which Western countries and institutions no longer enjoy the same amount of power and influence they once did. This includes negative narratives around the elite, the EU and NATO, and promoting a danger discourse (the rising extremist, migrant and Islamic terrorism threat), as well as positive narratives around Russia and its president, Vladimir Putin, as the saviours of traditional values.

2. *Amplifying Extreme Voices*

Far-right activists, conspiracy theorists and extremists are featured as commentators on Russian media outlets to encourage – as explained in a textbook taught in Russian military education institutions – 'all kinds of separatism and ethnic, social and racial conflicts, actively supporting all dissident movements: extremist, racist, and sectarian groups, thus destabilising internal political processes'.

3. *Rapid-fire Conspiracy Overload*

This promotes an overflow of images of violent protests, vandalism, fire, injuries and deaths intended to shock the nervous system and cause stress in the target audience. Repetition of triggering words and images, the rapid switching of stories and inconsistency are intended to result in depression, panic, fear and disorientation. With sufficient exposure, PTSD symptoms can develop and result in an inability to think critically and act rationally. In this state, propagandists enter people's minds with their solutions.

4. Influence by Suggestion

Suggestion is used to target groups that lack critical thinking skills – such as the very religious, undereducated, conformists, youth and people in a state of panic, fear or stress. Using the 'authority aura' effect, recognised leaders deliver emotionally charged speeches; and group environments, such as rallies and online forums, create the effect of 'psychological contagion' and help to consolidate people around the ideas presented.

In 2016, trolls from the Internet Research Agency, a St Petersburg troll farm, organised pro-Donald Trump rallies in Florida, Idaho and Philadelphia, targeting miners and low-income demographics.

5. Influence by Persuasion

This method uses logic, comparisons, arguments, multiple points of view, sociological polls and statistics to target groups prone to thinking critically, with a special focus on leaders and decision-makers in society.

6. The 60/40 Method

Invented by Joseph Goebbels, Hitler's Propaganda Minister, this theory posits that, if 60% of coverage is objective and reported to establish trust, 40% can inject disinformation at critical moments, taking advantage of the trust that has been established, in order to convince the audience.

7. Perspective

This centres on creating a single perspective by presenting only one point of view. According to disinformation expert Ben Nimmo, it involves selecting an 'interviewee on the basis of their beliefs, rather than their credibility, and not providing balancing coverage' and 'giving substantial airtime to pundits who validate the Kremlin narrative, and little or no airtime to its opponents'.

8. Distraction/Deflection

This reflexive technique of control shifts attention away from stories unfavourable to the Kremlin and towards school shootings, murders, catastrophes, terrorist attacks and natural disasters.

In the wake of the school shooting in Parkland, Florida, troll- and bot-tracking sites reported an immediate rise in tweets related to this topic from Russia-linked Twitter accounts. This took place in the same week that the media started reporting a story unfavourable to the Kremlin – on the ties between Donald Trump's former campaign manager Paul Manafort, the Russian oligarch Oleg Deripaska and the Russian Government.

9. Trolling

Trolling people Russia perceives as opponents in the West through online forums, social networks, portals, chat rooms and news sites is a long-established ploy, which includes aggressive, mocking or abusive messages. An example of this was a video produced by Russian state-controlled international TV network RT, with the title 'RT Exposed in Leaked Video: Watch How Evil "Kremlin Propaganda Bullhorn" REALLY Works'. By using sarcasm in this way, RT dismisses allegations, discredits opponents and distracts from its offensive campaign.

10. Repetition

One of the basic and most effective methods is the tireless repetition of the same statements so people get used to and begin to accept them – relying not on critical thinking, but on faith mechanisms.

11. *Positive Image Engineering*

This involves creating a positive image of politicians in order to popularise Russia's foreign and domestic policy agenda with foreign audiences. In 2016, for example, RT and state-owned news agencies Ruptly and Sputnik reported Putin's announcement that Russia had developed the most effective Ebola vaccine in the world – a claim described as 'shocking' and 'mind-boggling' by Professor Ira Longini, who helped develop the only Ebola vaccine to have passed the highest stage of testing. A year later, Ruptly produced a video making a fake claim that a New York restaurant had served a burger named after Vladimir Putin to celebrate his sixty-fifth birthday.

12. *Rotten Herring*

This prompts a direct association between a person, group or institution and a scandalous accusation. First, a false accusation is circulated on social media. Then, bots and trolls push the false accusation through related hashtags. Subsequently, the mainstream media reports the accusation as a story, which is then echoed by many outlets. A public discussion ensues. Experts, prominent figures and laymen join in with their opinions. After a certain number of repetitions, a negative emotional response is formed about the person, group or institution being falsely accused. Even if it is debunked, the negative association with the object remains, just like the smell of rotten herring.

13. The Big Lie

In this case, the fabricated narrative must have monstrous proportions. An example was the circulating of a false story by Sputnik about Emmanuel Macron being a 'US agent' lobbying in favour of banks during the French Presidential Election. According to cybersecurity expert Bruce Schneier, a single 'big lie' was more common in Soviet disinformation during the 1980s, but 'today it is more about many contradictory alternative truths – a "firehose of falsehood" – that distorts the political debate'.

14. Rumour

Rumours can significantly enhance certain stereotypes among target population groups and come in different categories: absolutely false; unreliable with elements of credibility; plausible; and authentic rumours with elements of improbability. They are also divided into categories by their emotional origin – rumour-desire; rumour-scare; aggressive-rumour – and are released at certain intervals.

15. Half-truths

Only reporting part of the truth to mislead the audience and advance the Kremlin narrative is illustrated by how RT emphasises negative events in the West and ignores positive developments, while hardly covering or criticising the Russian Government. According to Sara Firth, a former RT reporter, the channel is 'not interested in fact-checking and creating valuable, balanced journalism. Their main agenda is that it fits the narrative'.

16. False Equivalence

This involves comparing two or more things that appear to be logically equivalent, but in fact are not. Disinformation expert Ben Nimmo describes the use of this technique by RT's editor-in-chief Margarita Simonyan, who he says 'often cited the BBC Charter, stating that one of the broadcaster's missions is to "bring British values to the world" and accused it of British propaganda as a result'. In fact, the Charter states that the BBC's aim is 'to reflect the UK, its culture and values to the world'.

17. Gaslighting

This makes people doubt reality and facts. An example is Russia's self-declared information war against itself. The

Russian Government has accused the West of 'orchestrated campaigns aimed at discrediting the Russian press' with the aim of 'suppressing the voice of the Russian media'. Following Russia's use of disinformation to influence the 2016 US Presidential Election, Putin's press secretary Dmitry Peskov claimed that 'this was not an information war of Russia's choosing, it was a "counter-action"'.

5 March 2020

A woman in her seventies becomes the first person in the UK to die after testing positive for the novel Coronavirus.

Behind Closed Doors, Conservatives Ideologically Oppose the NHS

Shahmir Sanni

31 MARCH 2020

I have worked for Conservative lobby groups. I have worked for the Brexit campaign. I have drunk with the people running this country; partied with them; cried with them; dined with them; and loved them. They were a community that supported me, people who came to me for compassion and emotional support. I was the friend they called 'wet' for my liberal beliefs, but 'smart' for my prowess in the digital landscape.

Before the Coronavirus hit Britain, conservative thought leaders were reintroducing eugenics into political discourse, arguing in favour of its legitimacy under the guise of 'free speech'. The idea that one person is better than another because of their genetic make-up, or because of the cards they were dealt before they were even born, is an ideology rooted in the very fabric of British society. 'Better' in this day and age translates almost always as being more economically productive or 'smarter'. We have come far. But not as far as Britain would like to believe.

I have been in rooms with Conservative politicians and hacks where discussions around the NHS have centred around its privatisation. Behind closed (and sometimes even open) doors, the ideas are the same and often lack much nuance. Just pick up some research papers by Tufton Street think tanks and see for yourself.

Discussion centres around a simple idea that anything funded by the state is wrong. Many of these people reiterate the same one-liners to each other so often that they are convinced that there is no other way.

At private dinners, I have heard public workers depicted as enemies of progress, the civil service conveyed as pointless and many key public services that make Britain what it is referred to as a nuisance. Whether it is care workers, teachers, nurses, doctors, civil servants, it does not matter – all of their roles can be replaced by the private sector and, in the eyes of many Conservative politicians, they should be.

'The NHS doesn't need reform, it just needs to be sold off' is a phrase I have heard used at these private dinners. Along with: 'Publicly funded care workers aren't essential; if people are getting old they should have worked hard when they were younger. Why should taxes pay for their laziness?' I have heard them jest 'But what about Grenfell!' at the television whenever someone who asks for more funding for the NHS is being interviewed.

There is a deep-rooted culture, disseminated by influential lobbying groups who are platformed by the media, of seeing public funding as an enemy of progress. It is purely ideological, based not in economic theory or academia, but entirely on a regurgitation of political statements.

The public is cognitively dissonant to this because the actions of politicians are not critiqued by our journalists or media broadcasters. People are fed lies about how politicians are seeking to help them, rather than being told that there are vested ideological and financial interests in the policy decisions being made by these politicians.

As someone who has given up years of his life as a whistle-blower on the Vote Leave campaign's offshoot, BeLeave, and exposed electoral wrongdoing there during the 2016 EU Referendum, I have experienced so much trauma merely for trying to protect British democracy from corruption. I know that we are in the middle of not just a public health crisis, but a political one too.

Disinformation is rife, hypocrisy even more so. While we must all unite to come out of the Coronavirus crisis, we must critique the very systems that have made us ill-prepared, and also understand how our livelihoods can be put at risk as a result of political decisions.

Those running our country do not love the NHS, they are ideologically against the very fundamental idea of public healthcare. It goes against every research paper and book they love; against the desires of the millionaires who set up their lobbying groups and policy think tanks. It is fundamentally a project that does not fit in their free-market utopia.

I implore Conservatives to pull themselves out of this bubble and see the bigger picture, to understand the nuances of policy decisions that have been made and take action to protect the NHS. We must also appreciate that the hands that 'clap for carers' are the same hands placing a cross in the ballot box to vote in individuals who I believe do not have their best interests at heart, least of all when it comes to the NHS.

When this crisis is over, the current leadership will once again turn against the very things that we cherish most in times like this.

History Echoes: My Mother's Lockdown with Scarlet Fever

Stephen Colegrave

3 APRIL 2020

During lockdown, I have been re-reading my late mother's childhood diaries. Amid the Coronavirus crisis, they now seem more poignant.

It is easy to forget that it was only in the last decade that the number of deaths from communicable diseases finally accounted for more than half of worldwide deaths. Eighty years ago, when my mother was a child, there were many diseases that could and did kill, especially before the development of antibiotics. Isolation was often the only way to deal with these infections, as we are doing with the Coronavirus today.

Early in the Second World War, like many other children, my mother and uncle were evacuated from their small farm in Kent. Pam was ten years old and her brother just eight. They were lucky to have relatives in Musselburgh, near Edinburgh, even if they didn't have the experience of looking after children. Being free spirits, the children were used to roaming around the countryside with their older sisters, who stayed at home to help run the farm. They didn't take easily to life in a town and their Scottish school was definitely not their favourite place.

'My teacher's name was Miss Curie: yet another elderly spinster shaping my life!' my mother complained. 'Curled up on her desk was a tawse or leather strap. This was in constant use not only to instil discipline but to ensure learning. Two spelling mistakes brought them a cut from the strap.'

But my mother didn't have to put up with Miss Curie for long. After six months had passed, one day she and her brother woke up with red rashes all over their bodies and were diagnosed with scarlet fever. Before the introduction of antibiotics in 1945, this was a serious condition. It could lead to meningitis, pneumonia, rheumatic fever, liver and kidney damage, if you did not die from the original fever.

As it was contagious, they were both immediately bundled off to the fever hospital in an ambulance drawn by two horses with their stretchers swaying around in the back. They were to be hospitalised for six weeks in an isolation ward. All their school books were burned and the house where they had stayed completely fumigated.

'Fever hospitals in the 1930s probably differed little from the days of the plague,' my mother remembered.

Like today, they really were in isolation. They only saw two nurses, a formidable matron and a doctor when he did his rounds. Visitors were not allowed in the building but they had their own socially distanced visits – which were slightly more demanding than they are today. Visitors had to collect a wooden ladder and climb up it and talk through the glass of a closed window. All gifts had to be handed to the nurses, who then went through them to decide whether they were suitable. Several of the comics my uncle was sent were deemed inappropriate, Matron not being big on superheroes.

As they recovered, my mother and her brother felt terribly homesick. Occasionally, relatives climbed up the ladders to see them, but they hadn't passed on much news from home. Kent, the farm and their family seemed far away. Then, just when they were at their lowest ebb, they were told that their parents were on their way to see them.

'We both sat at the same window,' my mother wrote. 'Two ladders were erected and there were our parents. It was such an enormous relief to see them. What we both needed was for our parents to hug and kiss us. It was not allowed. They had to stay behind the glass windows as we sobbed and cried, overwhelmed with relief and happiness.'

If I had read this a few weeks ago, I don't think I could have fully understood how alone my mother must have felt at this time, especially at the moment when she could see her parents but not touch them.

When my mother's lockdown was over and her parents came to take her back to Kent, 'it was time for us to return home and back to war'. But her time in Scotland seemed to have made a bigger impact on her than expected.

'My teacher smiled at my newly acquired Scottish accent and I was encouraged to demonstrate rolling my "r"s,' she wrote. 'I had learnt to dance the Highland Fling and this was incorporated into our country dance lessons.'

Miss Curie also had a lasting effect, despite or perhaps because of the threat of her dreaded strap. My mother found her English grammar so vastly improved after her time in Scotland that she went on to study English at Sheffield University. This was a big step for a girl from a smallholding and led to a long career as an English teacher.

'Don't They See Our Suffering? Does What Italy is Going Through Count for Nothing?'

Kamin Mohammadi

9 APRIL 2020

Remember week one? That faraway time characterised by confusion and anxiety and a sort of elation? We in Italy were as confused as you are in Britain about what activities justified going out.

Teenagers – who had by then been out of school for two weeks – roamed the streets. Most businesses were still open, many people were still going to work, and so a decree was issued closing bars, restaurants, gyms and all non-essential businesses. Decree after decree limited our movements ever closer to home, closing parks when people were spotted walking cats and even goldfish in bowls; auto-certification was required by law to state why you were out, subject to fines and a criminal record if found to be untrue.

The Italian Prime Minister was on TV every night, sober, measured, focused. He urged his countrymen to stay at home. Celebrities appeared on television and social media, filmed at home in their tracksuits, begging people not to go out.

Everything stopped. Everyone was at home. Even with the

growing horror of the Coronavirus pandemic, this was unimaginable and we were in shock. We were also in mass grief for the numbers of dead, for the horrific images coming out of northern Italian hospitals, for funerals families could not attend, for lonely deaths encased in plastic. We shuddered at the sight of the Pope's solitary figure in the vast empty space of St Peter's Square. We wept every time we saw the Palazzo Chigi lit up in the colours of the Italian flag. We talked about all the plagues Italy has survived in the past and found the comparisons somehow unhelpful.

Italians trapped in their apartments in cities took to their balconies and windows at 6 p.m. every day to sing the national anthem together, to bang pots and pans, to shake tambourines and to sing popular songs, to applaud the healthcare workers. The sense of solidarity and unity was immense and gave us all a feeling of community that was surprising given the death of social life. Everyone suddenly found they had time to talk to friends and family all over the world. Social life via video calls blossomed. Parents tried to figure out home-schooling. Our homes became spotless as we did thorough spring cleans for perhaps the first time ever. I was charmed by the new-found politeness and reserve of Italians who now quietly asked, from at least one metre away, if you would mind moving your trolley so they could pass, whereas once they would have just walked over you, running their trolley over your toes, while talking loudly on the phone.

It was as if Italy matured overnight – the anarchic, rule-breaking Italian character morphed into one embracing social responsibility and the greater good over individualism. Kindness shone out everywhere and became our new modus operandi. We said 'Italy has found its heart again' and felt it to be true.

The news dominated our time and our talk from the moment we woke up to the moment we went to sleep. If we slept at all. We tried not to think about our lost incomes and just felt grateful to be alive. We signed up for courses, online communities, virtual tours of museums we had long ignored when they were on our doorstep. Rainbows drawn by children trapped at home and inscribed with '*andra tutto bene*' (everything will be okay) hung out of windows everywhere. They gave us hope and courage every time we saw footage of army trucks carrying away dead bodies at night from epicentres such as Bergamo and as the world-class hospitals of the wealthy Lombardy region teetered on the brink of collapse.

We all recognised that the healthcare workers needed protection, even as the state failed to supply them with adequate equipment, and so we took it upon ourselves to lighten their load by not getting infected, by applauding them from our windows. We applauded when Germany became the first European country to come to Italy's aid by taking some of Lombardy's intensive-care patients. We shared pictures of Venice's crystal-clear canals filled with fish, ducks sauntering down a silent Grand Canal, the dolphins visiting the coast of Sardinia for the first time in twenty years, the wild boar seen wandering down the street in Padua, the deer dancing with joy on the shoreline of Viareggio's beach, usually a chequerboard of sun loungers and umbrellas.

We realised that this was not going to end in a couple of weeks and that there would be no 'normal' again. That there was no going back.

Amid all of this, I watched my friends in London going to parties and getting on tubes and listened to the UK Government talk of 'herd immunity'. American friends here called me and cried bitter tears at the actions of the US President, crying out, 'But don't they see our suffering? Does what Italy is going through count for nothing?' We felt abandoned by the world.

Sometime around two weeks in, a hush descended. Reality settled on us like the layer of dust beginning now to gather on our pristine mantelpieces.

Now, consumption of news has had to be limited for the sake of our mental health. Warring couples have had to put aside their differences to get through this enforced togetherness. Many parents have had to abandon the earlier structured days of home-schooling, and day drinking has become the norm for some. This is not a holiday, nor is it a sabbatical.

As a writer, I had decided to treat lockdown as a writing retreat, but I realised it is also not that. Slowly it has dawned on us that we are here witnessing a great change in global human behaviour; a catastrophe that with every day that passes makes our habitual way of life increasingly impossible to contemplate.

Armed police have been deployed outside Sicilian super-markets to stop the hungry from walking out with unpaid-for trolley-loads of food. Unemployment is starting to bite and the state's promised help feels inadequate at best and scornful at worst. Poverty is the new reality for many. Tourism has been wiped out, a source of income that will not return any time soon.

This great leveller of a virus has also cruelly exposed our divisions – city dwellers going stir crazy stuck in small flats hit out at those posting pictures of springtime walks in rural iso-lation. Domestic violence has shot up by 80%, despite police launching an app through which victims can call for help, and rising incidences of homicide and suicide speak of rela-tionships that cannot be managed in isolation. Even the most die-hard businesspeople are talking of an unsustainable system which needs to change.

As I glance at Britain – my other country – I feel nostalgic for those days when we too thought that we had any real grip on this disease. Has Italy reached the peak? So they say. Are we flattening the curve? It looks like it. But let's be clear: it is esti-mated that the real figures are at least ten times as high as the official ones. What I now know and see reflected in those around me here is that we don't know anything. We are desperately clinging to science and statistics – our new god – but we in Italy know that this is educated speculation at best.

Italy admits that it reacted late, that its lockdown should have happened much sooner. We cannot understand why it took the US and UK so long to follow our lead when Italy's example was so very evident. And so we still ask: 'But don't they see our suffering? Does what Italy is going through count for nothing?'

I know I have been changed when I listen to a report from the UK stating that care-home residents are being asked to sign 'do not resuscitate' orders and I shudder, grateful that there has never been any such debate in Italy. The initial burst of elation might have calmed, but the sense of solidarity and community still exists, albeit with the volume turned down.

We are getting worryingly used to seeing so many police on the streets and the army closing off certain places. We have even reluctantly accepted the inevitability of tracking apps, surveillance, possibly health certificates as a way out, but are not quite ready yet to contemplate the darker implications of this. We are getting used to the feeling of living in limbo.

Most of all, we are becoming aware that we are all in mass mourning; that the grief that sits on our chests never quite leaves and so we are becoming kinder to ourselves, finding unexpected contentment in living at such a slow pace, letting go of ambitions that already feel like they belong to 'the world before'.

When it reconstructs itself, at all levels of society, there is a palpable desire to make sure Italy is led as much by its heart as it has been through this pandemic. And it is this visceral knowledge, this enforced exercise in empathy, which makes us feel determined to eventually build a society that is fairer and more equal.

The Coronavirus Briefing: An Exercise in Hypernormalisation

Hardeep Matharu

10 APRIL 2020

The daily Downing Street Coronavirus briefings are becoming increasingly terrifying spectacles for two reasons.

The first is the horrendous increase in deaths of people's brothers, mothers, fathers, friends, wives, sisters, colleagues, cousins, neighbours announced in monotone in front of Union Jacks and Georgian panelling.

The second is that, even as the politicians make these most awful of announcements and tell us that every death is a tragedy before relaying the numbers, we – the audience for whom these events are supposedly designed – know, can sense, that those behind the podiums are thankful to be dodging bullets of their own: namely, the briefing itself.

For what should be an exercise in incisive transparency and justifiable scrutiny serves only as a charade of lies, spin and half-truths; a daily theatre designed to connect us in this shared crisis, but which amounts to nothing at all.

Simply put: they're lying, we know they're lying, and they know that we know they're lying.

This little *mise en scène* we're all in is very dangerous. Never more so than now.

In his 2005 book on the last generation of the Soviet Union, anthropology professor Alexei Yurchak argued that everyone knew the Soviet system was failing, but no one could imagine an alternative to it so ordinary people entered into a play with those in power, to maintain a pretence of a normal society. Everyone knew it wasn't real, but it was accepted as so. The society, Yurchak argued, was in a state of 'hypernormalisation'; a fake reality.

I felt the terrifying shudder and shadow of hypernormalisation as I watched today's Coronavirus briefing. It's not that I haven't thought of Yurchak's concept in relation to the UK in recent years before but, unlike then, lives are now urgently at stake.

The Health and Social Care Secretary Matt Hancock was flanked – as is now a standard stage direction – by Deputy

Chief Medical Officer Professor Jonathan Van-Tam and Chief Nursing Officer Ruth May. A bright red and yellow sign resembling a traffic notice screamed 'Stay Home This Easter' but then a car crash did follow.

The subtle infantilisation of the British people, betrayed by apologetic language and a headmasterly tone, continued. We are necessary for this charade – but not on equal terms with those directing it.

Hancock declared that 'we all share a responsibility for tackling this virus by, first and foremost, staying at home'. As he said this, images of tens of thousands of racegoers at last month's Cheltenham Festival swam into my mind. Surely, this thought didn't just spring into the mind of Hancock – a man with a first-class degree in Philosophy, Politics and Economics from Oxford University? Surely he must have seen the photos of the crowds at the races back in March and had some common-sense response or gut instinct about it then?

Announcing his new plan for personal protective equipment (PPE) for frontline healthcare workers, he went on to say that 'everyone working in a critical role must get the PPE that they need' because 'we owe it to them'. But, he also repeatedly said that the workers should only use this equipment when they really need it, 'no more and no less'. We soon discovered why: 'Going into the crisis we did not have a major PPE manufacturing industry'. Hence (although he did not directly connect the two): 'Many items of PPE can be used for a whole session, not be changed after treating each individual patient. Everyone is still protected but there's enough PPE to go around'.

Next was a question from a journalist on why people from around the world are still able to fly into the UK's airports – where no Coronavirus checks are being carried out – and whether this will be stopped. 'We follow the science,' Hancock replied, as if it was obvious. 'We saw right at the start of this pandemic that the two countries that brought in the most draconian international travel restrictions, the United States and Italy, both of them have now got serious problems themselves so I think the science we followed on international travel has been borne out by events.' The use of the word 'draconian' was of note. Why are these measures 'draconian' when the aim is to save lives and the majority of people would likely support them?

But, Professor Van-Tam provided back-up. 'Our scientists have been very clear from the outset that that would not work as a measure to prevent the ingress of Coronavirus into the UK,' he told the journalist. 'Coronavirus is now in the UK and transmitting very widely. I understand the point you're making and I see where you're coming from in terms of when we get this under control, doesn't that change the situation? But we won't go from a position of widespread community transmission amongst our own people to a position of zero transmission amongst our own people.'

There was no mention of the evidence the scientists are basing this on. Again, something which seems to be a common-sense question the public has a right to ask was dismissed – and the journalist could make no comeback as he knew no further crumbs would be thrown to him by way of explanation. Nothing's going to happen to Hancock and the professor if they don't. It's an ordeal for them to get through, with the shedding of as little light as possible.

But, the most obvious cover-up came when Ruth May was asked how many healthcare workers have died because of COVID-19. 'We do have numbers of people who have died, whether they're nurses, midwives, healthcare assistants, doctors,' she said. One would expect the Government to have this. But, we weren't going to hear anything of it.

'It would be inappropriate for me right now to go into listing them and numbering them because we haven't got necessarily all the positions across England, with all of the people's families giving us the permission to talk about them,' she offered. 'It would be inappropriate for me to comment on any individual death that we've seen.' Again, she gave an answer to a question that wasn't asked and in doing so saved herself the trouble of providing the figures – which leaves us to presume that they are distressing.

My feeling towards all of this was a deep sense of anger, but also fear – that we will all simply become comfortably numb faced with this dose of constructed reality, day after day, at exactly the time that the UK is on a trajectory to record the highest Coronavirus death rates in Europe.

And once we have become numb, the charade will burst through and become our actual reality. The scene will not need to be set every day any more.

I do not claim to have the solutions, but we must all find a way to stay alive to the truth, to continue to fight for basic justice – even if that's simply within ourselves – and reflect on what role we are playing in what is unfolding.

As Dostoevsky said, 'Lying to ourselves is more deeply in-grained than lying to others.' Perhaps we all need to start there.

The Lessons of War

Otto English

5 MAY 2020

The lieutenant, a forward intelligence officer in the Royal Engineers, attached to the 10th Indian Division, had his orders: survey the basin of the river, find the shattered bridge and assess the possibility of constructing a Bailey to replace it.

As the German Army retreated north through Italy in June 1944, it was blowing up everything behind it and this was causing a massive headache for the advancing Allied Eighth Army. Bailey bridges were the solution – temporary, pre-fabricated, portable crossings, strong enough to support the weight of tanks, troops and heavy artillery. They could be swiftly constructed and allow the advance to Rome to continue.

The young officer had been allocated a bodyguard of two tough-looking Nepalese Gurkhas to accompany him, but experience taught him that it was better to go alone. More men meant more noise and stealth was of the essence. So he stood the Gurkhas down and crept forward alone into the night. As he passed the outer reaches of the frontline, some-one muttered, 'Rather you than me, mate.' They didn't know the half of it.

Some months earlier, the lieutenant had suddenly gone blind in his left eye and, despite the moonlight, he could barely see the path ahead of him in the dark. Matters weren't helped by the mud. June 1944 had seen a deluge of unseasonal rain and the mountainside was saturated. As he made his way along the narrow track, he slipped across wet rocks and risked losing his boots in the thick mire.

After an hour, he was down. It felt good to be off the treach-erous mountainside, but now he was close to German lines and faced the risk of capture – or worse. Soon, he reached the riverbank and crept towards the tangled remains of the bridge that the retreating Wehrmacht had blown up as it fled.

He took out a pencil, field notebook and torch; sketched the scene and scrawled some notes. After half an hour, and satisfied that he had got what was needed, he put his equipment away and headed back towards the mountain track. By now, any lingering concern had lifted. There were no signs of the enemy and he felt satisfied that the German Army was miles away.

It was almost pleasant to be out at night like this, walking through the Umbrian countryside. His mind drifted to the Italian girl he had met and the dog he had bought her in that market. He was in trouble for that relationship, but the lieutenant was an instinctive rebel and the girl had stolen his heart and he really didn't care.

Just a few weeks earlier, he had witnessed the full horrors of war close at hand during the Battle of Monte Cassino. It had affected him deeply. Any lingering faith in God was gone. Witnessing the brutal endgame and seeing bodies scattered across the hillside had reshaped his outlook on life.

The girl was worth far more to him than the whispers of his comrades and the promotion to captain that he now knew would never come. For the first time, he was truly in love. He wanted to survive the war and live out the rest of his life with her.

Then, suddenly, something to his right caught his one good eye.

Across the short expanse of a river, he could see another man, dressed in the uniform of the German Army Pionier battalion, making notes by torchlight. The Wehrmacht officer was so engrossed in his work that he hadn't noticed him.

What to do? The path up was just a few yards away – he could probably creep to it unnoticed and evince his escape. But wasn't he supposed to kill Germans? Wasn't that the point of war? Wasn't that why he was here?

He unbuttoned his holster, drew his service pistol and dithered. Firing his gun would attract attention but, more than that, he was overcome with the powerful sense that he really didn't want to kill someone. Unfortunately, this moment of pause meant that inaction was no longer an option.

On the opposite riverbank, the German soldier was now staring back at him in the moonlight. The lives of the two young men were now entwined in a moment of common fate. The lieutenant raised his pistol, pulled the trigger, and ran as fast as he could in the opposite direction. Behind him, he heard shouts and perhaps – although he could never quite remember – the return of gunfire.

He ran up the path, slipping and sliding with adrenaline coursing through him and his one good eye letting him down as he tumbled repeatedly into the rocks. He didn't stop until he was well away and up the mountain slope, and only then when he knew he was safely within reach of his own frontline.

When he got back to his campbed, he found it impossible to settle. Had he killed the man? He didn't know. He tried to get to sleep but eventually gave up. The following morning, news came that the enemy had retreated and, as work began on that Bailey bridge, he managed to get across the river. He scouted about, looking for a body or signs of blood and, finding none, convinced himself that he hadn't hit the man, let alone killed him.

And for that, he felt nothing but a deep sense of relief.

Forty years later, and now advancing into his late sixties, the man would tell this story to his teenage son as we walked through the fields.

I had grown up on the staple diet of war films and toys that boys played with well into the 1980s, and the story, repeatedly told as we trod the muddy footpaths of Essex, disappointed me intensely. This tale of fear, of reluctance to kill and relief that he hadn't was at stark odds with the narrative in my head. Why had he run away? Why had he been relieved that the German hadn't been hit? What was wrong with you, Dad? It made no sense.

A decade later, after he died, one of his old comrades told me other stories of my father's war – ones that shone a far more glorious light on his actions. But the story my dad chose to tell me – his son – was the one where he ran away.

The young lieutenant never married his Italian girlfriend and – many years later – met my mother and settled down with her instead. I was born when he was in his fifties and, as such, was out of kilter with most of the other children of my generation. It was mostly their grandparents who had been in the war and, in a way, I suppose knowing Dad had been there made me feel special. I was proud of him – even if the loss of that one eye caused him to drive ever more slowly as he aged, much to the amusement of my contemporaries.

Like millions of other ex-servicemen, as time receded, he looked back in fondness on the adventures of his youth and the comradeship of war. His closest friends were those who had been through it with him and survived. They were kindly, funny, decent people who had a type of wisdom that the generation that followed seemed to envy. These veterans were not incomparable super-beings but ordinary men forged by the exceptional circumstances of lives uprooted by events beyond their control.

It was only fifty years after VE Day that my dad bothered to put his service medals together and he only wore them that one summer, as he and his old comrades marched on that last great parade through London. He told me that same year that he hadn't 'celebrated' the original VE Day – which came while he was in Germany – because 'I didn't really see what there was to celebrate'. But he wanted to see his old friends again, so he went down to London for the day.

His views were solidly old-school Conservative. He believed in our place in Europe because 'I don't want you to have to waste your youth and risk your life doing what I had to do'.

He died in 1998 and would have been horrified by the tacky

appropriation of his war by tin-pot nationalists whose experience of the fear of battle extended no further than the cadets parade ground at Dulwich College.

This VE Day, I took my son for a walk in the park behind our house and told him once again about the amazing grandad he never knew and how lucky we are that, one night in June 1944, in a valley in Umbria, he ran away.

25 May 2020

George Floyd is murdered by Minneapolis police officer Derek Chauvin during an arrest after a store clerk had alleged he used a counterfeit $20 bank note.

White Complicity Matters: The Nazis by the Lake

Musa Okwonga

5 JUNE 2020

Like countless others, I find myself thinking of James Baldwin, and an old song that he quoted in a famous collection of his essays. That song, referring to the time in the Old Testament when the Earth was flooded as divine punishment, bore the following warning: *God gave Noah the rainbow sign, no more water, the fire next time.*

As we look at the United States, at a map where all fifty states are united in protest against the murder of yet another black person by a police officer, we see that this time we have the fire: that the tears of grief have been replaced by the flames of rage.

Some will argue that, in order to achieve a broader political goal, all this burning is unproductive, but in one sense they will be missing the point.

For a long time, black people were only tolerated in the

United States so long as they were quite literally productive: for as long as they filled a basket with cotton, or chopped a pile of wood, or laid yet another section of track. In a country where black people were bought and sold for their ability to turn their efforts into end results, it might be said that there is something poetic and even political about rage for its own sake. If someone has a nail driven through their foot, it seems perverse to tell them that their scream was inappropriately loud.

Of course, there has long been plenty of thought about how to make wider and positive change, and that thought has crossed borders. In recent weeks, we have seen the globalisation of protest against police brutality, with massive gatherings in Amsterdam and Paris.

In Berlin, I witnessed a smaller but no less passionate throng, led by a speech of magnificent anger by the artist and researcher Diana Arce. Arce, like many other black people in the crowd, was fed up with compromise, with gently walking white people through the stages of ending racial oppression. For her, it was no longer simply good enough for white people to attend these vigils and then congratulate themselves for having joined. It was now time for them to make the necessary and painstaking efforts in their own homes and communities.

There are some who might say that it is ineffective to call white people out for their refusal to engage with racism, that it is important to bring people gently along. Those people should note that, several years ago, James Baldwin called them out too. 'People who shut their eyes to reality simply invite their own destruction,' he wrote, 'and anyone who insists on remaining in a state of innocence long after that innocence is dead turns himself into a monster.'

If there are white people who, having watched the slow-motion murder of George Floyd, still need further evidence that there is something wrong with the criminal justice system's treatment of black people, then those people are monsters. They may bristle at this definition, they may point at all the lovely and kind things they do in their personal lives, but that will be no excuse. Their apathy is the fuel for further horror, since it is precisely their embarrassed silence upon which these murderers rely.

Recent events have seen two forms of unity.

The first is that of black people and non-black people around the world who care about us, who have been united by our fury at injustice.

The second is by those people in Europe, mostly white, who have seen the video of George Floyd's death and used it as a form of one-upmanship against the United States. Their revulsion at Floyd's murder has quickly turned not to compassion but to relief: they have comforted themselves that they are not as base or hateful as those Yanks, that these atrocities could not happen in their countries. These people are united by denial. Among these white people, the murder of George Floyd has not been used as a moment for introspection but as a sort of wine tasting of white supremacy, where Europeans take a sip of vintage American racism and proudly declare that it tastes much more sour than theirs.

I sometimes feel that, instead of asking black people how they feel about yet another gruesome death of a black person at police hands, the media should approach random white people in the street and demand: 'Yet another death due to police brutality. How does this make you feel? What can you as white people do to stop it?' After all, black people are constantly and collectively expected to be accountable for our trauma, to relate it as eloquently and concisely as we can for white people to digest – a little like the maid who chews the food so it is soft enough for the baby. I did an interview for a German media outlet where I chewed the food. I spoke for three minutes about a subject so emotionally exhausting that I turned aside my next three commissions – an act of spiritual self-preservation.

I do wonder: how much more do people need to see? Why was it necessary for me to go on television and give further context to a man being casually choked to death by a policeman's knee? Why was it necessary for me to go on there and become so nervous that I had not done the interview justice that I could not bring myself to watch it for almost two days? Why, for those two days, did I have to carry the burden of shame that I may have let down the black community? Why did I have the pressure of explaining oppression? Why, in order to make more white people care, do we black people have to make our deaths sound poetic?

I urge every white person reading this not to be someone for whom black people have to chew the food. I urge them not to look at the protests sweeping across many places and maintain that there is not a problem here. I urge them not to be those who point at injustice and then stand by.

A few months ago, I got into conversation with one of the locals here in Berlin. He told me that he often went to the countryside and, on one occasion, he went to the lake and found three young men, each of whom – as it turned out – were passionately enthusiastic about the work of a neo-Nazi band. As he told me the story, assuring me that – aside from that – they had been very pleasant, my stomach began to implode as it dawned on me that he had not said anything critical. Embarrassed, he swiftly moved the subject on.

Over the coming days, I thought more and more about what this man had done.

First, he had told me about a gorgeous, picturesque place he had been on holiday. He then informed me that it was not only frequented by some of the people who view me with an existential level of hatred but that, to give himself an easier life, he had said nothing and done nothing about people whose views he despised. Nothing at all. He had, in effect, become the marketing arm for these right-wing extremists – their message being that black people were not welcome in that beautiful part of the world, and even the good people would not put in a good word on their behalf.

In racial terms, he had perhaps seen me as some kind of Catholic priest for whom he sought forgiveness for not speaking out against bigotry, his confession tumbling from his tongue at the speed of white guilt. And, a couple of days after that, I felt calmer.

I thought: you know what? Maybe I am being harsh on him, maybe he was terrified too. Maybe he was scared to voice any kind of challenge. Maybe he was too worried even to say, 'ah, that music scene is not really for me'.

Yet, at the same time, maybe it is this silence – repeated millions of times by white people with quietly fearful hearts – which meant that millions of Jews looked around one day and thought: *how can this be? We have given so much to this continent, we have done everything they asked us to, we have lived and loved and laughed and danced and integrated, and still no one is coming to save us?*

So my last request is this. If you are someone who, when your voice is most needed, remains committed to that silence; if you are someone who, even after seeing what was done to George Floyd, still shrinks into their chair when they hear any hint of a racist rant from a friend, relative or stranger; then don't keep telling me and other black people that you are utterly unprepared to resist the terror which we most likely know is already there.

Don't tell me there are Nazis by the lake.

To Alabama and Back: Holding Up a Mirror to Racism

Hannah Charlton

25 JUNE 2020

It is pouring with rain. I'm standing outside the long, dark wall of a building in downtown Montgomery waiting to go through security, asking myself: why am I here? What right do I have to be here?

I'm in front of the National Memorial for Peace and Justice in Alabama. It is a visionary name for the first ever public commemoration for the victims of lynching and violent terror in the post-slavery period of American history when white supremacy forced black communities into subjugation and segregation: America's greatest wound, as yet unhealed and never fully acknowledged.

I'm feeling a complicated mix of emotions. Anxiety, confusion and the anticipation of deep shame, and of somehow being held accountable. I didn't yet know *how* to be here.

I had bought my ticket to both the memorial and its partner project the Legacy Museum across the road in a new building home to the Equal Justice Initiative (EJI). $3.50 was the price for a day that would lead me deep into the divided heart of America. It would also force me to examine my own personal British collusion.

Later, I came to understand just how privileged my curiosity was. The curiosity that would take me through Selma and along the road to Montgomery that the Civil Rights marchers took to demand the right to vote. But I needed to turn the inquiry on myself.

The first sight of the memorial is a long, low structure up on a slope, past a sculpture of enslaved people straining at their chains in terror. Under the roof were row upon row of steel coffin shapes, with just enough space to walk between. Each of these weathered steel caskets had etched into it the name of a county and below the names and death dates of those individuals brutally murdered during the years of violent terror. Walking through this forest of hanging headstones was to be confronted with waves of tragic deaths – women and men, sisters, brothers and the more poignant unknowns.

As I went lower through the memorial's spiral structure, the steel headstones gradually rose above me becoming hanging pillars so that I was looking up at the foot of the head-stone just as the lynching witnesses would have looked up to the body hanging from the tree. And I found myself mouthing each name listed – Charles Curtis, Hollis Riles, Cairo Williams, Hog Wilson, Bernice Raspberry, Smead Stith, Ballie Crutch-field – and perhaps in this way, recognising, infinitesimally, each victim.

I was surrounded by older white Americans, older African Americans, a group of Africans in their patterned dashikis. Everyone was quiet, absorbed in their own journey. I was uncomfortably conscious of how the design of the headstones pulled me, the visitor, into the position of the white voyeurs encouraged to come and witness the event. It reinforced the calculated desire of the white mobs to show that they had the power to terrorise entire communities of colour. It also made me painfully aware of the profoundly different experiences we, the visitors, were sharing – close physically in this moment but significantly distant in our own histories.

Along the wall was a series of small cameo plaques, record-ing the reason given for an individual lynching. To the weight of the steel caskets above was now added the weight of the stories on the wall – each one a life brutally terminated for slight infractions of white men's rules, with force, to humiliate black people for drinking from a white person's well, marry-ing a white man, marrying a white woman.

*

The man behind this initiative is justice advocate Bryan Stevenson. He has a bold vision of asking America to confront the true legacy of slavery and specifically of racial terror which he connects directly to today's mass incarceration and excessive sentencing.

For Stevenson, there is a continuation of the same racist narrative that mutated from the belief of white supremacy – that black people were inferior – into an extension that they were dangerous. 'Black codes' – introduced in the South for fabricated crimes such as loitering – legitimised the justice system to brand African Americans as felons and to continue slavery for white profit in the form of convict leasing. In a vicious spiral, this narrative, with felony and disenfranchisement at its centre, continues today.

A lawyer and activist, Stevenson founded the not-for-profit Equal Justice Initiative in Montgomery and guaranteed a defence of anyone in Alabama sentenced to the death penalty. Alabama was the only state at the time that did not provide legal assistance to people on death row.

The first EJI offices were near the landing at the Alabama River where slaves were unloaded on arrival. Stevenson looked around at the number of monuments devoted to Confederate heroes and found virtually nothing to mark – and recognise – the parallel history of slavery and its contribution to American development and wealth.

I found myself looking at the streets of Montgomery

through Stevenson's lens. Astonishingly, there is no statue commemorating Dr Martin Luther King Jr, the leader of the Civil Rights Movement. Although there is now a memorial trail of the 1965 march and an abundance of Civil Rights history sites, the Confederate presence feels palpably stronger.

The complexity and divisions in this city became more and more apparent at every turn. Alabama, it is clear, is both the most relevant place for Stevenson to start a new process of historical acknowledgement but also the toughest.

America has two historical narratives – one white, one black – and this division is rarely addressed, let alone shared and represented in the national landscape.

Following a long wall dedicated to the many undocumented victims, I continued to the centre of the spiral, called Memorial Square. Here is an unmarked spot from which it is unavoidable not to look down and imagine the crowds invited to witness, accept and welcome this public crime of killing.

I shared the central space with a Jewish teenager, one of a school group visiting the site. As we exchanged places on the square, I asked him quietly what it was like for him being in this place. He hesitated. 'Intense,' he said. 'Very intense.' He then murmured he was at a loss to answer. I said thank you and we both moved on. He came up to me ten minutes later, outside, and said he had given my question some thought. 'I'm Jewish and I know many Jews were active in supporting the Civil Rights Movement,' he told me. 'I can be proud of that.

But I'm also white. So I feel shame. I guess you'd have to say I have conflicting identities.'

I emerged from the central part of the memorial full of horror and guilt at what I had learned and how much I needed to question my own participation and privilege. I had come back to America at a time when many of the certainties of my life had been entirely capsized. I had left behind a UK that, since 2016, had changed and polarised in ways I had never imagined. With our isolationist policy, hell-bent on leaving Europe, a media-led group of Brexiters had used a distorted view of history to make the case for going it alone, at a time when global cooperation has never appeared more essential. Added into the mix was a rise of racist venom and hatred that I had not felt since the 1970s. Looming on the horizon, at the beginning of March, was the Coronavirus pandemic – revealing just how unprepared we were to deal with a global crisis.

I brought this mindset to Alabama, ready to absorb the pain of another country. But what I had not expected was that it consistently brought me back to my own context and my own history. And my white privilege – now sharply brought into focus globally by the death of George Floyd and the resulting protests and demands for equality and justice.

Outside the memorial building I found long rows of duplicate steel caskets lying in wait, with a rust-like patina on their surface. These are the caskets that Stevenson envisages will be accepted by each individual county and erected in their soil, not only to recognise the victims of lynching, but for each community to begin its own local process of acknowledgement and responsibility for the past.

He has talked of this Community Remembrance Marker project as being a way of creating a 'landscape of persuasion'. His concept is to populate the American landscape with a different representation of history and to begin a process of reflection and healing. But, the core of his vision is to address racial bias and make sentencing changes in the criminal justice system and to halt the insidious route towards felony and disenfranchisement.

It is a measure of the emotional and political distance that there is still to travel that few counties have accepted the invitation to take part in the initiative. Stevenson fully recognises the enormity of the task. He is shaping a journey of intimidating scale, but his vision invites all of us to take that journey with him, held by a compassion that makes it possible.

The Legacy Museum is close by and it continues the experience with some highly innovative storytelling, including two specific encounters that registered intensely with me.

The first was meeting a wall of transparent urns, filled with earth – the result of volunteers collecting soil from lynching sites and bringing it to the museum. Watching videos of people talking about taking the blood and DNA in the soil to a place where it will be respected rather than leaving it by the roadside is to meet truth in a stark, visceral and undeniable way. Stevenson has expressed the impact of this initiative as rooted in the earth: 'In this soil, there is the sweat of the enslaved. In the soil, there is the blood of victims of racial violence and lynching. But, in the soil, there is also the opportunity for new life, a chance to grow something hopeful and healing for the future.'

I listened to a story on the radio that brought this poignantly home, about a volunteer who was digging up earth on a lynching site in Alabama. A car pulled up on the road alongside her and a white man rolled down the window to ask what she was doing. She said that, for one moment, she fell back into a form of fear. But then she had the courage to raise her eyes to his and explain exactly what she was doing. He said that his family had owned this land for decades and had no idea about the lynching. He then opened the door, came over to her and asked if he could help dig. Together they filled the urn.

Montgomery's Civil Rights museums tend to focus on the past. The EJI seeks to go further and use the past to address the present and the future. Michelle Alexander's book *The New Jim Crow: Mass Incarceration in the Age of Colorblindness* outlined how the 'War on Drugs' enabled low-level crime to be over-punished, resulting in a significant number of African American men being categorised as felons and having their voting rights removed. The contemporary legacy of slavery is clearly outlined in the museum: 70% of American prisoners are non-white and one in nine black men under twenty-five are in jail or prison, on probation or on parole.

The second encounter to resonate with me was to turn from the wall of incarceration facts to the experience of sitting in a prison visitor booth and lifting the phone to hear the voice of a man on death row talking to me, while watching a life-size video of him, eye to eye, face to face.

Anthony Hinton was on death row for thirty years before he proved his innocence. Now a key advocate for EJI, he describes the daily burden of being unlawfully convicted and then asks, 'What would you do? What would you think each day? For all those years?' Most importantly, he asks the question 'Who do you think you would be when you came out?' This is an overwhelming piece of empathetic drama that emphasises the presumption of guilt forced onto African Americans. One of the guides told me that this is one of the strongest memories visitors, especially young people, take away from the museum.

I came out into the afternoon air and the voice of Anthony Hinton swirled round inside me. Not only did I question my own white privilege, I also wondered what my legacy museum would be. What would be inside a British museum dedicated to the entire history of the British Empire and the cost of our wealth?

But first I wanted to find out how voting on 'Super Tuesday' was going. The Civil Rights activists, led by Dr King, had fought for the right to register black voters in 1965. But in Alabama, it is still not easy to vote. In a grim echo of the fight for citizen rights over half a century ago, this state continues to be one of the most difficult places for an eligible voter to register and cast a ballot.

This voter suppression applies significantly more to African Americans through purged voter rolls, the shutting down of driving-licence offices (the easiest way to obtain the required photo ID), a closure of polling stations in mostly black counties, as well as felony disenfranchisement schemes.

I came across a school voting station, with its entrance a forest of voting signs, all in the same tones of red and blue. The system seemed impenetrable. We were handed an official guide ballot and rapidly drowned in a sea of print – eleven ballots, forty-six names, options of politicians, judges, education board at national, state and county level.

It is feared that voter suppression, especially among African American communities, will be a key element of Donald Trump's campaign for re-election in November. The Democratic nominee for the presidency, Joe Biden, had come to church in Selma for the fifty-fifth anniversary of Bloody Sunday and spoke of the new rise in hate under Trump: 'If you give hate any breathing room, it comes back.' Biden won the vote, largely with the support of the black churches.

As the scale of Stevenson's task grew clearer, so did the realisation that I needed to go on my own journey – both back through my life and also back to Britain, to look with different eyes at my own history and the narratives that are still so heavily perpetuated. Time for home truths.

Since returning to London and being in self-isolation, I have embarked on a late-in-life white-supremacy journey.

Layla Saad and her book *Me and White Supremacy: Combat Racism, Change the World, and Become a Good Ancestor* have been a revelation, along with Bryan Stevenson, Akala, Afua Hirsch and Kalwant Bhopal. Saad especially has directed me, stage by stage, with piercing accuracy, to examine all the many aspects of white privilege, fragility and silence as well as shattering any notion that it is people of colour who have the responsibility to 'dismantle white supremacy'. The work starts with me.

I went to Alabama with a mindset of white, privileged curiosity and the desire to tell a story about 'somewhere else'. But the experience took me on a much deeper journey back into hard truths about my own whiteness, our dark imperialist past, and how we have turned a blind eye to our legacy.

We need to be much closer to all aspects of our past, to stand below the weight of the steel caskets, to intone the names of the dead, to stand face to face with a statue the same height as ourselves. We need to process these experiences in our bodies as well as in our minds in order for them to disturb us enough for change. The journey, Saad says, to be a good ancestor requires truth, commitment and the courage to love on a greater scale than we have ever done.

What would a British memorial to equality and justice look like? What would be our markers within each and every community affected by our colonialism? What would it take to have the courage together to address the systemic racism deep in our cultural DNA? To bring the legacy of Empire – so far away from our small island – closer to our consciousness? To have a new 'landscape of persuasion' across Britain so that, individually and collectively, we can address our past and move towards a greater level of equality and justice?

Should Special Forces be Policing Our Cities?

CJ Werleman

23 JULY 2020

Several years ago, I was in Israel and the Palestinian Territories conducting background research for a book I planned to write on the psychological and emotional impact soldiers experience after carrying out their first confirmed killing at close distance.

It was a challenging undertaking for many reasons – not least because so few now actually get close enough to the enemy due to the advanced technologies of modern warfare and the hit-and-run nature of insurgency and counter-insurgency conflict. Armed drones, satellite technology, laser-guided missiles and weapons allow soldiers to 'paint' the target with a laser, rather than engage with it directly, making the act of killing a task carried out by combatants that are often located a continent away from the battlefield.

But the personal testimonies I gathered, alongside other published material on the issue, provided enough information for me to hypothesise that members of elite or special forces are high-functioning psychopaths. This is not a moral or ethical judgement, but rather an observation of the emotionally dissociative state of those who are trained to kill and kill again at face-to-face distance to the enemy. It is also not controversial, given that special forces operatives are often known to describe themselves as 'compassionate psychopaths'.

I use this hypothesis not to denigrate the military's most elite soldiers, but to discuss how their training and combat experience might have an effect in shaping the way in which militarised police departments exercise force upon those protesting illiberal, failing and corrupt governments.

Much has been written about the broad trend towards the militarisation of police forces in Western democracies since 9/11, particularly the way in which surplus combat equipment has been procured and assigned to local police departments.

It is a conversation that has been amplified now that President Donald Trump is deploying armed border-patrol officers to what he calls 'Democrat cities'. Court documents reveal, for instance, that Trump deployed a secretive federal unit, which undergoes training designed to mimic special forces, to crush anti-racism protestors in Oregon under the mission name 'Operation Diligent Valor'.

For the acclaimed historian Timothy Snyder, author of *On Tyranny: Twenty Lessons from the Twentieth Century*, 'this is a classic way that violence happens in authoritarian regimes, whether it's Franco's Spain or whether it's the Russian Empire. The people who are getting used to committing violence on the border are then brought in to commit violence against people in the interior'.

Therefore, if we are to have an honest conversation about the militarisation of police departments and the domestic deployments of armed units trained and staffed by special-forces soldiers to cities, we must consider how their psychological states might threaten the lives of citizens and the future of democracy.

In Tel Aviv in 2016, I met a former member of the US Army's Delta Force – one of its prized assets and tasked with carrying out specialised operations against high-value targets. Covered from neck to wrist in tattoos, with many referencing Christian Crusader iconography, he told me that his unit was one of the first dropped into Afghanistan after 9/11 to lay the groundwork for Operation Anaconda, which took place from 1 March 2002 – the first large battle against Taliban and al-Qaeda forces since the Battle of Tora Bora two months earlier. Despite the fact that an estimated 800 enemy forces were killed during seventeen days of fighting, he would have to wait a further four years to take part in his first confirmed kill.

'Most of the time we were guiding air strikes onto enemy positions or engaging with them at night and at long distance, so confirmed enemy KIAs ['killed in action'] are impossible to tell,' he said.

In late February 2006, as US forces sought to clear the Iraqi city of Ramadi of insurgents, his unit was tasked with clearing an enemy supply point. 'I pushed open a slightly ajar door and the door swung gently back towards me, which is often a sign someone is standing behind the door,' he said. When he stepped inside and peered behind the door, a fourteen-year-old boy stood there, trembling and paralysed with fear. 'I held my finger to my mouth to make the "shush" gesture, pulled him towards me, so he was facing away from me, covered his mouth and then stuck my knife into his neck, killing him,' he said. When I asked him how he felt then and now about killing the boy, he replied: 'No regrets. It was unfortunate, but that's war and the mission was successful.'

This man claimed to have carried out 'dozens' of similar missions in Iraq and in Afghanistan before leaving the military and becoming a US air marshall in 2012. He said that a number of his former team members are now actively employed in US law enforcement.

The concerns this raises are not confined to America, however.

New revelations have emerged regarding the conduct of Australia's special forces in Afghanistan, with one investigation revealing a photo of two Australian SAS soldiers holding a Confederate flag emblazoned with the words 'Southern Pride' while on operations there in 2012.

'Two SAS troopers holding a Confederate flag in Afghanistan suggests that the culture is breaking down,' former Australian soldier Ben Wadham, a professor in sociology, has said. 'What it indicates . . . and, we've seen this over time, is that there is a strong race politics in the Australian Defence Force.'

Flags and symbols of racism and hatred are one thing, but the murder of unarmed and non-threatening non-combatants is another altogether. It is now evident that overt displays of white supremacism are affecting the way Australian forces carry out military operations abroad, as revealed in the leak of hundreds of pages of classified Australian Defence Force documents in 2017.

The documents not only provided an unprecedented view into how members of the country's elite forces carried out clandestine operations in Afghanistan from 2001 to 2013, but also the growing unease among the military's upper ranks towards systemic 'problems' within its elite forces, a 'warrior culture' and a Mafia-like code of silence rewarding or ignoring acts ordinarily considered war crimes. More troubling are revelations that members of Australia's special forces deliberately shot and killed unarmed men, women and children before planting weapons on their bodies to conceal their crimes, with one document revealing how an SAS corporal severed the hands of dead Afghan insurgents because of 'tactical necessity'.

'When you're back at the unit, people would make jokes about the size of the rug that they've swept everything under, and that one day it'll all come out and people are going to be thrown in jail for murder or anything else that they've done,' Braden Chapman, a former SAS operative deployed to Afghanistan, told an Australian news outlet. Chapman revealed that a 'culture of impunity' exists among special-forces units and how he witnessed former team members executing civilians in 'cold blood'. Former members of these units are increasingly being recruited into Australian state police departments, particularly in a counter-terrorism capacity.

'Those units are trained by the Australian Defence Force,' John Sutton, a lawyer and former Australian Defence Force officer, has said. 'They are armed with weapons systems very similar to what the Australian Defence Force use and, in some instances, there are lots of tactics, techniques and procedures which are given to those police units from the Australian Defence Force.'

The behaviour of Australian special-forces units mirrors that of their American counterparts. A 2011 investigation revealed how US Ranger, Delta Force and Navy SEAL units murdered innocent civilians with a sense of impunity in Afghanistan.

The number of American soldiers fighting under the leadership of special-forces units has doubled since 2001 and, with the 'War on Terror' winding down, a greater number of these soldiers are likely to be recruited into the country's police forces to carry out counter-insurgency operations against their fellow citizens if Trump's current clampdown on protestors in 'Democrat cities' becomes a new normal for suppressing activism.

In Chicago, public defenders, attorneys and activists are 'bracing for their neighbourhoods to be hunted, not protected', according to Flint Taylor, a Chicago lawyer.

The question citizens of the US and other Western democracies must now ask is whether they wish to have their streets and communities patrolled by 'compassionate psychopaths', who hold little or no emotional or physical connection to the city to which they have been deployed, on behalf of increasingly authoritarian governments.

The Generational Fears Holding Young Asian People Back

Pruthvi Khilosia

30 JULY 2020

The South Asian story in the UK imitates its own culture – bringing a vibrant contribution to the nation alongside its struggles.

A better understanding of acceptance and ethnic integration has paved a safer path in society for many first-generation families, and the creative arts and media have been a platform to turn to. But many young South Asians still find it difficult to get into an industry that isn't the norm within their culture – preventing stories of identity, struggle and acceptance from being heard and fostering a systemic racism that should be examined.

It is simplistic to point the finger at a 'lack of ambition' or 'interest' by people from these backgrounds in taking creative paths – the problems run deeper than that. As the award-winning *Killing Eve* actress Sandra Oh recently said, her professional development had been 'behind' and 'slow'.

For South Asians, it is about understanding why it is a struggle for them to make it into such an industry and how the pressures of culture and society can be accommodated. Under 20% of South Asian minorities are in skilled or managerial roles

– a position of power within the creative industries that can put their stories in the right hands, enabling an authentic cultural understanding.

I was fortunate to meet Britain's Asian film icon and director Gurinder Chadha, known for films such as *Bend It Like Beckham*, for a student project – a short documentary on how South Asians make it in the media. A British Indian woman who came to the UK with her family, Chadha's is a story many ethnic-minority people share in this country. Her struggle to fit into British society has only made her more passionate in expressing her views.

National Front riots were one of the many hurtful memories of her upbringing that led to her earlier works such as *Bhaji on the Beach* and *I'm British But . . .* – a landmark exploration of what it meant to be a young British Asian in the new cultural environment of the 1980s, depicting identity struggles South Asians still face today.

'I needed to be able to tell my own stories, so I went into television and then into film,' Chadha said, talking about her journey as a director.

My project explored why it is a challenge to break into a creative career from my background and how making it can open up doors and inspire others alike.

Growing up in an Asian community, you bring your cultural taboos with you. And these taboos are often built on fear. One of the most common fears young people from these communities often hold is that being creative 'isn't a traditional career – an Asian career', Chadha said. This often stems from worries that the previous generation had about whether to play it 'safe' and take the first job they were given when they came to Britain, or take their chances and do something bigger. This mindset is something many young people in Asian communities internalise and agonise over, something that is part of their very culture – and so important that it can limit their futures, regardless of where their passions lie.

Support from families and the wider community can be the first step to having the confidence to do what you want to – something journalist Adnan Riaz agrees with. 'They never had it easy by far,' Riaz said of his family when I interviewed him for my project. 'I had a lot of freedom compared to other Asian children. [The] support network was very important.'

The ugly truth is that it takes extra measures to accommodate the cultural pressures, the systematic bias and racism minorities face in order to give them the same opportunities as people from non-ethnic-minority backgrounds. Microaggression, generational poverty, as well as pressures from within their communities as a result of cultural fears, all need to be understood by the industry and those high up within it, who will not be familiar with these concerns in their own lives.

'If I wanted to see people like me in the media then I had to be part of that change,' journalist Siddra Asghar told me. 'It's really hard, especially for an Asian person because you do come up with a lot of challenges in terms of cultural pressure and societal pressures. Another element for me was being a woman of colour because the experience of a woman is different in the Asian community.'

The work of those such as Gurinder Chadha have shown what it means to be 'British', especially for first-generation minorities. 'I have a bank of work that will stand the test of time and will always be there as a record of how our community has developed,' Chadha said.

Such work is important because, in itself, it highlights the questions of identity and societal pressures young people from these backgrounds have to grapple with, but it also gives hope and courage that they *can* do it – including to a British Indian twenty-one-year-old in the white suburbs of Lancashire, who wants to believe in being able to do something he always wanted to without fear holding him back.

The People Rejecting Mainstream Living

Douglas Whitbread

31 JULY 2020

Matthew Watkinson trudges up the slopes of his off-the-grid property in Pembrokeshire, West Wales. 'We didn't really trust the rest of the world to look after us properly,' he says about why he and his family left their suburban home in Essex. 'We weren't really predicting a viral pandemic like this, but we were concerned.'

The 2008 financial crisis was a wake-up call. 'Mainstream science was telling us there's a big problem environmentally,' he says. 'It just struck me that I didn't want to be that reliant on all these massive corporations when there's a different way.'

Today, his mostly timber home – built from a recycled horse lorry – a camper van and two flatbed trailers blend into the landscape. But, amid the fern and gorse, the family of four have enough resources to satisfy their basic requirements. Solar panels, a wind turbine, firewood and a biogas digester provide their energy. A spring supplies fresh water, and honey and egg sales generate income. Within a few years, the land should also provide most of their food.

'We don't have a mortgage, we don't have utility bills,' Matthew says. 'We're not totally separate from society … but we're more insulated than most.'

While this might seem like an exercise in individualism, Matthew's situation stems from a radical Welsh planning policy which set a new precedent for rural existence. His property is a One Planet Development (OPD) – a subsistence-based smallholding built in open countryside. There are forty-two dotted throughout Wales. The planning status comes with conditions: a household's ecological footprint must be a fraction of what most produce; its occupants must meet 65% of their minimum needs after five years; and their premises must be carbon neutral and allow for an on-site business.

'If people were going to have access to purchase land at agricultural prices in the countryside, they had to give back big time in terms of their stewardship functions of that land,' says Dr Jane Davidson, the ex-Welsh minister responsible for the policy.

The sustainable development scheme, launched in 2009, tied factors such as national prosperity and public health to citizens living within their environmental limits and later inspired Wales's landmark Well-being of Future Generations Act. 'This was about a different form of governance,' Jane explains. 'Environmentalism, [viewed] by traditional economists, is seen as preventive and stopping actions. I don't see this at all in that way. For me, it's about . . . changing to new actions.'

But by allowing people to live on agricultural land – covering three-quarters of Wales – the OPD concept wasn't without controversy. 'It flew in the face of conventional planning wisdom [which has existed] ever since the Second World War and the attempt to preserve greenbelt around cities,' says David Thorpe, a writer and journalist. His book *The One Planet Life* argues that mass job creation, food security and the replenishment of soils would result from 'recolonising the countryside' with labour-intensive OPD farms. But he also suggests small settlements, and even cities, could adopt their principles. 'There's two different kinds of community,' he says.

'One is a cluster of houses, where they're all still responsible for their own management plan and they live fairly separate lives ... [another], where it's a genuine village, where a lot of the services are combined.'

Tucked away amid Pembrokeshire's Preseli Hills, Lammas eco-village – formed in 2009 under the scheme – shows how this could work in practice.

'In a sense, we were a continuation of the low-impact development movement that has been evolving in this country for decades and decades,' says Tao Wimbush, a founder. 'But instead of acting outside the planning system, we were attempting to create a niche and operate within it ... The current social, political status quo has to transform. And it can either choose to embrace that transformation or it will be forced upon it. Why? Because the ecology will require it.'

Lammas began as a collaborative enterprise, whereby stakeholders made joint decisions about community needs. Over the years, this system evolved.

Tao cultivates indigenous crops that flourish without the need for fertilisers. Proponents say that this model, known as permaculture farming, yields up to five times the produce of industrial practices, while increasing biodiversity. But volatile weather remains a challenge. 'It's a constant dance,' Tao says about working in this way. 'Last year we had "the beast from the east", which brought in some really heavy frosts in late

March, beginning of April. That had a knock-on effect right through the growing season.' Tao doesn't just rely on plant-based protein, however. From his window, he motions to a 'wether', a castrated male goat, in a nearby paddock. 'It's walking around at the moment,' he says, '[but] I'm just waiting for the right time to kill him and chop him up.' For city-slickers, bred on a diet of cellophane-wrapped meat, this may sound alien. But Tao insists that OPD life isn't about disavowing society altogether. 'Most of us do a bit of part-time work in the mainstream ... whether it's nursing, a bit of mechanics, a bit of planning consultancy,' he says. 'We drive vehicles. We use a bit of fossil fuel. But by and large ... our lifestyles are balanced, and in a way, that's what the planning policy does.'

On the border of Caerphilly and Cardiff lies Dan and Sarah Moody's OPD.

As teens, they felt inspired by John Seymour's *Complete Book of Self-Sufficiency*, a bible for those wanting to live off the grid. 'We couldn't afford to live in the house that we were in,' says Dan. 'So we just moved onto the land, with five home-educated kids, and lived in a Mongolian yurt and a gypsy caravan and an old lorry that was set up as a living space.' Over time, they added a barn and shipping container, along with a wooden cabin, the basis of their current home. But, in 2012, their off-the-grid dream was threatened. No Welsh council had accepted an OPD proposal at this point and the policy had effectively stalled, with applicants unable to prove their viability to sceptical local authorities. In 2014, after a lengthy process, the Moodys became the first to be approved.

Dan and Sarah learned to optimise their land's resources over many years, without any formal training. 'We started growing our own food, and then, the kind of realisation of how important organic and good food is, and looking after the environment, and looking after the soil, and looking after all that sort of stuff [took place],' Dan says.

As more people work remotely, the idea of swapping clogged cities for palatial eco-homes may sound appealing. Ryan Anderson (not his real name) was someone who made this trade. 'Basically, we were looking for a different way of life,' he says. 'We weren't on the housing ladder. We didn't want to get into mortgage debt. So we were looking for gaps, possibilities.'

This began when he moved with his family to Wales in 2013 and put down roots in a community. Three years later, they found a site that fitted the planning criteria. But, since moving onto the land last May to build their home, it hasn't been easy. 'We've been living in sheds over winter, and it's been freezing and quite challenging with all these big storms,' he says. 'We've got two kids, [and] we really want to get in our house by next winter.'

His land will also require a lot of work to bear fruit. Unlike others living on OPDs, who are now managing a multi-layered ecosystem, Ryan and his family are just beginning this journey. 'We've been working the land, planting apple trees, which take a good five years to really be quite productive, so there's a time factor,' he says. In the eyes of those pursuing this route, however, the hardship is worth bearing. Ryan is not part of the 'cottagecore' trend of romanticised country living and views this action as essential in preserving the world's resources. 'Everybody really needs to be doing "one planet living",' he says. 'Because if we're going to sustain ourselves, we've only got one planet.'

Despite the support offered by the Welsh Government, there hasn't been an explosion in OPD properties and the concept still fills a minor role in the country's environmental policy agenda. But, as the Coronavirus pandemic uproots economic orthodoxy, a social security net arising from nature, not capital, may be the only way forward.

The Crushing of Cardiff's Thriving Tiger Bay

Chris Sullivan

5 AUGUST 2020

Tiger Bay was a unique multicultural area, in Butetown and around Cardiff Docks, dating back nearly 200 years.

'In Butetown there existed a total racial harmony,' recalls

fifty-six-year-old Richard Cordle who was born and bred in the area. 'It was pure heaven. You had every race under the sun; everyone knew each other, including every last shop owner and landlord. Everybody helped each other out if they were in trouble. It was like one big extended family made up of people who were proud of their community. I am and always will be proud to be a docks boy.' Unfortunately, the picture painted by Cordle – of harmonious diversity – has now been lost in the name of progress and 'regeneration'.

By 1870, Cardiff was a major iron and coal export port and, by the 20th Century, one of the world's biggest docks. Sailors brought their cargo, mores, music and culture. They caroused, drank and brawled in the area's bars and spent their wages in the gambling dens and brothels of the free-thinking, egalitarian Bute Street.

Back then, there were Basque, Italian, African and Somali cafés alongside clubs and all-night shebeens playing black dance music in Tiger Bay. In 1911, the area was described as one of the most colourful and cosmopolitan communities on Earth.

'Caribbean and soul music was everywhere,' says Cordle, whose father was from Barbados and his mother Welsh-Maltese. 'We even had our own Notting Hill-type carnival that started as a *mardi gras* in the late 1950s. There were at least fifty-seven languages spoken in our small area. I went to school with kids whose parents or grandparents came from all over the world, including Yemen, Latin America, Morocco, Estonia, Spain and beyond, and I have cousins of Italian, Maltese, Polish and Bangladeshi extraction.'

But the city establishment was not so happy. Cardiff's Chief Constable David Williams campaigned in 1918 to stop black men from playing cricket, concerned that 'white flannels are more revealing than corduroys and make black men more attractive to white girls'. 'Young Cardiff girls,' he proclaimed, 'should not be allowed to admire such beasts.' This prejudice turned to violence on 11 June 1919, when white veterans from the First World War, from all over Cardiff and south Wales, attacked the residents of Tiger Bay. 'They wanted to lynch and burn everyone from the docks, no matter their colour,' explains Cordle. 'So everyone from Tiger Bay barricaded Bute Street and told the police that they would defend themselves. Many were ex-servicemen, mainly Somali, Yemeni, Afro-Caribbean, and had guns. They held them off for three days and nights.' The conflict involved more than 2,000 people. An Arab lodging house was burned down and a Somali priest was attacked by the mob, which also stripped a white woman married to an African man and knocked her teeth out. One newspaper described it as a night of 'guerrilla warfare', while the *South Wales News* headline read 'Blacks Hunted by a Furious Mob'.

Tiger Bay continued to be a constant source of anguish for Cardiff's council and well-to-do residents, who believed the worst about a community that, although not perfect, was an inspiring model for community spirit and multiculturalism. 'That stigma obscures the fact that the majority of the men who lived there were hard-working members of the community, not pimps running whores,' said the late long-time resident, author and historian Neil Sinclair. 'The reality is far from that, as everyone looked out for one another and nobody ever locked their door . . . It was stigmatised. Another example of good old-fashioned racism.'

During the Second World War, Cardiff suffered its own Blitz, directed at the docks, and Tiger Bay took a battering. At the invitation of the Government, more immigrants arrived after the war, filling an employment shortfall. Disembarking on ships such as the *Empire Windrush*, they gathered at the Caribbean café on Bute Street. And, just like Notting Hill, Soho, Brixton and the East End of London, the area exploded with vitality.

'There were parties all the time, house parties and shebeens, and illegal drinking joints,' laughs Cordle. 'Lots of black GIs came here and had never seen black and white people mixing like this. The authorities tried to ban them from the pubs but the landlords and locals refused, as that's not our way. Tiger Bay was the hottest spot in Wales, perhaps similar to London's Soho, and was not without a certain notoriety, and raised many a Welsh Presbyterian eyebrow.'

Sinclair recalled how 'come four o'clock when the whistle blew, they didn't go home and slap the money on the table for their mams, they headed for the pubs and the place was jumping'.

But then the social cleansing began.

In the early 1960s, the council razed Tiger Bay to the ground, destroying forty-five streets of 19th-Century town houses and cottages; filled in the historic Glamorganshire canal with cement; and deployed unprecedented cultural vandalism. In their place, lifeless concrete council houses were erected. Today, just three of the original streets remain while historic buildings such as the Wharf in Schooner Way, built in 1893, have recently been completely demolished.

More damage was done in the early 2000s by the Cardiff Bay Development Corporation, which spent £2 billion on regeneration. The money could easily have been used to rejuvenate the dilapidated housing and dockside; to retain the area's character; maintain the community; and create a unique historic and cultural attraction. After all, dwellings of a similar age had been rejuvenated and modernised for a fraction of the cost in other areas of Cardiff such as Splott. But, then again, none had suffered the institutional prejudice that Tiger Bay had.

'The regeneration has destroyed something unique and ecologically valuable and replaced it with something boring, generic and depressing,' regrets Cardiff-born urban designer and planning consultancy boss Adrian Jones. 'There's very little of Cardiff in Cardiff Bay.' Many of the district's great historic pubs, featuring proud Victorian interiors, have disappeared and instead been replaced by Nando's, Subway and Wagamama restaurants, alongside luxury homes locals cannot afford. The original Butetown area of Tiger Bay has been squeezed into a smaller space – isolated and neglected.

In 2019, Butetown had the highest rate of child poverty in Cardiff, at 46%. Still a melting pot of races, cultures and religions, it is also home to simmering fury. One resident, Elbashir Idris, who was born in Sudan but has lived in Butetown most of his life, speaks of a wall that runs the entire length of Bute Street.

'We call it the Berlin Wall,' he says. 'On the other side of that wall is Atlantic Wharf, which is a much more gentrified area of the ward of Butetown. And over there is the seat of power at Cardiff Bay. We feel segregated and marginalised from the rest of Cardiff . . . this Berlin Wall of ours is a device that, for decades, has made the people of Butetown feel like a separate community.'

Why Would Russia Want to Interfere in British Politics?

Misha Glenny

5 AUGUST 2020

The Russia report makes clear two things – the Conservatives get a lot of money from Russian oligarchs and Parliament's

Intelligence and Security Committee believes that there should be an investigation into Russian interference in the 2016 EU Referendum.

But one thing the report skirted over was the question of Russian motivation: why might Brexit be in Russia's interests?

The UK was the one country that linked the intelligence-sharing union of the Five Eyes (itself, the US, Canada, Australia and New Zealand) with the criminal and intelligence databases of the European Union. Brexit breaks that critical link in the Western alliance. To understand why Russia gains so much from that, consider how the world looks from Russian President Vladimir Putin's perspective – and why he might welcome the weakening of the EU.

Russia under Putin is not the same as the Soviet Union under any of its leaders from Stalin to Gorbachev. It is a capitalist economy, albeit one in which a small clique often overrides genuine market competition, but it is more integrated into wider global trade relations than the Soviet Union ever was. Russia's foreign policy is therefore not merely driven by politics but by the requirements of its trade relations. Last year, the EU imported some 30% of its oil and 40% of its gas from Russia – 60% of all Russian exports to the EU. The main consumers of Russian energy are Germany, Italy and the Netherlands. The EU is by some measure its largest trading partner. The UK, however, imports very little of its oil and gas from Russia, and the British relationship with

Russia has always been about money and security politics, not trade.

Putin's rule has become progressively more authoritarian especially since Russia's urban middle classes began making their feelings felt in mass protests since 2011. The country remains overdependent on the sale of hydrocarbons, which represent around 60% of its exports and 40% of revenues to the federal budget last year. Furthermore, it faces a serious long-term demographic crisis and the long-term forecast is that Russia's population will sink to around 110 million from 146 million today. Focusing on foreign policy is a way of deflecting attention from these troubles.

Putin's aim is to present Russia as one of the four decisive forces in international politics, along with the US, China and the EU. It suffered a profound domestic trauma during the gangster capitalism of the 1990s, in which living standards collapsed – except, of course, for those of the oligarchic and criminal classes. One of Putin's great talents after he became president in 2000 was to exploit that widespread social insecurity and eliminate his opponents using what, in the communist takeovers of the late 1940s, were known as 'salami' tactics. This was also personal for him. As a KGB officer serving in Dresden in the 1980s, he could have expected the benefits of promotion had the Soviet Union not collapsed. His generation benefited least from the ruptures of the 1990s. The main reason he has become more authoritarian is that his coterie has, in resorting to violence, intimidation and extreme wealth accumulation, begun to resemble the oligarchs of the 1990s, rather as the pigs in *Animal Farm* started to resemble the humans after a few years in power.

Russia also has the hostility of the West to contend with. Russians, and their security elite like Putin, experienced the expansion of NATO and the West's increasing interest in Ukraine after 2004 as an aggressive strategy. For Putin, this was especially galling as he believed that he had bent over backwards to accommodate Western interests in the first few years of his rule. In Afghanistan, for instance, the Russian President ordered his military to allow the US to use Russian facilities in Tajikistan to prosecute its war against the Taliban. What Putin has been left with, however, are US and European sanctions – which have had both a psychological and economic impact on Russia.

The overall picture is that Putin faces immense social, political, geopolitical and economic challenges in sustaining Russia's status as a great power. What, though, of its military power?

As the Russian military's chief of general staff, Valery Gerasimov, pointed out, the nature of warfare has changed and Russia must adapt towards the new hybrid strategies that embrace 'information warfare' as a central plank. He didn't spell it out but Russia has nothing approaching the economic capacity and infrastructure to maintain parity in weapons technology and military investment with the US and China. Because of this, it started to examine how it could exploit the West's societal and political vulnerabilities.

The Russia report suggested that nihilism drives Russia's foreign policy, with commentators arguing that the Russians want to destroy our way of life. I would argue that Russia seeks to drive wedges between and within Western countries to weaken them and their ability to coordinate policy over issues such as Ukraine or the Nord Stream 2 pipeline, which takes oil directly from Russia to Germany, bypassing Poland and Ukraine. This is where trade and security politics intertwine.

The UK was always an easy and popular target for Russia and, since the 1990s, it has been a primary place for Russians to stash their money. They observed how successive governments from Tony Blair's onwards actively avoided investigating Russian money. For two decades, oligarchs have used British lawyers, courts, PR companies and politicians to cajole and intimidate their domestic enemies along with independent investigators or journalists. They have exerted influence in buying newspapers and football clubs.

Blair used a lot of angry rhetoric after the Russian defector Alexander Litvinenko died on British soil from poisoning by radioactive polonium in 2006, but there was never the least suggestion that the UK would start to investigate oligarchs such as Roman Abramovich, who enjoys a close relationship to Putin. It wasn't until after the Skripal poisonings in

Salisbury more than a decade later that Theresa May felt moved to deny Abramovich a work permit as a snub aimed specifically at Putin.

While Russians enjoyed the light-touch regulation of the City, the UK was a particular irritant to Moscow by dint of it being the only country to both belong to the EU and enjoy the full trust of the US intelligence community as embodied in the Five Eyes relationship. In the debate about Brexit, few people raised the issue of security – but its implications are profound.

One of our greatest unsung successes in recent years was Europol – the EU's law enforcement agency – under its British director, Rob Wainwright. On leaving the EU, the UK left Europol and it will now be able to access the immense data banks held by Europol and EU states with regard to terrorism, espionage and organised crime only through a lengthy application process, which will in most cases render the information obsolete by the time it arrives.

Regardless of how often Boris Johnson says 'our European friends', the stark truth remains that, by leaving the EU, the UK has exchanged its relationship of collaboration with the rest of Europe for one of competition. It is that competition, both political and economic, which Russia views as beneficial.

The other world figure to have damaged Western relations is, of course, Donald Trump. Together, he and Brexit are doing just what Russia wanted them to do – loosening the economic, political and security ties within Europe and between Europe and the US.

With a patsy like Trump in the White House and a Conservative Party so clearly in hock to Russian money, it is too easy an opportunity for Putin to pass up.

This essay was first published by *openDemocracy*.

Brexit and the Paradox of Victimhood

Chris Grey

13 AUGUST 2020

The most surprising feature of Britain since the Brexit referendum is just how unhappy Brexiters have been.

On the face of it, you would expect there to have been joy and jubilation, especially on the day that Britain actually left the EU. In fact, any celebration has been muted if not non-existent, while Brexiters seem to be angrier than ever.

A complex political psychology has played out since 2016, the consequences of which are having a major impact on British political culture. But there is a danger, due to the swirl of events and the rapidity with which even very recent history is being rewritten, of this being forgotten.

Almost as soon as the EU Referendum result was announced, Brexiters such as Nigel Farage began to talk about their fear that it would be betrayed. Meanwhile, within the Conservative Party, a battle was underway to define – as the Vote Leave campaign had not – what Brexit actually meant. At the time, that was principally about the distinction between a 'soft' and 'hard' Brexit. In practice, it was about the difference between seeking to retain Single Market membership or not.

But the key point to understand is that, whatever concession was made to the hardcore of Brexit Ultras – Conservative MPs in the European Research Group (ERG), Farage, Brexit Party MEPs, committed activists within these parties and their many supporters in the media and various think tanks – they would always demand another.

The numerous historical opt-outs they wanted – such as from Schengen and the Euro – were achieved but just led to new demands. As soon as David Cameron offered them a referendum, they started agitating about the wording of the question, the framing of the response and who should be able to vote in it.

They got their way on all these things, mainly to head off the possibility that if – as was expected – they lost, they would cry foul. But there were bigger issues at stake.

Until fairly recently – although not during the referendum

campaign itself – Farage and UKIP were quite happy with the Norway model of Brexit. And, during the campaign, many in Vote Leave said that this was exactly what Brexit would mean. But, as soon as they had won, this was not enough. Brexit, they now insisted, had to mean a hard Brexit: leaving the Single Market but also any form of European Court of Justice jurisdiction and negotiating a free-trade agreement with the EU. In other words, the Canada model.

It was this which was the subject of the internal battle in the Conservative Party in the second half of 2016, during the period when Theresa May would only offer that 'Brexit means Brexit'. It was not quite the meaningless slogan it seemed as it denoted that Brexit would happen and that the referendum result would not be revisited. But her public utterances were ambiguous about whether that meant Single Market membership or not.

That ambiguity ended partially with her party conference speech in October 2016 but definitively with her Lancaster House speech in January 2017. Brexit now, unequivocally, meant a hard Brexit – reportedly on the whim of her advisors rather than by any wider discussion.

Briefly, the Ultras were placated but, very quickly, they started demanding that a true Brexit meant no deal at all – and that anything else would be a betrayal.

That demand intensified as the pragmatic realities of hard Brexit became clear, culminating in the Chequers proposal of

July 2018. Notably, in the same period, 'no deal' Brexit began to be renamed as 'hard' Brexit, with what used to be 'hard' Brexit re-badged as 'soft' Brexit, and what used to be 'soft' Brexit dismissed as not being Brexit at all.

Already weakened by the ill-judged General Election of 2017, May's Withdrawal Agreement limped on until her demise. By that point, the Ultras' principal demand was the removal of the Irish backstop from the Agreement. This Boris Johnson has done – by reverting to the previous – rejected – means of an Irish Sea Border. This was the 'oven-ready deal' on which he won the 2019 General Election. With the support of the ERG, he got this deal through Parliament and signed it with the EU.

But now things have changed again.

Hardly had the ink dried on what was now a binding international treaty than the Brexit Ultras began to repudiate it. Suddenly they discovered that, despite having voted for it, it was a 'poisoned pill' which betrayed the Brexit referendum's vote for sovereignty.

At one level, there is an obvious pattern: trying to give Brexiters what they want in order to appease them proves to be pointless because, whatever they are given, they come back – like blackmailers or protection racketeers – with even more extortionate demands. But beneath that is something much stranger and far more dangerous. The Brexit movement was always one of campaign and complaint, feeding on a sense of victimhood. It thrived on the idea of being the powerless 'silent majority', forbidden by the 'PC elite' from 'saying what we really think'.

Given such a mindset, winning the referendum was actually a disaster for them because, from then on, they were in charge and their policy has defined British politics. Ever since then, they have sought to regain the comfort zone of victimhood. Their driving force is not, as it might seem, the constant fear of betrayal but the constant need and desire to be betrayed.

Given that, it would make no difference if 'Remainers got behind Brexit', for that is the last thing the Ultras actually want and would just lead to them saying that this is 'Remainer Brexit', not a 'real Brexit'.

Indeed, when Theresa May did so – with a conviction that shocked Remain voters – they destroyed her for being 'Theresa the Remainer'. Now that they have Boris Johnson, they are saying that he has struck a deal that isn't 'sovereignty compliant'.

Invariably, the Brexit Ultras claim that they are speaking for the 17.4 million people who voted to leave the EU in 2016 – but this is nonsense. Not only was no definition of what Brexit would look like put forward at the time, but there has never been a polling majority for leaving the Single Market, still less for exiting all the various EU agencies and programmes that the Ultras revile because they have some lurking role for the European Court of Justice.

But, bogus as it is, that claim matters – because it has the effect of creating an insoluble paradox. On the one hand, Brexit must be done because it is the 'will of the people'. On the other hand, any actual form of Brexit is a betrayal of the will of the people. That is a consequence of the Brexit Ultras constantly asking for more and – at a profound level – of their need for the victimhood that comes from not being given more.

Since the referendum an entire nation has been shackled to the political psychology of a relatively small number of people who – like rebellious teenagers secretly wanting to be set boundaries – demand total victory while craving defeat. It makes it impossible to turn Brexit into a workable policy because, at heart, it is not a policy demand at all, but a demand to be thwarted.

It is an old joke that the cruellest sadist is one who refuses to inflict pain on a masochist. That joke is now being played out in the politics of Brexit Britain. The thing is – it is not very funny.

The Sham of Conservative Meritocracy – Education's Oldest Algorithm

Sam Bright

14 AUGUST 2020

The self-impressed security of adulthood makes many forget the traumatic memories of being a student at exam time. A war between your brain, nerves and writing speed, in the space of just a few hours, shapes the course of your life. The late nights cramming, parental nagging and occasional sobbing are all forgotten when you reach the stable plod of middle-age employment.

While every student year group has it hard, none has been lacerated like the class of 2020.

Fretting about the possibility of grade inflation if exam results were based on predicted grades alone, during the Coronavirus crisis which meant that exams could not be sat in person, the Government coded an algorithm to 'standardise' the outcomes of kids across the country based on two central factors: the past performance of schools, and teachers' assessments of their students.

The Conservatives believe in empowering the individual; they supposedly hate blunt, bureaucratic state instruments that treat everyone the same. Yet, the latter is exactly what the Government initially deployed to decide the A-Level results of thousands of young people this summer. As a result, the grades of private-school students were boosted – a side effect of their educational ascendancy for generations – while students from deprived areas were spiked. The algorithm cannibalised the veneer of fairness that coats the education system. But that's not all it did.

The algorithm scandal exposed the fallacy of meritocracy that characterises education and attainment in the UK. In doing so, it laid bare the innate inequalities of the system, which are usually masked by the overachievement of occasional underdogs. The entire concept of 'standardisation' suggests that there is a standard – a social formula – that underwrites the performance of students. But, as the Government's algorithm showed, this guiding formula is not unbridled meritocracy.

In his 2012 Conservative Party Conference speech, Britain's then Eton- and Oxford-educated Prime Minister David Cameron remarked, 'It's not where you've come from that counts, it's where you're going.' This notion of meritocracy – the process by which people 'succeed' – hasn't really changed since 1958, when it was first theorised by political scientist Michael Young in his seminal text *The Rise of Meritocracy*. Young posits that meritocracy is itself based on a simple algorithm: 'IQ + Effort = Merit'. In other words: to achieve what you want in life, all you need is hard work and talent. Anyone can succeed, regardless of their background, if they simply have brains and grit. The exam-results debacle finally took a sledgehammer to this myth.

The strong correlation between school performance, local deprivation and exam results, built into the Government's standardisation formula, revealed what lots of people already knew: that social background is a central force in the performance of students. Essentially, the authoritarian algorithm created a hyper-exaggeration of a system that already exists, whereby kids from good schools and good homes generally go to good universities and a few of their peers from less advantaged backgrounds follow them. In usual circumstances, however, conservative-minded individuals can use the few disadvantaged people who make it out, so to speak, as evidence that anyone can make it. As Akala writes in his book *Natives* in the context of race: 'A few successful black people also do very little to alter the race-class dynamics of the UK, and can even help to cement it. These successes can and will be used . . . to beat other poor people that "didn't make it" over the head. They can be used to pretend that the system is just and there are enough seats at the table – "if you just work hard and pull your socks up you can be like me" – rather than simply being honest about the way things actually work.'

This year, however, the exceptions – the teenagers who get the grades despite all their social and economic barriers to success – were forced to conform to the rule. Their grades were dragged down, because the algorithm judged, correctly, that people from their station typically underperform.

There is plenty of evidence that educational stratification relies heavily on social background; that people, more often than not, become the very thing that they come from. The 2018 'Access to Advantage' report by the Sutton Trust, which examines social mobility in Britain, has a few facts that are worth listing in this regard.

It found that, over a three-year period, eight of the UK's top schools received as many Oxbridge acceptances as 2,894 schools and colleges combined – the latter total representing three-quarters of UK schools and colleges. Independent school students are seven times more likely to get places at Oxbridge than students from non-selective state schools, and more than twice as likely to go to a Russell Group university. Roughly 1.5% of Oxbridge applicants from the south-east, south-west, London or east of England attend the famed institutions. You are approximately half as likely to go to Oxbridge if you're a higher-education applicant from the north or the Midlands.

The report unsurprisingly concludes that 'in the UK, whether someone goes to university, and if so at which institution they study, is highly impacted by an individual's socio-economic background, the school they attended and where in the country they are from ... Whether looking at Oxbridge, the Russell Group or top tariff institutions, our most highly regarded universities are not equally accessible to all young people in the country.'

While this year's exam-results fiasco has been galling, it is simply an amplification of the insidious sorting process that sees the rich and privately educated miraculously succeed every single year. The Government's algorithm was a stark failure of public policy and one that should attract derision. But, if the education system is to fundamentally change, to prevent students from endless trooping in the footsteps of their parents and peers, campaigners must look beyond this isolated failure. Fairness in education relies on eroding the structural inequalities that line the boots of people who aren't white, middle class, southern, and/or privately educated.

There has been an algorithm sorting children for centuries – it just wasn't created by a computer.

Boris Johnson: The Anti-Prime Minister

Jonathan Lis

28 AUGUST 2020

Boris Johnson emerged from his holiday not to tackle the A-Level results crisis, but to joke about it. On a visit to Castle Rock School in Coalville, the Prime Minister declared: 'I'm afraid your grades were almost derailed by a mutant algorithm.' It was an appropriate phrase, for it describes not the exam-results scandal but Johnson himself, for his entire career has been one of mutation.

In the 1990s and early 2000s, he was a 'hang and flog 'em' social conservative, crusading against single mothers, gay people and anti-imperialists. In the late 2000s and 2010s, he was London's own lovable rogue, advertising conservatism with a liberal wink on its face. And, since 2016, he has been the scorched-earth demagogue prioritising Brexit and power over the country's democratic institutions.

Like an algorithm, Johnson does not simply act at random. He does not 'go rogue'. The algorithm works like any computer game: it performs the functions someone has programmed for it. It may seem out of control, but it is in fact doing exactly what it has set out to do. Just as love means never having to say you're sorry, Johnson's self-love means never having to take responsibility. Everything is the fault of someone or something else: voters, foreigners, computers.

Virtually everything Johnson says follows the same pattern.

In a speech in June about a prospective trade deal with Australia, he bellowed: 'How long can the British people be deprived of the opportunity to have Arnott's Tim Tams at a reasonable price?' It was vintage Johnson: the grand discussion of something trivial to reassure people they were in on a big joke. War-time Churchillian rhetoric to describe biscuits.

No other prime minister has or would speak in this way. Others would consider it infantile, demeaning, the wrong register at the wrong time. Johnson knows that, and the knowledge of his own exceptionalism is what excites him. But it goes even deeper. Johnson doesn't know or care if it is the wrong register for a British prime minister or for Britain's interests. It is the right register for him. The show may entertain others, but he actually performs it to entertain himself.

Investigating historic child abuse was 'spaffing money up the wall'. Procuring ventilators was 'Operation Last Gasp'. It is at one and the same time the insecure panic of someone who doesn't know how to empathise, and the public-school confidence of someone who knows he doesn't need to. Because he cannot identify with other people's emotions he chooses not to try.

Brexit is an amusement to accommodate Johnson's personal interest and whim. In some ways, it has quite explicitly functioned as a game – guided not by concrete improvements to anyone's life, it has become a game-show challenge to achieve something complicated within a strict time-frame.

Here, then, is the difference between an exam and real life. In real life, tackling something important, you will take as much time as you need. If it looks nearly impossible, you will seek to extend the time. In an exam – an A-Level, say – you have three hours and then have to submit, ready or not. For Johnson, Brexit is less important than an exam. If it doesn't work, it doesn't matter. He will blame someone else and it was fun to try. And so the key to this game is failure. Johnson does not set out to fail per se. Rather, failure is just another route to winning. He sabotages things because he can.

This thinking sounds perverse because it is and it must be understood within the framework not of governing, but of a game with one necessary victor. Success, stability and predictability are boring. Why not see how far you can push the people who support you? If you can still win with the most danger, the most excitement, inflicting the most damage, why not try? It is here that the strategies behind Johnson's premiership begin to make sense. Of course, he would unlawfully prorogue Parliament. Of course, he would rewrite the lockdown rules to exonerate his chief advisor Dominic Cummings. Of course, he would lie to people's faces about care homes, testing and personal protective equipment. Everything must be outrageous, shocking and unprecedented. Everything must outdo every predecessor. This is governing as teleology: it is not the premiership that is important, but how he feels at the end of it.

It doesn't matter that it would be easier not to play this game. It doesn't matter that more people might appreciate him if he at least tried to succeed. This is not the point of the exercise. None of the failure matters because he is simply working to a different metric of success.

Johnson wanted to become prime minister but never to be prime minister – at least, not in the formal sense of doing what leaders are appointed to do. For him, power is about breaking precedent, cheating the system, scoring the con to end all cons. When you are so purely solipsistic that only the self exists, you are capable of centring, considering, governing only for yourself.

Cronies cling to you for the scraps of self-interest they can pluck in your wake. This is corruption at its most decadent: botching a crisis or destroying a national infrastructure not for political gain, nor even for financial reward, but ultimately for pure personal sport.

This is why Boris Johnson is the anti-prime minister. He isn't there when his country needs him to be – and he doesn't know how to be. He is there to do a different job: not to be prime minister but to be Boris Johnson. And it's not that Johnson wants to harm people – it's that the concept of harming them barely enters his imagination.

The public knows this. When, during the 2019 General Election campaign, Johnson was asked about honesty or empathy, people jeered and laughed: this is a game we are playing too. When Johnson wants to parade a veneer of cleverness, the media lets him parade it. When he seeks the indulgence of voters' approval, voters indulge him.

Despite all of its levels and dimensions, this game has just one rule and allows for just one winner. It dictates that the United Kingdom, and its people, currently exist for one purpose and one purpose alone: Boris Johnson, the mutant algorithm.

The Strange Relationship Between British and English Nationalism

John Denham

15 SEPTEMBER 2020

The Union was forged at the heart of Empire and, remarkably successful abroad, its strength at home rested on constructive ambiguity.

For England, the Union was the extension of English interests and institutions: its Parliament, monarchy and capital city. This facilitated an Anglo-centric 'British nationalism' in which Britain was the expression of England and there was no separate England or English identity.

Within the Union, Scotland maintained its distinct national identity in law, education, history and culture while benefiting equally from Empire. Wales too, through language and faith, maintained and even developed its own sense of national identity.

That the English view of the Union differed from that of its other nations didn't matter until the end of Empire eroded the Union's purpose. In the post-war years, Scotland and Wales began to further assert their own identities, while the unresolved legacy of Empire broke out in Northern Ireland.

Though ties of kinship and shared history remained strong over the years, each part of the Union developed its own political culture, with devolved elections in each contested and won by different parties. In this way, there was no 'British' politics any more – but, England, the nation at the heart of the Union, has struggled to understand this changing world.

Those who blame 'English nationalism' for recent political convulsions are wrong, because Boris Johnson and Nigel Farage's Brexit project has been an example of British nationalism writ large. Rather than moving towards English nationalism, Johnson's Government is doubling down on British nationalism. This can be seen in its aim of reversing huge swathes of devolution through the new Internal Market Bill and recent studies which show that today's Conservative MPs have a highly centralised, unitary view of the British state.

Johnson's British nationalism certainly has an English view of the Union – but he is not an 'English nationalist'. In his politics, there is no room for England or the distinct interests of English people.

Support for the Conservatives has rested on a patriotic, Anglo-centric British nationalism. But, to win the EU Referendum, Johnson and Farage needed the votes of people who put England and Englishness first.

According to the British Election Study, the decisive voters in Brexit were those who feel they are 'more English than

British'. Many of these people will have been on the losing side of every social and economic change of the past thirty years. They feel they have lost out and that others have louder voices than theirs. My own research shows that they believe that England has distinct interests that political parties should protect. Far from being British nationalists, they put England's interests ahead of the Union and want English MPs alone to make their laws. This 'political Englishness' is not reflected in any nationalist movement.

Many of these people, who have left-of-centre economic views and live in poorer areas, recently backed Johnson. The apparent paradox of voters making choices that appear inimical to their own interests has fed claims that they are driven by a reactionary cultural politics. Yet, their aspirations seem political: national sovereignty, including control over migration and a voice for people like them.

The appeal of 'Get Brexit Done' was strongest for those who thought that they had already voted for it once before. The alignment between political Englishness and Johnson's British nationalism is not inevitable; but he offered more of what they wanted than his opponents.

England's liberal-left is dominated by a different and more powerful minority who feel that they are 'British' rather than 'English'.

If political Englishness is only about twenty years old, these Britons are a relatively new phenomenon too.

Their 'emergent Britishness' is inclusive and cosmopolitan, belongs to younger, more mobile and highly educated people, and to the business, government and the media elite. It is, in part, a product of state-supported British multiculturalism – a genuine success story in its own right, which only really ever happened in England, constructing a new Britishness but never engaging with English identity. This emergent Britishness shares fundamental assumptions of all British nationalism: that the nation is Britain and that it is Britain that matters; that English identity should be marginalised; and that England must have no democratic institutions of its own.

Westminster's English parties are British nationalist in outlook, providing no national forum to debate the future of England. But where the political English go next will determine England's future and, for as long as it lasts, the Union.

The United Kingdom is an imperial union that no longer has an empire. The pretensions of British nationalism cannot hold it together. A re-founded union is both possible and desirable, if England, Wales, Scotland and Northern Ireland come together as nations sharing much common interest. It is British nationalism, not English nationalism, that stands in the way.

A Tribute to Sir Harold Evans

Peter Jukes

24 SEPTEMBER 2020

I woke up to an email that put a lump in my throat. My former editor Tina Brown wrote that her husband Harry Evans had died in the night 'surrounded by his loving family'. She quoted the prologue to the fourth act of Shakespeare's *Henry V*: 'A largess universal, like the sun, His liberal eye doth give to everyone.'

At that moment, instead of breaking with sadness and a sense of misfortune, another feeling entirely overwhelmed me. Joy. Celebration. We were so lucky to have ever had him.

I only got to meet Harry a decade ago. He became an advisor to *Byline.com* and opened our small New York festival. But you didn't have to meet Harry to feel his spirit and generosity. It infused everything he wrote and edited. He was everything a journalist should be: open, inquisitive, sceptical at times, but never cynical – always enthusiastic and positive.

Maybe part of that generous energy was down to Harry's background, which reads like a textbook lesson in all the possibilities of post-war British social mobility. The son of a railwayman from Eccles, he left school with no qualifications and started working in local journalism at the age of sixteen, rising to the pinnacle of the best British newspaper of the last century, *The Sunday Times*.

No wonder, with this trajectory, Harry seemed to approach every day, and every person, with a sense of good fortune and mischief. Whenever you met him, you felt a little miracle could be in the making.

But he never forgot how lucky he was and how unfair his home country still is. Unlike others who have ascended the rungs of the British class system, he always pulled the ladder back down to help others – from the victims of Thalidomide, those targeted by the secret state or the Murdoch empire, to other journalists in need of support and advice. Among the closed courtyards and fenced-off defensiveness of British journalism, he was a rare thing: not a gatekeeper but a gate-opener.

During his fourteen years editing *The Sunday Times*, Harry opened the gates for so many people who probably will never even know his name. I think particularly of one fourteen-year-old boy down on his luck in the 1970s.

He'd moved three times in two years thanks to his bipolar father's multiple bankruptcies. By 1974, the boy's parents had separated, and he and his kid brother and sister had only been saved from homelessness because their mother had just trained as a social worker and obtained a job in a large, grim Victorian mental health facility, and had been given a council house in the grounds of the hospital. It was a lifeline of sorts.

But that boy still started going off the rails in that tiny, pebble-dashed semi with no father around and a tired, over-worked mother.

With the long commute to school and a broken family, he started drinking and smoking with other disaffected teenagers in his village. There were weekly school detentions for bad behaviour and threats of suspension. He veered from half-hearted suicide attempts to wild nights out and dropped from near top of his class to near the bottom.

But despite those straitened times – no holidays, one cheap pair of shoes a year, living off frozen hamburgers – every Sunday morning, Harry Evans' *Sunday Times* dropped on the doormat. The paper under Harry's editorship was like a window into another world. Though he didn't read much, the teenage boy did love to draw in pencil, and he began to sketch the faces out of the 'Review' section: an old woman painting, a man fishing in a river, a 19th-Century Frenchman with an amazing moustache and huge bags under his eyes. He didn't recognise the names but started reading up about Jonathan Raban and Gustave Flaubert. He began to follow the television reviews by someone called Dennis Potter.

Then the boy got interested in the news section, especially by the graphically narrated 'Insight' team: stories of Israelis recovering their hostages in a raid on Entebbe and army shootings in Northern Ireland. Slowly his pebble-dashed prison fell away, and the boy's mind was opened.

He started doing better at school. Within a few years, inspired by this panorama of culture, politics and international affairs that Harry Evans and his writers had revealed to him, the teenager won a scholarship to Cambridge University, started writing dramas, and appeared on the front page of *The Sunday Times* 'Review' section for one of his student plays.

That boy was me. I still bear the scars on my left wrist of those dark days living in the grounds of the psychiatric hospital, but the torch Harry passed over outshines them by megawatts. And I'm just one person inspired by his work: Harry touched the lives of hundreds of thousands, maybe millions.

'The true measure of a man is how he treats someone who can do him absolutely no good' goes the famous maxim and, from my personal experience of meeting Harry four decades later, he was a giant.

I was a nobody, but he wanted to meet me in 2012 because of my tentative first steps into journalism writing about Rupert Murdoch and the phone-hacking scandal. Given his track record, I expected someone grand and difficult. But he spun into the hotel foyer with an elf-like magic: small and wiry but surrounded by an outsized electrical field of energy. There was no deference expected to his status, no long stories about past glories. He was curious and inquiring and fun on stilts.

Soon Harry introduced me to the *Daily Beast*, then edited by his partner Tina Brown. They both stood by my writings despite personal hit jobs against them in retaliation by editors working for Murdoch's News Corp. But they also emphasised fairness and objectivity, even towards Murdoch, and every time Harry wrote for the publication, he extensively declared his interests – the kind of transparency so woefully lacking from British journalism today.

It would be easy to say that Harry's successors in the British press represent everything he was not: editors who punch down rather than up, monstering minorities, demonising the poor or disadvantaged; newspapers that sacrifice transparency and truth for the interests of a small clique of friends; journalists not speaking truth to power, but bending the truth for the powerful.

But that would be too cynical and despairing. All those cabals and cliques were there in newspapers long before Harry burst onto the scene. He showed us a different way, an example even more vivid in his absence, to be remembered long after the time servers, sycophants and stenographers have gone to their well-furnished oblivion.

So that's why my heart broke, not with sadness but joy. We were so lucky to have him. And like that hushed moment in a theatre when the curtain falls on some tremendous, life-affirming drama, even though there are tears in your eyes because there will be no encore, you just have to stand and applaud until your hands hurt.

Sir Harold Evans, 28 June 1928–23 September 2020

3 November 2020

Democratic candidates Joe Biden and Kamala Harris receive more than 81 million votes in the highest voter turnout by percentage for a US Presidential Election since 1900 to defeat the Republican incumbents Donald Trump and Mike Pence.

Will the End of the Queen's Reign be Britain's Deepest Crisis of All?

Chris Grey

10 NOVEMBER 2020

As the US elects Joe Biden as its new head of state, there is a profound sense of a historic change and even the closing of a chapter of unprecedented political turbulence. That comes after a mere four years of the Donald Trump presidency. How much more historic, then, will be the very different change to Britain's head of state when that time comes?

The 21st Century has seen the UK endure successive and deepening internal crises.

The Iraq War polarised the country and intensified a sense that politicians couldn't be trusted because it broke an implicit understanding that, precisely because intelligence information had to be secret, it – unlike all other kinds of policy data – would be used with complete honesty. The MPs' expenses scandal, the 2008 financial crisis and its long legacy followed. Then, of course, came Brexit, exposing and exacerbating deep divisions of age, class, education and region, and renewing the possibility of both Scottish independence and, conceivably, Irish unification. With that still playing out to a very uncertain future, the Coronavirus arrived with its own divisiveness between generations and regions, even within England, and income groups.

Throughout all of this, familiar institutions and conventions of the law and the constitution have been exposed to extraordinary stresses. It is neither hyperbole nor particularly original to say that the political system and constitution of the United Kingdom, and its very existence as a united kingdom, are now fragile in a way that was almost unimaginable a generation ago.

But what is almost never said – perhaps because it would be considered bad taste to do so – is that, at some point fairly soon, the country is inevitably going to face the death of its head of state, Queen Elizabeth II.

You don't have to be a flag-waving monarchist to see just how remarkable and important her reign has been in providing a unifying continuity that is so familiar as to be taken for granted. We don't tend to use this terminology, but this second Elizabethan era has lasted longer than the Victorian one. It is a reign that has encompassed the Suez Crisis, decolonisation, devolution, joining and then leaving the EU, and profound social and technological changes. Her longevity matters, not just domestically but internationally, so that world leaders – even one as bombastic and iconoclastic as Trump – find kudos in meeting her. She plays a pivotal role in the Commonwealth and, when she is gone, it seems likely that Australia and, perhaps, other countries will decide to no longer have the British monarch as their head of state (as Barbados is planning to do next year).

The Queen is one of the last remaining binders of the four parts of the United Kingdom. She is also one of the last ways that generations are bound together and, in particular, one of the last significant institutional links between the Second World War and the present day. When in her address to the nation during the first Coronavirus lockdown she invoked Vera Lynn's 'we'll meet again', it was meaningful in a way that would have been impossible had anyone else said it. And though it is routine for politicians to reference – and in some cases to seek to imitate – Sir Winston Churchill, it was the Queen whom he served as one of the fourteen prime ministers during her reign so far, and who knighted him.

As Brexit especially has shown, the Second World War still has an extraordinarily powerful role in contemporary British identity and politics. It is constantly referred to, both as a critique of the EU and particularly Germany, and as a rationale for 'standing alone'. Dunkirk and the 'Blitz spirit' remain meaningful historical reference points, even though they are highly mythologised and even though almost none of those invoking them were alive at the time. The Queen, however, was, and her existence serves to embody a connection between the war years and the present. As a result of all this, it seems certain that, when her death comes, it will provoke an intense and complex national reaction.

Undoubtedly, the Government and media have locked in office drawers the ceremonial plans for this moment, but what cannot be planned for are the cultural and political manifestations. As, for very different reasons, the death of Princess Diana showed, these could take surprising and perhaps deeply emotional forms.

In particular, the passing of the Queen can hardly fail to engender a profound and possibly fractious meditation on national identity, on the Union, on Britain's history and its place in the world, and to give focus to all the existing doubts and dilemmas of those things. That is not to anticipate the end of the monarchy as an institution, for there is very little republican sentiment in Britain. Rather, it is about the impact of the person of the Queen, so long present in the background as a source of continuity for the majority of those alive today, no longer being there.

If this is so, it may be uncomfortable, but it need not be a bad thing. Such a meditation is long overdue and, now, urgent. So it could well be that the final public service of the Queen's long reign will be to initiate a national conversation not just about the past, but about the future.

Citizens Disunited: The End of the Transatlantic Trumpist Alliance

Peter Jukes

17 NOVEMBER 2020

For most of the past forty years, British domestic politics has been out of sync with the United States. Though Ronald Reagan and Margaret Thatcher composed a formidable Cold War alliance and promoted the 'Anglo-Saxon' model of privatisation and deregulation, the reality of everyday cultural life around politics in the US was very different from the UK.

I lived in Boston as an exchange student at an American high school in the early 1980s and, compared to the Punk-era Britain I had left behind, the political scene was much more consensual and polite. My teachers were a mix of small 'c' conservatives and former Vietnam War protestors, but discussions were fluid and, unpredictably, likely to arrive at an agreement. Among the pupils, few would think of not dating someone because of political allegiance. In Congress, politicians would cross the floor and vote across party lines. There was still a belief in bipartisanship – in contrast to the grim, grey UK I returned to.

Under the cosh of Thatcherism, nuclear rearmament and radical industrial restructuring, there was no way you could snog someone for long as a British student in the 1980s without ending up asking the question: whose side are you on? The dirty war in Northern Ireland, the miners' strike, the Conservative Party Brighton bombing, Rupert Murdoch's Wapping dispute, CND women at Greenham Common, the Big Bang, yuppies, 'Sloane Rangers' and the 'Loony Left' – during that decade it was almost impossible to chat with a London cabbie or have a family Sunday lunch without an unpalatable political argument.

Twenty years later, all that had reversed. When I returned to live and work in the US again in the early 2000s, the polarisation of Britain's Thatcher years seemed to have been exported there. Issues such as gay marriage, abortion, gun control and religion were now intractable discussions for Americans. Their political culture had polarised and cocooned, with Democrats telling me they'd never date a Republican, and vice versa.

Meanwhile, in Britain, under the premierships of Tony Blair, Gordon Brown and even self-styled 'heir to Blair' David Cameron, the idea of a 'culture war' over matters of sexual orientation, religious observance or the role of socialised healthcare seemed unlikely and vaguely absurd. I remember remarking to an American friend around that time that I was glad our Conservative Party wasn't infected by the atavistic, vote-suppressing extreme politics of the American Conservative right.

How blind I was about what was to happen.

*

The key moment for the unleashing of hard-right US Conservatism into UK politics was the US Supreme Court ruling in the case of *Citizens United versus the Federal Election Commission* in 2010.

Citizens United was an activist group chaired by David Bossie, who would later be Donald Trump's deputy campaign manager. In 2010, Bossie managed to revise a law which prevented for-profit and not-for-profit corporations from advertising or broadcasting political messages during elections or primaries. The legal judgment was based on the constitutional First Amendment right of free speech and the Supreme Court effectively ruled that these corporations were 'people' and had the same rights to political self-expression as individuals.

Whatever the metaphysical import of this ruling, the practical effect was to unleash unlimited spending on political campaigns by American corporations and rich individuals – and that wave of money soon hit the UK and jolted British politics to the right.

The networks to receive this influx of cash were already in place. Sir Antony Fisher, an Eton-educated businessman, having made his money from US-style intensive chicken farming, and the founder of the Institute of Economic Affairs in London in 1955, set up the Atlas Economic Research Foundation in the US in 1981. Funded by the oil-industry giants, big tobacco and other right-wing not-for-profits such as the Koch

Brothers Foundation, it acted as a transatlantic umbrella for a range of libertarian and free-market think tanks.

The Atlas network's role in pushing for Britain to leave the EU was apparent when leading Brexiter and former Conservative MEP Daniel Hannan delivered its 'toast to freedom' in New York in 2018 and celebrated the factory-farmed 'broiler chicken' as a symbol of liberty. The lowering of food-hygiene and factory-farming standards to US levels has been touted as one of the main benefits of Brexit – at least to those in the food industry.

But the Citizens United overspill, and its emphasis on 'free speech', went much further than these obvious commercial and lobbying networks in the UK, and had a toxic effect on the culture of British politics.

One hidden channel for right-wing US thinking and practice was the Young Britons' Foundation (YBF), a self-described 'Conservative madrasa' and a UK offshoot of the Young America's Foundation, which was funded by the hedge-fund billionaire Robert Mercer.

For twelve years, until it was closed down over allegations of bullying after the suicide of a young Conservative activist in 2015, the YBF hosted some of the key figures who led Britain to Brexit. Hannan was the YBF president. Matt Richardson, who went on to be the secretary of Nigel Farage's UKIP, was the executive director. Matthew Elliott, of the TaxPayers' Alliance at

55 Tufton Street and destined to become executive director of Boris Johnson's Vote Leave campaign, hosted talks and panels.

Apart from the potential channels for US dark money, the striking thing is the change of tone ushered into Conservative politics through the YBF. A key moment was its tenth-anniversary conference at Churchill College, Cambridge University, in 2013. Steve Bannon, then the managing director of the alt-right website *Breitbart*, was a major presence, discussing the role of online campaigning with the *Guido Fawkes* site's political editor Harry Cole, and recruiting their fellow panellist Raheem Kassam to run his London branch. Bannon had also just co-founded the notorious digital campaigning company Cambridge Analytica which would target individuals based on their fears and paranoias. Bannon called this combination of news and psychometric targeting his 'weapons' which he would use – in the UK too it would seem – to 'flood the zone with sh*t'. Also billed to appear that weekend was Douglas Murray, associate director of the Henry Jackson Society, to talk about 'Jihad, Islamism, Israel, the War on Terror and Neo-Conservatism'. Its founder, Dr Alan Mendoza, was also a regular attendee. According to a founding director and former associate director of the Society, around this time, it began to become a 'far-right, deeply anti-Muslim racist organisation'. It was also a recipient of dark money from key donors in America who began to back Donald Trump.

*

British political discourse began to degrade with the arrival of American right-wing conservatism via both the funding of activists and new media outlets which propagated their message. And 'free speech' was the wedge by which formerly marginal expressions of xenophobic nationalism, racism and Islamophobia could become central in Britain's public debate.

It didn't matter if many of the voices expressing these opinions online were paid for by multiple accounts, boosted by digital analytics, or indeed often outright replicants run by troll farms hosted and funded by hostile foreign countries. And we fell for it. Millions of Brits and Americans read and believed opinions and facts effectively generated by robots. The pioneer of computing, Alan Turing, once suggested that artificial intelligence would arrive when, during a conversation, we failed to spot the difference between a computer and a person. We failed the Turing test, politically, in 2016.

The media of the 20th Century was once described by philosopher Noam Chomsky as 'manufacturing consent'. By the time of Britain's EU Referendum and Donald Trump's election in 2016, with most people receiving their news and opinions through algorithms devised by social-media giants such as Facebook and YouTube, this was effectively replaced by the 'automation of consent'.

Some people seek to minimise this, pointing to the existing racial and economic fissures in British and American society that made them both ripe for populism, particularly after the financial crash of 2008. But just one in fifty of the votes cast in the EU Referendum, or 70,000 votes in the US Rust Belt states in the 2016 Presidential Election, won the twin shock victories either side of the Atlantic. Did dark-money-funded culture war interventions make enough of a difference to tip things over the edge?

The protagonists certainly thought so. Nigel Farage raised a pint after the EU Referendum victory to thank Bannon and *Breitbart* – 'we couldn't have done it without you' – while Trump declared: 'I'm Mr Brexit plus plus plus.'

The failure of Donald Trump to secure a second term is a severe setback to that transatlantic alt-right alliance of libertarians and neo-nationalists. The prospect of a UK trade deal with the US under Joe Biden, though it was never going to be that favourable to Britain, is likely to now be even more problematic given his different priorities in the White House and Congress's demonstrable objection to anything that would undermine the internationally binding Good Friday Agreement.

On a personal level, Johnson has many fences to mend with Biden, because of his perceived proximity to Bannon and Trump, and his frankly racist remarks about Barack Obama's attitude to Brexit stemming from his antipathy to Britain because of his 'part-Kenyan' ancestry. Biden has called Johnson Trump's 'physical and emotional clone'.

More profoundly, the media and lobbying networks around the Make America Great Again movement and Brexit will have much less influence in Washington, where they matter. Steve Bannon is currently indicted for fraud and, with a Biden nominee leading the Department of Justice, an unredacted version of Special Counsel Robert Mueller's report on Russian interference could reveal more transatlantic connections with Vladimir Putin's Russia. Other ongoing FBI investigations into campaign finance and counter-intelligence is likely to expose more about Trump's various business dealings with hostile foreign powers and those could entrammel some key Brexiters.

Many on the UK right were heavily invested in a Trump second term. We could soon discover why. But, beyond any criminal or intelligence liability, the simultaneous arrival of Biden and Brexit in January next year will make the UK even more irrelevant to the global considerations of a new US Government. As a result, British think tanks will be of less interest to US for-profit and not-for-profit corporations.

With no place at the EU table and a declining economy, hit by the dual shock of leaving the Single Market and the worst Coronavirus impact of the G7 nations, Britain is simply not – in crude financial terms – such a key asset. And right-wing British activists will receive fewer remittances of dark money as a result.

*

The US culture wars were always designed to create 'wedge issues' around guns, religion, education, race and class to get working-class Americans, particularly in the South, to vote against their economic interests and for tax cuts for a wealthy elite because, at least, they shared the same nominal values.

This 'Southern Strategy' was echoed by Johnson and Dominic Cummings in the 2019 General Election and could be seen in the collapse of the Labour 'Red Wall' in north-eastern constituencies. It led to a stunning tactical victory, but the long-term strategic consequences are still moot.

Trump's Rust Belt defence collapsed after one term. This does not bode well for the Conservative Party's current rhetoric pitting working-class voters against 'metropolitan elites'. When it comes to Britain's role in American culture wars, as Bannon identified early on, the UK was a bridgehead in the battle for the populist right. With its reputation (at least in the US) for prudence, propriety and stiff-upper-lip sobriety – as Bannon told his head of research at Cambridge Analytica Chris Wylie in 2014 – Britain was an exemplar. If the UK fell for Bannon's brand of nationalist populism, the US would be likely to follow and the EU collapse: Brexit would be a lesson to everyone.

Well, Brexit was a lesson to everyone. The country's reputation for transparency and reasonableness is permanently tarnished; both its economy and soft power influence are badly trashed. The disparate nations of the United Kingdom are more in danger of breaking up than they have been for decades; and their people are restive, divided and destined to continue battles about 'wokeness' and 'cultural Marxism' long after they have lost any wider resonance.

In that way, the transatlantic alliance of dark money and polarisation is over. We are now on our own. Britain served its role as part of a larger offensive but it is now abandoned like a rusting aircraft carrier waiting to be sold for scrap. We may remain a 'rump Trumpocracy' in the UK and our think tanks will still receive dribbles of cash from the US Conservative right. But we will be increasingly irrelevant and rapidly ignored – and then will finally have to confront our own demons without blaming or relying on monsters from abroad.

The Powerful Lure of the Soft Fascism Within

Hardeep Matharu

1 DECEMBER 2020

For many, this year has been weighed down, struggling with a heaviness it hasn't been easy to shake off. Following four destabilising years, the pandemic has brought a different level of disorientation. The ground beneath us has shifted, out of our control.

A line in a book I read recently, Jason Stanley's *How Fascism Works*, struck me. With Donald Trump on his way out, I wanted to understand the workings of an 'us and them' politics and what the rise once more of these hollow strongmen says about our societies.

'Fascism is not a new threat, but rather a permanent temptation.'

In these words was a reminder that the darkness of division is not a force to be found outside of ourselves, but its potential to flourish within. The question wasn't 'what makes Trump act like this?' or 'why do people support him?' – but rather 'why do I not?' and 'could I?'

Writing in 1945, George Orwell articulated brilliantly this uncomfortable truth. 'What vitiates nearly all that is written about anti-Semitism is the assumption in the writer's mind that he himself is immune to it,' he observed. 'The starting point for any investigation of anti-Semitism should not be "why does this obviously irrational belief appeal to other people?", but "why does anti-Semitism appeal to me? What is there about it that I feel to be true?" If one asks this question one at least discovers one's own rationalisations, and it may be possible to find out what lies beneath them.'

While some dismiss comparisons between our current political problems and the 1930s as exaggeration, there is no doubt that fascistic elements have reared their heads in a number of societies in recent years – many of them democracies. Rather than jackboots and paramilitary movements on the streets signifying the return of heavily militarised states, the frontline of the conflict between the authoritarian and the liberal mindset has shifted. In a digitised information age, there is a psychic war being stoked and raging within ourselves; a 'soft' fascism being nudged into our hearts and minds – at the hands of social media companies, corporations and rogue actors intent on weaponising people's worst instincts – and their most human of vulnerabilities – for personal and partisan gain.

It is a battle in which we are all on the frontline. Searching for simple answers in an increasingly complex world to feel better, more secure, about who we are, we are bombarded non-stop with information and ideas. Through algorithms and constant comparisons on Facebook and Twitter, we are encouraged to doubt and distrust. Marginalisation and victimhood fester.

'Foreign politicians blame Russia for meddling in elections and referenda all over the planet,' observed Vladislav Surkov, a close advisor to the Russian President Vladimir Putin, last year. 'In fact, it's even more serious than that: Russia is meddling in their brains and they don't know what to do with their changed consciousness.'

Do we?

America may have sent Donald Trump packing, but the recent US Presidential Election did not represent a decisive repudiation of his toxic brand of authoritarian populism.

In the UK, Boris Johnson's Government – a transatlantic 'rump Trumpocracy' – has shockingly denigrated accepted norms such as the rule of law and political accountability in ways never seen before. Meanwhile, Narendra Modi's plans to 'return' India to its rightful civilisational destiny as a Hindu nation continues each day. The future for the country's minorities, particularly Muslims, and where this will lead is a devastating development in the world's largest democracy.

In these globalised societies – in which improvements in life outcomes have gone hand in hand with gross inequality – leaders feeding people lies have become commonplace. A political discourse has been normalised, designed to stir emotions and evict rationality, and has found an all too receptive audience in many.

Much has been said about the tactics – digital and otherwise – used by the Leave campaigns during the 2016 EU Referendum in the UK: fuelling fears of brown and black immigrants, an angry xenophobia, and hopes of a lost Great British identity which would return if the exceptional UK cut itself free from Europe's oppression. But, what must also be appreciated is that these messages resonated – there was something within the people to whom they appealed which meant that the fear, anger and misplaced hope they whipped up made sense.

Such concerns, I would suggest, go beyond feelings about Britain on the world stage, a Westminster elite, or the immigration system – they spoke to people's feelings about themselves and their lives; to their need for a more spiritual sense of who they are.

The appeal of conspiracy theories has similar echoes. In the wake of the Coronavirus, which has fundamentally unsettled our lives as we knew them, QAnon – which falsely posits that Donald Trump is saving the world from a cabal of cannibalistic paedophiles – has flourished.

As Stanley writes in *How Fascism Works*: 'Conspiracy theories ... provide simple explanations for otherwise irrational emotions, such as resentment or xenophobic fear in the face of perceived threats. The idea that President Obama is secretly a Muslim pretending to be a Christian in order to overthrow the US Government makes rational sense of the irrational feeling of threat many white people had upon his ascension to the presidency.' The emotional pull of such 'explanations', preying on our need for archetypal myths and storytelling, means that whether it is easier to be a fascist or a democrat is not as clear-cut a consideration as we may like it to be.

Just as Plato recognised democracy's inherent vulnerability to a demagogue winning power and destroying the system by appealing to people's darker instincts, Stanley rightly points out that being a democratic citizen requires 'a degree of empathy, insight and kindness that demands a great deal of all of us' and that there are 'easier ways to live'. For him, a central question is: 'How do we maintain a sense of common humanity, when fear and insecurity will lead us to flee into the comforting arms of mythic superiority in vain pursuit of a sense of dignity?'

This year has carried a mental and emotional weight for me; throwing up difficult questions, rooted in past and present. A type of psychic warfare has at times felt very real, speckled with black holes filled with fear, anger, regret, frustration, injustice, victimhood and sadness.

In these moments, Gollum, the corrupted hobbit in *The Lord of the Rings*, came to mind – a character fighting a psychic war within himself.

In J.R.R. Tolkien's epic – about the all-consuming nature of power compelling and crushing individuals – Gollum emerges after his former self, Sméagol, kills a friend for the ominous One Ring. In the second film of the trilogy, 2002's *The Two Towers*, Gollum and Sméagol are shown having a fight.

'You don't have any friends,' Gollum tells Sméagol, eyes wide and full of malice. 'Nobody likes you.' To which a sad and disturbed Sméagol replies: 'I'm not listening, I'm not listening . . . I hate you. I hate you.' 'Where would you be without me?' Gollum rants back. 'I saved us. It was me. We survived because of me.' In the end, Sméagol sends Gollum away. But, those familiar with the story will know it doesn't last.

The genius of the film's direction lies in the same physical character being depicted as two distinct personas within consecutive frames which move seamlessly through both perspectives – showing them to be distinct and one and the same. Taunting the naive but basically good side of himself, Sméagol, Gollum is shown to be ruthless and nasty, but the audience also sees what he could be; *his potential to choose something better* – and in this lies a poignant presentation of the complexity of what it is to be human.

When he was asked why the story's protagonist, Frodo, isn't able to destroy the One Ring – the central quest of the series eventually, unwittingly, achieved by Gollum who destroys both the ring and himself in his obsessional need to possess it – Tolkien said that *The Lord of the Rings* wasn't a fairy tale with a 'hero' who triumphs over evil, but about a choice of values. By showing mercy towards Gollum earlier on in the story, those around him ensured that he survived and, in the end, only Gollum is able to destroy the ring. 'Do not be too eager to deal out death in judgement,' the wizard Gandalf advises Frodo in the trilogy's first film. 'Even the very wise cannot see all ends.'

At any given juncture, when destabilising feelings rise up and the ground beneath us starts to shift, we can fall down our black holes or decide not to let their darkness in. Which one we choose can have repercussions for us all.

In the Nuremberg Trials, the world confronted the horrors unleashed by Nazi Germany, carried out by men and women who could be described as 'ordinary'.

Ivor Perl was thirteen when the first trial began seventy-five years ago. He and his brother, who survived Auschwitz and Dachau concentration camps, were the only members of their Orthodox Jewish family of eleven who were still alive at the end of the Holocaust.

In 2015, Ivor – now in his eighties – was asked to give evidence in the trial of Oskar Gröning, a former SS guard known as the 'Bookkeeper of Auschwitz'. He initially refused, before changing his mind.

'I was absolutely horrified,' he recounted. 'An old man was wheeled into court with a nurse on either side of him. I wanted to hate him but I just saw an old man. I could feel something draining away from me. I can't describe what I felt, but it wasn't hatred.'

Ivor chose not to allow vengeance to flow to a man who had shown no such mercy himself – it was a choice to learn the lessons of the history he had lived through.

Three years after the end of the Second World War, the Universal Declaration of Human Rights was adopted, affirming the dignity of all people. The aim was to enshrine in law the notions of equality, justice, tolerance – essential for the functioning of liberal democracies, but which the world had seen substituted for darkness in the name of blood and nation.

Perhaps the strongmen who have found their moment in recent years will begin to lose their grip, maybe they won't. Donald Trump will be leaving the White House, but his millions of supporters will continue to carry within themselves the feelings which his darkness spoke to. Meanwhile, the unhealthy ends to which social-media platforms can lead and the days of Big Tech giants monetising our personal information are far from over.

Recalling seeing Gröning in the courtroom, Ivor Perl said, 'I don't want revenge. I want people to learn from history.' Using our awareness of hardships of the past to inoculate ourselves against the virus of hatred seems like a good place to start.

For the black holes within us are there to be filled and, when our psychic conflicts seek to load them with fear, hate and anger, we all have to choose. Real power – to cultivate darkness or light – lies within us. We give it away at our peril.

Humanising the Dehumanised: Notes from Calais

Kevin O'Hara

23 DECEMBER 2020

There is a humanitarian crisis in a small but prominent corner of Europe and our eyes are blinded to it.

Hundreds of desperate people are simply trying to survive

this grim winter. Among them are young men in flip-flops, thrown out of their flimsy tents in dawn raids by the police, beaten and attacked with rubber bullets and tear gas, left with nothing but the clothes they are standing in.

Cold, wet, hungry and scared, these people are ignored; driven to the margins of society. Yet, their plight is of our making – they are just a thirty-five-minute train journey from our coastline, in Calais, and the harsh treatment they receive is jointly funded by our own Government.

I went to Calais to see for myself the plight of the estimated 1,000 asylum seekers currently sleeping rough in the area. Volunteering with the Care4Calais charity, I was overwhelmed by the good grace of the individuals it helps and left in awe at the courage and resilience the people have despite the horror of their daily lives.

The official line is that there are no camps in northern France. 'The Jungle', which at its peak provided a place to live for around 10,000 asylum seekers, was destroyed in 2016. In the effort to fell the camp, woodlands were chopped down and mile upon mile of steel fencing and barbed wire erected across the Normandy landscape. But new, unofficial camps emerged and, in Calais and along the coast to Dunkirk, hundreds of desperate refugees remain and new ones continue to arrive – despite the hostile response of local authorities.

At a site nicknamed BMX – due to its location beside a bike park – live around 180 Eritrean refugees. I was taken aback when first visiting the site, at the care with which the asylum seekers looked after themselves despite their dismal living conditions.

We gave them food to cook and provided them with the opportunity to charge their phones – their only means of contact with families thousands of miles away. We brought a large speaker so they could play music, gave them tea, coffee and biscuits, alongside clippers and scissors so that they could cut their hair. As they trimmed away, played football and volleyball, enjoyed card games, Jenga and Connect Four, I got to know something of their lives.

All the time, we were watched by two intimidating van-loads of the French national police, the *Compagnies Républicaines de Sécurité* (CRS). The week before, there had been a particularly brutal raid by the CRS at this site. They destroyed the asylum-seekers' belongings, slashed tents and removed sleeping bags. The officers even deployed several tear-gas canisters and rubber bullets. One young man, running from the CRS and blinded by the gas, lurched into the road and was hit by a car. He died later in hospital. A second young man was hit in the face by a rubber bullet. He remains in hospital in a serious condition.

In the shadow of the CRS, I laughed with these resilient young men as they revelled in the brief respite from their persecution. These refugees, mainly young men escaping the brutalities of conscription back in Eritrea, were remarkably respectful, polite and caring, inundating us with gratitude for the small help we could give. As we prepared to leave, I watched as they started to drift back to their small fires, lean-to tarpaulins and leaky tents – their remaining shelter following the latest eviction by the CRS. That night, the temperature dropped and I cried for the first time as I sat in my warm flat, writing up my notes.

Visiting Dunkirk was grim. It had rained all night and a freezing wind lashed in from the Channel. I found myself talking to a British nurse volunteering in the area for a few months and asked her to describe the most common issues she faces. 'In Dunkirk, we deal with a lot of trench foot,' she said. 'They simply can't get dry.'

As I stood in my many layers of warmth, guarded by a face mask, giving out biscuits to accompany comforting cups of tea, I was approached by Ali – a man who had no coat, dressed in a pair of long johns, without any trousers. That morning there had been another eviction. The CRS, heavily armed and in large numbers, drove through the site, pulling asylum seekers from their tents. Ali awoke to the noise and managed to grab his boots on the way out. They were all he had left, aside from the clothes on his body. His few belongings, the small tent and sleeping bag, a few items for cooking, and of course, his trousers, were all taken or destroyed. He told me that he was simply grateful to have both of his shoes. In past evictions, the CRS have taken single shoes from refugees – a particularly senseless and vindictive form of abuse.

Maslow's 'Hierarchy of Needs', a model for the physical and psychological requirements of humans, starts at the base level with physiological requirements – food and shelter. Safety is one level above. The Calais refugees aren't just being denied these simple needs, their human rights are being actively stripped from them.

The CRS policy is to import officers from across France and require them to serve for just two weeks at a time. The thinking behind this is that, if the tours of CRS officers go on for any longer, they will start to humanise the refugees – to feel empathy towards them. The system is therefore designed to dehumanise asylum seekers, taking away their most basic rights.

The UK is not innocent in this matter. It takes just 5% of refugees seeking a safe haven in Europe – a small percentage compared to other large, developed states. Home Secretary Priti Patel harangues asylum seekers crossing the Channel by boat, branding them 'illegal', but there are currently no so-called legal routes open to them.

The UK closed its doors to refugees at the beginning of the Coronavirus pandemic and has announced further increases in financial support for the security efforts of the French Government – the work of the CRS. The UK has created a system whereby the only option is to stow away on a lorry or to risk the death-defying journey in a dinghy.

It doesn't have to be like this. Britain could choose to work with France to create safe, comfortable places for asylum seekers to stay, free from violence and senseless evictions. If we don't want people to be smuggled into the country, the Government could provide legal, legitimate ways for people to seek asylum. A basic initial assessment, on the French side of the Channel, could identify those with genuine asylum cases, destroying the opportunity for illegal trafficking in one fell swoop. But the UK Government shows no appetite to resolve these issues.

Just a few months ago, the CRS corralled a group of asylum seekers before loading them onto buses, with only the clothes that they happened to be wearing at the time. The buses headed south, into the night. The asylum seekers had no idea where they were going. These people had fled some of the most dangerous places in the world, often former British colonies, with the intention of making it to the UK. Disoriented and scared, they were bused all the way through France, to the Pyrenees, and dumped on the border with Spain. Some of them realised what was happening and, on a couple of buses, pretended to fight among themselves, causing the bus to pull over and giving them a chance to escape. One of the volunteer leaders at Care4Calais received a call telling him of their plight. He spent the rest of the night driving around a cold and wet Normandy trying to find small groups of escaped asylum seekers to bring them to some kind of safety. When they got back to their tents, there was nothing there. The CRS had taken everything.

These people are treated like human cattle. In fact, if cattle were treated in this manner, there would probably be uproar – on both sides of the Channel.

The Rise and Rise of the Big Tech Empire

Matthew Gwyther

30 DECEMBER 2020

2020 was a great year for the American Big Tech empire. COVID-19 meant it consolidated its position across its dominions worldwide: digital thrives when we are unable to leave our homes and have to socially distance when we do. It takes over from the face-to-face.

Amazon, Apple, Google/Alphabet and Facebook had an extraordinary third quarter, with $38 billion in profits on nearly $240 billion in revenue. Amazon's profits are up 200% on the previous year. Google's grew by 60% and Facebook's by 30%. Even Microsoft made $14 billion in profit during the same period as its cloud computing business has boomed.

So what's been bad for restaurants, theatres, cinemas, airlines, higher education and countless other industries has been good for the world's biggest tech companies. And there is plenty left to conquer and power to consolidate. For we are now subjects of the American Big Tech empire.

Technology today is no longer a sector. It has gone way beyond the traditional distinctions of software and hardware and become an omnipresent layer; a foundation that impacts on all other sectors – ranging from media to agriculture and food, transport to financial services.

Data is the new oil and powerful, data-driven Big Tech companies increasingly challenge the positions of governments, exercising undemocratic power and remaining reluctant to cough up anything much in the way of tax to exchequers.

The author Franklin Foer has argued that Big Tech is different from the sort of imperial monopolies run by robber baron oil tycoons and bankers in the previous two centuries. 'More than any previous coterie of corporations, the tech monopolies aspire to mould humanity into their desired image of it,' he observes. 'They believe that they have the opportunity to complete the long merger between man and machine – to redirect the trajectory of human evolution.'

This is a task of imperial hubris and has a lot in common with the vision of the Romans, who were convinced of their intellectual, technological, military, cultural and societal superiority. They looked at ancient Brits and believed that they were doing them a favour by taking over. *The Aeneid* spells out this arrogance: 'You, O Roman, govern the nations with your power – remember this! / These will be your arts – to impose the way of peace, to show mercy to the conquered and to subdue the proud.'

Big Tech thinks it has the answer to everything. The woes of modern cities? Google will build a new city from the ground up, as it wanted to in Toronto. The vision was to have a city bristling with technology, from autonomous cars to innovative ways of collecting rubbish, and hundreds of sensors collecting data on air quality and the movements of people. Buildings would be sustainable and built in radical new ways, and cycle lanes would be heated. Citizens would all be living in Google's version of *The Truman Show*.

Meanwhile, Facebook has become a centre point of civil society, as a company with 2.7 billion users that operates in almost every country in the world. It has developed into more than just a place to share photos and plan family events: it is where people read news, arrange protests, engage in debate, play games and listen to music. It is a Forum, Coliseum and Temple of Apollo. We live in its world, according to its algorithm.

Luciano Floridi, professor of philosophy and ethics of information and director of the Digital Ethics Lab at Oxford University, was born in Rome and knows the imperial playbook. He is one of the leading European thinkers weighing up the effects of tech in our lives.

He believes that tech is *sui generis* when it comes to regulation and that Big Tech is taking over 20th-Century sovereign power, but without any true accountability. The counterpart of political accountability – voting in a democracy – is competition in business and that is lacking.

'It's a habitat, an ecosystem, a landscape,' he says. 'You don't lean on tech and the internet the way you do on radio, TV or a newspaper. Mark Zuckerberg wants us to think of him as half newspaper, half telco. No, that's just too convenient. What he provides is a public square and that's a different story. You cannot shout whatever you want in public space. We cannot accept that it's a matter of "online versus offline" harms. That is so 1990s. It's not bullying in the school classroom as opposed to bullying on Facebook. There is no longer any divide.' He even provides an equation to illustrate this: 'Online + Offline = Onlife.'

And when start-ups try to resist by doing something different, Big Tech neutralises any potential threat by buying them out. Since 2005, Alphabet, Apple, Amazon and Facebook have acquired 385 other US companies. Alphabet alone has acquired 185.

But, with the Coronavirus pandemic allowing it to further consolidate its power and leaving these companies with even more influence than before, the advance of Big Tech is finally causing some degree of unease.

Italy's data-protection regulator has launched a formal case against TikTok, alleging that the Chinese-owned video-sharing app violates privacy, especially of children; and this autumn, the US House Judiciary Committee's report into anti-trust was published, concluding: 'Companies that once were scrappy, underdog start-ups that challenged the status quo have become the kinds of monopolies we last saw in the era of oil barons and railroad tycoons.'

Action to hold the seemingly unstoppable new Big Tech empire accountable looks increasingly likely.

Repression and the Empire Men: The Sweet, Just, Boyish Masters

Jake Arnott

1 JANUARY 2021

The 'Empire Man' was the male embodiment of the British Empire. This heroic adventurer was the celebrity of his age, commemorated in countless bronze effigies now the focus of 'culture wars' over our imperial past. The debate rightly concentrates on the actions of these men rather than their character, but an examination of the true nature of this archetype reveals some of the powerful contradictions in the very psyche of imperialism.

An infantile, conflicted figure, particularly in emotional and sexual matters, Empire Man was the child who never grew up.

In 1922, George Santayana offered this tribute to the British Empire: 'Never since the heroic days of Greece has the world had such a sweet, just, boyish master.' Whatever we might think about the accompanying qualities of 'sweet' and 'just', it is 'boyish' that resonates with a disturbing sense of arrested development. Both narcissistic and self-hating, with a terrible fear of the adult, and therefore sexual, self, the archetypal Empire Man conjures a roll-call of supremely repressed and sexually ambiguous individuals. Gordon of Khartoum, Lord Kitchener, Cecil Rhodes, Robert Baden-Powell, Hector MacDonald, T. E. Lawrence – come on, spot the happy heterosexual. It would be foolish to attempt to 'out' any of these men; it is what they didn't do sexually that becomes as significant as what they did, and how this denial was sublimated into great power through a heroic sense of stoicism.

Often this manifested itself as corporeal self-disgust. General Gordon declared that he applied promises to his soul but curses towards his body and admitted that 'I wished I was a eunuch at fourteen'. He had a fondness for street urchins and rough sailor lads, whom he would invite to bathe at his house in Chatham, where he would ritually scrub them clean. He developed a suicidal mania that culminated in his 'martyrdom' at Khartoum, a Freudian death-wish that clearly opposed his sexual or life instinct.

Kitchener barred married men from his officer corps in the

Egyptian army, surrounding himself with a coterie of young subalterns, known as the 'Band of Boys'. There were rumours about his sexuality even in his lifetime. A Reuters correspondent commented that he 'has that other failing acquired by most of the Egyptian officers, a taste for buggery'. He became famous for subjugating both himself and his surroundings, supervising forced labour in the Sudan and a system of concentration camps in South Africa. He cultivated a series of intense male friendships, culminating in his attachment to Captain O. A. FitzGerald, his constant companion until his death in 1916. He remains the consummate authority figure of Empire, an icon on the panoptical recruiting poster: moustachioed, accusative, avuncular (clearly a precursor of George Orwell's Big Brother).

Cecil Rhodes also employed many young unmarried men on his staff. As soon as any of his lads married, he would dismiss them. Even Rhodes' official biographer described a relationship with one of his private secretaries in these terms: 'He liked Johnny to be near him. The two had many little quarrels, on one occasion for a couple of days they hardly exchanged a word. They were not unlike two school boys.' Another of this empire-builder's companionships was observed as 'an absolutely lover-like friendship'. Again, there is no evidence of any consummation of this desire but the rewards for self-denial were very great. Never mind the astonishing wealth he accumulated, Rhodes had two whole countries named after him.

The land grab that he instigated in what is now Zimbabwe still has disastrous implications.

Robert Baden-Powell, founder of the Boy Scouts, displayed a certain candour when he wrote that 'a clean young man in his prime of health is the finest creature God made in the world'. He formed an attachment to a handsome fellow cavalry officer that he referred to as the 'Boy' and had a keen interest in regimental theatricals, his speciality being 'skirt-dancing' (essentially a drag act). But as pedagogue of Empire he passed on the need for repression, warning against 'beastliness' (masturbation). 'The use of your parts is not to play with when you are a boy,' he wrote in a passage meant for *Scouting for Boys* (later excised on the advice of his mother), 'but to enable you to get children when you are grown up and married. But if you misuse them while young you will not be able to use them when you are a man: they will not work then.' Perhaps he grimly foresaw his own difficulties in achieving procreation. After his wedding in 1912, he suffered from agonising headaches that lasted until the birth of his third and last child when, duty having been done, he left the marriage bed for good and slept on a field bunk on the balcony.

T. E. Lawrence was the last and probably best-known Empire Man who used a repressed nature as a weapon of conquest. A modern strategist with the stoicism of a medieval martyr, he encouraged the Arab Revolt against Turkey by finessing guerrilla tactics and insurgency, putting himself in constant discomfort and danger. Again, there is a continuing debate about his sexuality. Adopting local dress and customs, Lawrence transformed himself into the object of his own desire, openly addressing his romantic attachment to the Arab cause in the dedication of his magnum opus *Seven Pillars of Wisdom*: 'I loved you, so I drew these tides of men into my hands / and wrote my will across the sky in stars / to earn you Freedom, the seven-pillared worthy house.' The betrayal of the Arab Revolt remains a central cause to most of the conflicts in the Middle East ever since.

The repressed Empire Man diligently policed his own desires but there was a real danger in being found out. In 1903, Major-General Sir Hector MacDonald loyally blew his brains out in a Paris hotel room after a homosexual scandal in colonial Ceylon. It was his class rather than his sexuality that probably proved his downfall. Having risen through the ranks, he lacked the social contacts or elite circle that might have protected him.

The closet of Empire was a forcing house where sexual repression wasn't just an end in itself but a means to power. The two things that gave the British such potency were the Empire and steam technology. You get power by building up pressure. Just as the steam power that had made industrialis- ation possible depended on this pressure being restrained, so the national male psyche was harshly subjugated so that men of adventure would be propelled into a dangerous world with the fierce energy of sublimated passion. This was the very fuel of expansionism.

And regression was just as important. A wilful immaturity and forced playfulness that allows some strange presumption of innocence about the whole bloody affair, even as we look back on it now. 'We seem, as it were, to have conquered half the world in a fit of absence of mind,' observed essayist John Robert Seeley in 1883, adopting a passive, almost petulant tone still used today by Empire apologists.

The legacy of Empire sees a failure of development, not so much in the colonised but the colonisers. This deliberate emotional retardation in the male continues to haunt the consciousness of the Western imagination. And the public school system that maintained it still persists in churning out politicians who see themselves in the mould of Empire Man. Our imperialist, old Etonian premier Boris Johnson seems able to get away with arcanely racist remarks about 'flag-waving piccaninnies' and 'tribal warriors' with 'watermelon smiles' simply because they are so appallingly regressive and childish. His sister recalls that a four-year-old Johnson declared his ambition in life to be 'world king'. That he has achieved something of this infantile ambition shows that we are still plagued with 'boyish masters'.

6 January 2021

A violent insurrection at the US Capitol Building during the certification of the 2020 presidential vote leaves five people dead and 140 injured.

Trump's Presidency Has Been Defined by Male Supremacist Violence

Sian Norris

8 JANUARY 2021

In the hallway of the US Capitol Building, a bookcase containing writing about women in politics lay smashed up, the books scattered on the floor.

Perhaps the culprit was the man who debates whether women should be allowed to vote or belong in politics. Maybe it was the newly elected member of the House of Representatives who has a restraining order for harassing women during anti-abortion protests. Or it could have been the man who invaded House Speaker Nancy Pelosi's office, sending a message to women politicians that, no matter how powerful you are, a man can take your seat.

While it is categoric that the violence at the US Capitol last month was about race and white supremacy, for the past few years there has been a growing consensus that terrorism is linked to gender-based violence. In case after case, men who commit terrorist acts have been found to have a history of domestic or sexual abuse against women and girls.

From day one, Trump's presidency was linked to male supremacist violence.

There was his own history of misogyny and his support for men accused of gender-based violence. There were the voters he attracted because of his alleged sexual assaults of women. And there was a policy platform that stripped away protections for women victimised by men.

As men with violent views about women stormed the heart of US democracy, once again we saw how misogyny and terrorism are inextricably linked. But how did misogyny play out throughout Trump's administration? And can we draw a line between the legacy of male violence and support for male violence over the past four years, and the domestic terrorism on display in DC?

Let's start with the man himself. Dozens of women have accused Trump of sexually inappropriate behaviour including rape. While Trump denies the allegations, he famously boasted about grabbing women 'by the pussy' in a tape released before the 2016 Presidential Election.

The comment and allegations won Trump support from men in the online male supremacist *Red Pill* forum. This community celebrated his misogyny and, according to compelling analysis of the forum in the run-up to the election, helped to put him in the White House. Male supremacists within the *Red*

Pill saw Trump as essential to winning the 'war on men'. One thread set up to encourage votes for Trump was called '"Sexual Assault" Is Why I'm Endorsing Donald Trump for President of the United States'. One member posted in the thread: 'When somebody accuses a powerful or famous figure like Trump of "sexual assault", I don't look the other way. I don't denounce them or their behaviour. Instead I run towards them, because there is no truer signal which side somebody is on, than when they're given a bogus accusation by the establishment. This is our beacon to find allies in the war.'

Rather than something that would turn voters away, Trump's alleged assaults of women galvanised his supporters within a violent misogynistic subculture to go to the polls. This was exacerbated during the confirmation hearings for Trump's Supreme Court nominee, Brett Kavanaugh, after the judge was accused of historic sexual assault. While Trump was very careful not to say that he disbelieved Christine Blasey Ford, who claimed Kavanaugh attacked her at a party in the 1980s, he mocked her during one of his many rallies. Once again, the signal was sent to his misogynistic base: alleged male violence was acceptable and a route to power. Men on extremist misogynistic 'incel' forums still praise Kavanaugh today because 'he fought the feminists and won'. According to some incels, Kavanaugh is 'the supreme representative' of their community.

Trump's alleged violent acts towards women won him

support in extremist circles. They were a signal to his misogynistic voters that he was 'their man in the White House' and the 'ultimate alpha'. He responded by building a policy platform that appealed to their male supremacist beliefs – developing laws that attacked women's rights and undermined women's safety.

Take, for example, Trump's support for anti-abortion legislation and Supreme Court judges. Banning abortion is a key way of undermining women's safety and leaves them more vulnerable to male violence. In the worldview of Trump's misogynistic supporters, access to safe, legal abortion is responsible for the perceived decline and 'degeneracy' of society that is signified by women's freedoms over their own bodies and access to public space. Banning abortion reasserts male supremacy and male entitlement to women's bodies.

One poster in an online thread on another forum, *Purple Pill*, explained that they wanted to ban abortion because 'I've learned to hate women, feminism and their sexual choices so much'. On an extremist incel thread, another writes: 'I care about abortion [because] women have to suffer.' These supporters also blame abortion for one of the key tenets of white-supremacist conspiracy theory – the 'Great Replacement', which posits that a white majority is being 'replaced' due to low white birth rates and immigration. Trump's attacks on women's rights served both to punish women and fuel racist conspiracy theories of a fascist far-right.

A second piece of legislation that bolstered Trump's misogynistic base was the decision not to re-authorise the Violence Against Women Act. Undoing gender-based violence laws is a key aim of male supremacist movements, which believe that women should be subordinate to men in the home and that men should have sovereignty in the family. Trump's administration also narrowed the definition of sexual harassment in Title IX, the law that protects against sex discrimination at federally funded schools, while expanding the rights of those accused of sexual misconduct. The move was praised by men's rights activists.

It is no surprise that a president accused of violence against women, and whose supporters voted for him because of those accusations, should attempt to dismantle protections for women and girls from male aggression.

While the mobs descending on the Capitol were white nationalists, waving the Confederate flag in the halls of American democracy, it cannot and must not be ignored that the majority of them were men, who stormed the building goaded by a president who had fanned the flames important to them over four years.

Addressing male supremacy – which is inextricably linked to far-right white-supremacist movements – is not an attempt to distract from the violent racism that Trump encouraged. Instead, it is about recognising that Trump's administration was a white, male supremacist presidency that legitimised male violence against women and weakened protections for women while strengthening the rights of male abusers, and was welcomed by violent misogynists.

Gender-based violence and white male supremacy were at the heart of Trumpism – in Trump's personal life, in his supporters and in his policy. At least some of the Trump supporters invading the Capitol shared a misogynistic and male supremacist worldview. When we know that gender-based violence is so often an indicator of terrorism and violent extremism in other spaces, Trump's incitement to violence and the response of his supporters in Washington DC was all part of a sadly predictable pattern.

False Balance is Killing the BBC

Patrick Howse

13 JANUARY 2021

It is hard to overstate the BBC's importance to our culture, politics and society.

It has helped to cohere British national identity through a

century of turbulence. It is one of the largest and most trusted news-gathering organisations in the world and has enabled the UK to punch above its political and cultural weight for decades.

To the ire of its right-wing detractors, the broadcaster is still politically and culturally influential. But there are malevolent forces raging against it.

Too often in recent years the BBC has been hamstrung by fear and doubt. This began with the departure of Director-General Greg Dyke after the row with Tony Blair's Government about the Iraq War, but it has continued and grown apace as critics have gained volume and confidence.

Instead of fighting back, however, the BBC's response has been one of appeasement. It lost the ability or the inclination to hold lying politicians and commentators to account. Rather, it gave equal air time to experts – people who base their views on evidence and logic – and those who were deliberately trying to stoke fear through misinformation.

When it is faced with a major political moment, which focuses attention on the coverage of the broadcaster, the BBC retreats to this false position of 'balance'. But the truth is not the midpoint between a fact and a lie.

There are some encouraging signs that the BBC has started to realise this. Last month, for example, BBC Reality Check scrutinised the claim by Health and Social Care Secretary Matt

Hancock that Brexit allowed the UK to approve a COVID-19 vaccine more quickly than EU nations. Hancock's comments were followed by a flurry of supportive tweets by the usual line-up of Brexiter Conservatives, including Jacob Rees-Mogg, Nadine Dorries and Michael Fabricant. However, as Reality Check pointed out, the claim was false. 'The idea that Brexit enabled the UK to press ahead and authorise [the vaccine] is not right,' Reality Check's Chris Morris wrote. 'It was actually permitted under EU law, a point made by the head of the UK's medicines regulator.'

Reality Check has been a beacon of honest, rigorous journalism at the BBC for some time. Yet the problem with the BBC's coverage has often been that blasts of reality are tucked away in dark recesses of the *BBC News* website, rather than being used to challenge lies in real time, when millions of people are watching.

Ultimately, in order to survive the 'culture war', the BBC is going to have to rediscover its principles and its courage – prioritising the truth above all else.

Talking to former colleagues within the BBC, I believe that there is a determination to get this right. However, whether it can do that with a new chairman – who is likely to be conservative and might even be someone who has been openly hostile to the broadcaster in the past – is certainly open to doubt.

From Wellness to Alt-Right Conspiracy: The Strange Marriage of New Age and Far-Right

Sian Norris

18 JANUARY 2021

There is a sickness at the heart of the wellness community, whereby a movement of people who often share very real and understandable concerns are merging with a far-right conspiracist culture that is harming health and democracy.

'The anti-vaxx movement was one of the main bridges between the "woo-sphere" and the far-right movement,' explains Katya Weiss-Andersson, a holistic wellness practitioner whose podcast, *Kumbaya Confessional*, explores the overlaps between what she calls the 'woo-sphere' and issues around white supremacy, capitalism, homophobia and anti-Semitism.

'In the woo-sphere, anti-vaxxer has gathered so much steam that when it was mirrored back in the far-right movement there became more and more crossover between ideologies and practices from one side to the other,' she says. 'Now they have become closer to one big circle than a Venn diagram.'

These ideologies and practices range from a scepticism about Big Government and Big Pharma, to QAnon conspiracies that the Coronavirus vaccine is an attempt at mind control, or that the 'plandemic' is a hoax designed to trigger division.

Krystal Tini merges the common tropes of wellness and New Age rhetoric with conspiracism, commanding her followers to 'live fearlessly' in the face of a mainstream media and politicians who want to 'put fear and anger in your heart'. She claims that the Coronavirus is a 'crime against humanity' and public health measures to protect people are a form of 'mind control' to keep populations in a state of fear and at war with one another. A warped notion of truth is central to her message – she tells her followers to 'never allow someone to take your truth away from you'. Such rhetoric gets to the heart of some of the overlap between wellness and alt-right conspiracy: a belief that there is no empirical truth and one's own intuition is more valid than, say, data, science or medical fact.

'There's this idea in the wellness community that your truth is a valid truth,' says Seyward Darby, writer of *Sisters in Hate,* which looks at women on the far-right. 'On the surface this is not a bad thing. But it gets perverted by people who are trafficking in false equivalences.'

Weiss-Andersson agrees: 'There's a lot of doctrine and ideology in the woo-sphere that intuition is the one and only thing we need to be using in order to determine what's true and in order to make decisions about our lives. Intuition is a very valuable piece of the puzzle. But it can also encompass our own cultural programming. We need to practise discernment and acknowledge when we make decisions about things that maybe it's intuition and maybe it's our own internalised prejudice.'

A faith in one's own truth and intuition links to a wider issue of individualism within the woo-sphere. Such an attitude has definite resonances with the far-right and white supremacists who, as Weiss-Andersson explains, 'foster this value of individualism above all else'. Krystal Tini tells her followers, for example, that 'we need to stand on our own as individuals and not as a society. We were brought here to be different and to think on our own.' Her videos can feel like watching Thatcherism in yoga pants.

This has profound implications for attitudes towards the Coronavirus.

'There's this really big obsession with individual agency,' Darby explains. 'This idea that you can control your own well-being, it's up to you. This turns people away from thinking of themselves as being part of a community or a collective in any meaningful way.'

'They say you can get enough vitamin D and your zinc and your colloidal silver and you'll be fine and if you get COVID you won't get a bad case,' Weiss-Andersson says. 'But if you aren't following health protocols you can still go out and spread deadly cases to anyone you encounter. And there's no cognisance of that. There's no realisation that it's not all about me.'

Once this individualistic stance is embedded, it is not a

huge leap to start victim-blaming those who do fall seriously ill from the Coronavirus.

'There's almost a eugenics quality coded into it,' Darby says. 'Because the second obsession here is one of purity. This idea that you can cleanse yourself from negative influences. When you are immersed in these communities you start to see these influences everywhere. That can spiral into thinking about conspiracies and thinking there are forces behind these toxic influences you can't see.'

Here is where we see another overlap with the far-right, where the idea of not being polluted by those deemed 'other' is a hugely important concept.

'It's not so many mental leaps of thinking "I don't want these toxic influences in my life",' Darby explains, 'to "what are the other ways I am being polluted by people who aren't like me?"'

Both Darby and Weiss-Andersson share a frustration that the conspiracist end of the wellness community is undermining concern with very real issues that require our attention – including healthcare provision, government corruption and food production.

'I'm all for midwifery, doulas, eating organic and supporting small farmers,' Darby says. 'What becomes problematic is when people can't differentiate between what is progressive and what is retrograde.'

She also believes that there is much overlap between the

'notion of the divine feminine and the idealisation of mothers by the far-right'.

'If you believe your ultimate power is rooted in your femininity, it's only a few steps to join a group that literally says you are the key to the future, you can have the babies and raise the children, your maternal feminine energy is important to the future of the white race,' Darby adds.

Weiss-Andersson is hopeful that things could shift back to a healthier, more inclusive and collective woo-sphere – not least because discussions about these darker aspects are now taking place. 'I am so happy that more people are having these conversations,' she says. 'I think from there we need to be able to engage with nuance and complexity.'

How the Murderous Past of Armenian Genocide Flourishes Today in Denial

Peter Oborne

3 FEBRUARY 2021

The day after the Azerbaijan war ended last November, I paid my respects at the genocide memorial on the Tsitsernakaberd hill high above the Armenian capital of Yerevan.

The spot commemorates the deaths of more than a million Armenians at the hands of Turkey during the death throes of the Ottoman Empire at the start of the 20th Century. Historians estimate that half of the population of Armenia died in camps, in systematic massacres and forced deportation.

This was all documented at the time. The United States did not join the First World War until 1917, so its diplomats were free to send details back to Washington during the height of the killing, as did missionaries and reporters. But barely thirty countries have recognised that the Armenian Genocide took place, Britain and the United States not among them. Nor the nearby states of Saudi Arabia, Iran or Israel. Like many neighbouring powers, they appear to feel they can't upset the Turks, who refuse to accept the truth.

It is understandable perhaps, but unforgivable – the way that genocide denial is sanctioned. By refusing to acknowledge the past, we make it more likely it will repeat itself. It is no coincidence that Armenians are once more threatened with genocide.

Though ignored by foreign correspondents who covered the recent war, hate speech was an obtrusive feature of the conflict. Local social media was rampant with favourable references to the massacres of Armenians. Here is one example from a recently published report by Armenia's Human Rights Ombudsman: 'Your mom, sister, daughter and wife on their knees. In 1915 we didn't f**k you good enough you should get more.' Another: 'It is necessary to kill both the mother and the child of an Armenian.' Of course, in times of war, hate speech on social media is perhaps not so surprising. There are cases of Armenians using similar language, though as far as I can tell on nowhere near the same scale. But what is shocking about Azerbaijan is the way in which hate speech is not only sanctioned by the authorities, but how it starts at the top.

Azerbaijan's President Ilham Aliyev explained the situation long before the war: 'Armenia as a country is of no value.' In his victory speech, Aliyev – who denies the Genocide – labelled Armenians 'savages'.

The media manager of the Azerbaijani premiership football club Qarabağ posted this: 'We must kill Armenians. No matter whether a woman, a child, an old man. We must kill everyone we can and whoever happens. We should not feel sorry; we should not feel pity. If we do not kill [them], our children will be killed.' While UEFA has banned the offender for life, and the post has been deleted, this sentiment is common and well documented.

Matters are not much better in Turkey itself, which supported Azerbaijan during the war and where hatred of Armenians is endemic.

'I don't dare to turn on the television at home – but the hate speech is out there and the portrayal of Armenians as an enemy disturbs me extremely,' Silva Ozyerli, an Armenian living in Istanbul, told Agence France-Presse during the conflict.

The Turkish Hrant Dink Foundation showed that Armenians were the most targeted group in hate speech in Turkish media in 2019 – much of it related to the Genocide. Hrant Dink is named after the celebrated and astonishingly brave Turkish-Armenian campaigner who was assassinated in 2007. Photographs later emerged of the assassin flanked by smiling Turkish police and gendarmerie, posing with the killer side by side in front of the Turkish flag.

Turkey's President Recep Tayyip Erdoğan uses dismissive and derogatory language about Armenians, including the toxic phrase 'leftovers of the sword'. As the Armenian Member of the Turkish Parliament Garo Paylan noted: '"Leftover of the sword" was invented to refer to orphans like my grandmother who survived the Armenian Genocide. Every time we hear that phrase, it makes our wounds bleed.'

To put it another way: the murderous past is still alive – and flourishing.

Take Ramil Safarov, an officer of the Azerbaijani Army, who was convicted in 2004 of murdering Armenian Army Lieutenant Gurgen Margaryan. Safarov, then twenty-six years old, broke into Margaryan's dormitory room at night and attacked him with an axe while he was asleep, almost hacking his head from his body with sixteen blows. He admitted to the murder, with his defence claiming that Margaryan had insulted his country's flag – a claim which was repeated widely in the Azerbaijani media despite the court uncovering no evidence for it. He said that he was sorry that he had not had the opportunity to kill any Armenians earlier. Eight years later – shortly after a visit by Hungarian Prime Minister Viktor Orbán to Baku – Safarov was extradited to Azerbaijan, where President Aliyev pardoned him, promoted him to the rank of major, gave him eight years of back-pay and a new apartment. The famous Azerbaijani singer and former parliamentarian Zeynab Khanlarova said, 'Safarov is not just a hero of Azerbaijan, he is an international hero! A monument should be set up to him. Not every man could do this. There are two heroes – Mr Ilham Aliyev and Ramil Safarov. I would have done exactly as Ramil did. He did the right thing to take the life of an Armenian.'

The term 'genocide' was coined by Raphael Lemkin in 1944 just as Hitler's Holocaust was getting into full swing. The concept described how extreme nationalism directed against racial or religious minorities could lead to their attempted annihilation and was enshrined in the Genocide Convention of 1948.

Lemkin, who was Jewish, developed his ideas of genocide with the Armenian case in mind. So, too, did Hitler. In August 1939, speaking at his villa in Obersalzburg of his plans to massacre the Poles, Hitler remarked: 'Who, after all, speaks today of the annihilation of the Armenians?' A good question.

At the end of the Second World War, Turkey immediately became a core ally of the West and part of the NATO alliance. It threatens to deny its airbases to countries which use the 'G word'. Well-funded scholars have denied it ever happened and have blamed it on the Armenians themselves. (US President Joe Biden has promised to recognise the Genocide. Other presidents have done the same, but been dissuaded once in office.)

According to the celebrated QC Geoffrey Robertson, who has written a forensic study of the Armenian tragedy, this denialism (with which Britain and the United States collaborate) 'amounts morally to the last act of the 1915 Genocide'. According to Genocide Watch: 'The Azerbaijani Government promotes hate speech and officially honours violence against Armenians.'

Without an acknowledgement that the Armenian Genocide took place, there is always the fear it could happen again. And that is why the genocidal language and hatred inside Azerbaijan, and indeed in Turkey, is so horrifying. It is time the world acknowledged the truth of what Turkey inflicted on Armenia a century ago.

Additional research by Martha Harrison

From Folklore to Wokelore: How Myths of Britishness are Turning Totalitarian

Peter Jukes and Hardeep Matharu

18 FEBRUARY 2021

Humans are narrative-hungry animals and though, to survive, we need an acute appreciation of reality (when to sow crops, where to create a shelter, what predators and parasites to watch out for), we also need overarching stories to give us purpose and meaning. In a time of crisis or alarm, when our purposes and place in the world are unsettled or obscure, these narratives can turn into consoling fantasies that cannot compensate for reality.

That's where Britain finds itself as the Government's 'War on Woke' is launched.

With a hard Brexit combined with a deadly pandemic, Britain is seen by many, especially overseas, as suffering a convulsion of grandiosity and insecurity – a delayed reaction to our post-war identity crisis. Having lost our imperial role seventy-five years ago, the UK has spent most of the last half-century trying to put ourselves at the heart of Europe – only to suddenly and resentfully wrench ourselves away. Added to that strategic break is Britain's poor handling of the Coronavirus, which adds recession and lockdown to dislocation.

In normal times, this combination would be deadly for a government. But these are not normal times. Since the ruling political party cannot win on its record or its promises for the future, it is resigned to campaigning over the past and misrepresenting reality. If you can't fight on truth, you have to fight on myth.

Rather than facing up to reality, the British Government and most of its institutions have gone through a looking-glass world in which 'fair is foul and foul is fair'.

Though Britain has suffered one of the highest per capita Coronavirus death rates in the world and one of the biggest economic recessions, we are told – and seem to believe – that this was under the aegis of a government which 'truly' did everything it could.

Though the UK, in search of some kind of indissoluble sovereignty, has actually created a border within itself in the Irish Sea and seen business after business bear the impact of a hard Brexit as a result of which exports to our main market in Europe have shrunk by 60%, this has been done to 'take back control' – in the same way a man controls the gun which shoots him in the foot.

Meanwhile, as Britain's idea of the past is dominated by a generation only old enough to remember Airfix models, *Eagle* comics and the mythologisation of the Second World War, we elevate the heroism of a 100-year-old soldier who walked laps of his garden to raise money for the National Health Service (in one of the richest countries in the world), forgetting his comrades who voted in the Labour Government of 1945 to create a health service that didn't rely on charity.

We will likely not reach the sunlit uplands of a post-Brexit Global Britain. We cannot recreate the conditions for a British Empire 2.0. So what do we do?

Our collective story is in crisis. But, just at the moment that history is needed more than ever, the study of it is under question, with the Government insisting that it should shape and control what historians write about our national past, and the creation of a freedom-of-speech tsar patrolling our re-examination of ourselves.

British history was always prone to legends and fairy tales. But what is new is the state sanctioning of confabulation; of an army of think-tank commissars and commissioning editors ready to enforce it. From the 'take-it-or-leave-it' fairy tales and legends of our past, we are moving into the area of religion and myth – an absolutist version of a collective narrative that requires unconditional assent.

From King Alfred's defence of Britain against the Danes, to the defeat of the Spanish Armada, and a quarter of the world ruled over by the Empire, the legendary status of our collective past has always shaped the way Britain sees itself.

The Brexit years, in particular, have seen a revival of the exceptionalism at the heart of Britain's colonial exploits and war-time successes. That we stood alone – a plucky, great nation which saved Europe from fascism – and have always punched above our weight, need nothing or no one apart from our own superior abilities, drove the Vote Leave campaign's 'take back control' mantra.

Forgotten in this love-in with our past are inconvenient truths – that Churchill effectively sacrificed a subjugated Empire in order to defeat Hitler's quest for his own, for instance, or that Britain relied on thousands of soldiers from its colonies in Asia and Africa to win both wars.

Alongside these historic legends, Britain has long been trapped in a fairy-tale image of itself – one beloved by Americans who lap up the quaintness of *Downton Abbey* and *The Crown*, Kate and Wills, and the 'People's Princess' – Tony Blair's populist embellishment of the late Diana.

This image of Britain that fascinates the US is the stuff of make-believe, and therefore can be opted out of. Tea at Buckingham Palace, audiences with Etonian prime ministers and state carriage rides are magical because they are unreal. President Joe Biden hinted at this very thing after the storming of the US Capitol in January when he said 'we're a government of laws ... they are the guard-rails of our democracy, and that's why there is no president that is a king, no congress which is a house of lords'.

The emotionally triggered vitriol directed at Meghan Markle, wife of Prince Harry, by large sections of Britain's right-wing media is sadly predictable because Meghan is the Woke Princess who held up a mirror to British society. While the marriage of the Duke and Duchess of Sussex was at first lauded for its fairy-tale credentials – a mixed-race American divorcee and actress marrying into British royalty was seen as a modernising masterstroke for The Firm – things quickly turned sour when Meghan was perceived as not toeing the line of keeping her mouth shut, staying humble and unambitious. She didn't know her place. Even now, as she sits in a mansion in California with Prince Harry, having fled royal duty, the British right-wing press still can't let it lie. Meghan ruined our fairy tale.

While these stories have loomed large in British consciousness, we have been able to buy into them or not. Our belief in these narratives has not been a condition of loyalty to or acceptance by the British state. At the same time as the Queen celebrated her Silver Jubilee in 1977 the Sex Pistols song 'God Save the Queen', with its memorable lyrics about the 'fascist regime', was top of the *NME* charts and number two on the BBC Top 40 singles chart. Britain was famed for this kind of pluralism: a contradictory collage of punk and royalty, heritage and modernity. And, with a choice of fairy tales and legends on offer, none required more than conditional assent.

Myths, on the other hand, are more monolithic. They tend to demand absolute assent.

The difference between a plural set of national fictions or legends and monolithic-absolutist national myth were seen most clearly in the *Kulturkampf* – the culture wars – of early 20th-Century Germany. What began as a search for a collective set of heroes and symbols soon became a campaign against 'cultural Bolshevism' – which has an unsettling echo of the current campaigns against 'cultural Marxism'.

An ominous example of the transformation of voluntary fiction into compulsory myth is the story of Richard Wagner and the Bayreuth Festival. Wagner, himself a vitriolic anti-Semite, tried to create a distinctly Germanic pantheon of heroes and mythic narratives for the new unified nation. But he hired a rabbi's son, Hermann Levi, to conduct the premiere of *Parsifal*, who remained principal conductor of the festival for two decades after the composer died. By the 1920s, Adolf Hitler was a regular attendee and formed a close friendship and alliance with the composer's daughter-in-law, Winifred Wagner. She was a key figure in the *Kampfbund für deutsche Kultur*, a well-funded movement which successfully extirpated modernist music and works by 'degenerate' artists in Germany.

People still debate the legacy of Wagner and his role in the rise of the Nazis. But it is perfectly possible to sit in a theatre (for hours), listen to his shimmering harmonies, suspend your disbelief about his long-suffering heroes, and then completely abandon the mumbo jumbo and psychological baggage as soon as the curtain falls. But, in the 1940s, when the Bayreuth Festival was turned over to the Nazi party and soldiers returning from the Eastern Front were forced to sit through Wagner lectures, no such choice existed. The conditional fiction had become an unconditional myth.

Walter Benjamin – the Jewish historian and cultural critic who committed suicide when encircled by the Nazis – believed this myth-making to be a defining trait of 20th-Century fascism. The Nazis, he said, had succeeded in 'aestheticising politics'.

By turning politics into a culture war, a mix of irrationality, identity and emotion, the normal means of conflict resolution in civil society – the rule of law, open debate, the ballot box – were replaced by titanic misty figures clashing in the skies. And those myths led to war and genocide.

The War on Woke is a kind of 21st-Century form of the *Kulturkampf* and, as such, cannot be dismissed as a mere distraction to avoid the more pressing issues of a hard Brexit and a brutal pandemic.

Many dismiss the notion that some kind of campaign to fight back is worthwhile or even preferable as this detracts from the evidence of failure and fights the opposition on their ground. Ultimately, for all the outrage and comment they cause, it is argued that culture wars don't profoundly affect the real business of politics; they are the gladiatorial element of the 'bread and circuses' used to entertain the restive citizens of ancient Rome: a distraction from the real struggles in the Forum and Senate.

But culture wars do matter when it comes to mass psychology and the ethos and temperature of a nation. The divisions stoked along identity lines through the Brexit project are testament to this, with the same imperial tactic of 'divide and rule' now being carried forward in the Vote Leave Government's War on Woke.

Donald Trump's former campaign manager Steve Bannon – one of the leading figures in the 'alt-right' populism of the past decade, who advised Boris Johnson as he planned to take over the Conservative Party – understood this well. 'Culture is upstream of politics' and, as Bannon proved, his 'weapons' would lead to a hyper-nationalist, nativist uprising inside the heart of American democracy itself.

Though Trump has left the White House, the War on Woke is a British variant of the kind of conspiratorial thinking that led to the insurrection of 6 January in Washington DC and the raid on the Capitol.

Yale Professor Jason Stanley, author of *How Fascism Works: The Politics of Us and Them*, has lamented that Trumpocracy seems alive and well in the UK, if waning in the US, and noted that the suggested appointment of a state-backed 'free speech champion' to patrol campuses fulfils authoritarian preconditions.

The first problem is that this doesn't solve anything. Combating 'cultural Marxism' or patrolling free speech is just a shadow play, which will do nothing to tackle material issues. As discontent deepens, so too can the appeal of fake palliatives and even more dramatic shadow plays. The reactive cycles of disillusion and delusion can end up in a reactionary national psychosis.

The second problem is that the mood that powers all of this is paranoia and vindictiveness. The dynamics of this kind of mythic thinking, Stanley points out, rely almost entirely on an 'us and them' narrative of existential threat: native people being invaded by foreign hordes, noble rebels fighting 'deep states' and dominant empires. The words 'anti-woke crusade' evoke this kind of apocalyptic divide into the sheep and goats of the final battle.

A paranoid style has tainted Britain's cultural landscape throughout the five years of the Brexit debate, which at first created the 'enemy without' – the EU Commission, immigrants and Turkish accession – as the main focus. But, there was always the suggestion that the enemy without was aided by an 'enemy within'. This was tragically proven during the 2016 EU Referendum campaign itself by the assassination of the British Labour MP Jo Cox by a man shouting 'Britain First'.

This intemperate evocation of betrayal, and a demonisation

of opposition, didn't stop in 2016. The polarised, binary battle between 'Brexiteers' and 'Remoaners' continued, while judges were denounced as 'enemies of the people'. Since riding into power 'to get Brexit done' at the end of 2019, Boris Johnson and his Vote Leave Government seem unable to buck the divisive rhetoric. Instead, it's amped up. These attitudes have been internalised by Conservative MPs and their communications teams, as they block their constituents on social media, attack 'activist lawyers' and condemn historians merely doing their jobs for 'rewriting history'. Given the Government's majority in Parliament, the Uncivil War first unleashed by Vote Leave now has all of the apparatus of the state behind it.

And this is why Johnson's *Kulturkampf* cannot be ignored.

The War on Woke won't improve Britain's pandemic response or ameliorate its recession, heal its social divisions or growing poverty, nor solve its rupture from its major trading partners in Europe. It will just make things worse. But, as the delusions of exceptionalism fail (which they are bound to, because they are delusions), the explanation of betrayal, the 'stab in the back' and the foreign enemy, mounts.

The escalating narrative can only resolve itself in a final, apocalyptic battle – not a conflict between two opposing forces, but between reality and myth.

As Walter Benjamin suggested, the only solution to Boris Johnson's attempt to turn politics into mythology is to expose the politics of his myths.

Who the Hell are the Disabled?

Penny Pepper
26 FEBRUARY 2021

In the early days, I watched every Government Coronavirus announcement and realised there were new labels placed upon me and millions of others. The sick, the elderly, the disabled . . . the vulnerable. What an interminable hollow mantra of pseudo-caring.

So, I'm more vulnerable – and disabled people feature too high in the COVID-19 death tally. Why? Answers may lie outside the obvious mainstream thinking.

The first question is: who the hell are the disabled?

There's a likelihood of every human being experiencing impairment and perhaps disability in their lifetime (yes, they are different states), but you wouldn't know it from our presence in mainstream life.

Official Government figures stated in 2014 that there are more than 11 million people who fall within their definitions, which includes those with mental health issues, diabetes and invisible impairments. We are the largest minority group in the UK, if not the world. But oh, the disabled are tragic. Or sporty brave. Or embarrassing. They're ungrateful. They're a burden. More recent history condemned us as scroungers. How we reclaim our place within the human family – explicitly and fully included – underpins much of my work.

Many of us have fought to move the oppression of these markers we never chose, including the new, smothering Coronavirus blanket of the extra vulnerable. We start with the realisation that impairment comes easily with the intricacy of our complex human biology – the human animal breaks easy. But, we who live with disability know it is the confrontation with the imposed barriers and breakdown of societal organisation that makes us disabled.

This is the 'social model' of disability. It has been around for more than forty years and continues to liberate the minds of disabled people. It underpins our civil rights movement. Developed in the 1970s by disabled anti-apartheid refugee Vic Finkelstein, this led to the formation of the Union of the Physically Impaired Against Segregation and the intellectual foundation of the social model in the 'Fundamental Principles of Disability', the manifesto for any self-respecting disabled activist to this day. It defined us as oppressed. Now we knew – not what's wrong *with* us, what's wrong *for* us.

The simplest way to demonstrate the social model is to use me as an example. I became a wheelchair user at fourteen after childhood illness. I didn't have the language of the social model, but I was soaked in rebellion even as a baby writer, able to see that endless tweaking of me medically would never make a difference to whether I could get on a bus. I saw the barriers and instinctively knew they should be removed.

By the time I went through punk and found my tribe, I was fortunate to live through the emergence of the social model, particularly in disability culture. Vic Finkelstein took an early role in the London Disability Arts Forum, where later I served on the editorial committee and received early writing commissions.

I understood, at last, that it was not my fault I couldn't get that job in an office up four flights of stairs or use the tube to get there. The fault was caused – disability was caused – by society's failure to competently and comprehensively ensure our equality and inclusion. Not only in how the environment is arranged but in attitudes that continue to marginalise by the lack of access which can be defined loosely into three key areas.

Firstly, the environment – perhaps the most obvious in explaining the social model. An example is the requirement that buildings are not reliant only on stairs.

Secondly, information – a barrier is printed material in inaccessible formats. While technology should have made these barriers easier to remove, in some cases it has multiplied them. But this isn't merely about printed or online material. Access is created through audio as well as print. British Sign Language as well as verbal language.

Thirdly, negative attitudes – from which all the other barriers manifest and magnify, which are the toughest to dismantle. A rallying cry, 'Nothing About Us Without Us', reflects our frustration at what is imposed and, while our activism grows, we remain marginalised in the big Out There.

Sometimes, just sometimes, I wake up and I am not disabled in my fully accessible, barrier-free home, with a personal assistant employed to the choice and control concept developed by disabled people. When I leave home, the first barrier – a lack of dropped kerbs – reminds me quickly I am disabled again.

The sombre truth is that the social model highlights how the failure of governments to fully respond within this framework brings us firmly to the current Coronavirus impact – that the unnecessary barriers still experienced cause such an excessive number of disabled people to be affected, beyond any existing comorbidities. My own experience with the virus highlights this. Me, the gobby old punk, entirely charming but scathing in the face of injustice and barriers.

I've needed two tests over the past year and the first saw me set off with my PA to the testing centre, where I was assured – on the phone – of access and parking. When we arrived, I was confronted with a flight of steps and nowhere to get out of my car (environmental barrier), and no signage as to where I could actually get in (information barrier). Negative attitudes opposed me at the No Entry gate when I was blanked by security staff and let through only after my PA was lectured – the old 'does she take sugar?' trope. The second was a home test. I couldn't open the packet or read it as the font was too small. Fortunately, my PA removed those barriers and, when it came to my vaccine, ironically, there was not a single barrier. But I am an old rebel. I know how to fight.

I've screamed at my TV hearing the reports about the disproportionate death toll of the Coronavirus among people with learning difficulties and within the disabled population as a whole. The statistics are grim, showing up to 60% of Coronavirus deaths are within our community.

If accessible information is not available, if there are barriers to care or transport, then these are the horrific obstacles – removable obstacles – to access a vaccine. It sounds basic and it is obvious, but little action is being taken. We don't need yet more enforced circumstances that create a specific vulnerability arising from our social exclusion.

If I don't scream, I weep. Yet, along with other activists, I've learned how to fight through my words and have a responsibility for those disempowered to speak, who have faith that I raise their concerns and share their stories. The social model, if put into full practice, would not only liberate disabled people from oppression (including those yet to come), it would transform outmoded concepts of the human condition.

Progress is evident but equality remains elusive – as the Coronavirus horror shows. I fight on, the social model my eternal touchstone from those that went before me.

From 9/11 to Insurrection: How Trump Went to War with His Country and America United to Fight Back

Anthony Barnett

26 MARCH 2021

It is fitting that two events watched live around the world have bookended the final two decades of the era when market values dominated American politics: the first was the levelling of the Twin Towers; the second was the storming and occupation of the US Capitol.

Both were forms of 'propaganda of the deed', initiated by cunning, fascistic narcissists – Osama bin Laden and Donald Trump – each of whom apparently spent hours watching TV. Both were taboo-busting shocks played out on US landmarks; one destroyed, the other desecrated.

Threads of violence and frustration link 9/11 to 6 January 2021.

The connections are symbolised by thirty-five-year-old Ashli Babbitt, a veteran of fourteen years' service in the US Air Force, who did tours of duty in Afghanistan and Iraq. During that time, she earned twelve medals and ribbons, including the Global War on Terrorism Service Medal, the Iraq Campaign

Medal, the Air Force Expeditionary Service Ribbon with gold border, and the Global War on Terrorism Expeditionary Medal.

Babbitt, a former Barack Obama supporter, switched her support to Trump in 2016. 'I think Obama did great things,' she tweeted three years ago. 'I voted for him!..and I voted for trump. I could not vote for Hillary.' By 2020, she was branding her tweets with slogans from the baseless conspiracy theory QAnon, which posits that Donald Trump was sent to save the world from Satan-worshipping cannibals – including high-profile members of the 'liberal elite'.

In January, she flew from her home in San Diego, California, to Washington DC. 'Nothing will stop us,' she tweeted. 'The storm is here and it is descending upon DC in less than 24 hours.' She joined the 'Stop the Steal' rally outside the White House, watched President Trump speak, then marched on the US Capitol with her fellow believers. As she tried to scramble over a makeshift barricade that blocked the glass doors to the Speaker's Lobby entrance of the House of Representatives, a lieutenant in the Capitol police shot her dead.

In effect, Babbitt recycled Bin Laden. Like him, she was trained by the US, served in Afghanistan, turned against American power, declared that a storm would fall upon it – and was killed.

The assault on Capitol Hill unleashed a double earthquake that will transform politics around the world.

The first quake is on the right. When Donald Trump won the presidency in 2016, the desire of the traditional power structures was that he would be tamed by office. But he refused to bed down and continuously fired staff who crossed him, was blatantly corrupt, abandoned any pretence of support for human rights, recklessly trashed the principles of environmental safeguards, and prepared to turn the US into a fortress of authoritarianism directed by his family.

For four years, the political establishment – for want of a better term – hoped it would not get any worse. When he lost the 2020 Presidential Election in November, they were relieved: surely he and his supporters would now play by the rules. Instead, Trump escalated. He repudiated the legitimacy of the process and told his supporters to 'fight like hell' and 'take back our country' in a process that culminated in the Capitol insurrection.

It was bad enough that Trump was personally willing to use force to retain the presidency. The bigger shock was that a majority of the Republican Party, its legislators and activists, supported him and still do. The threat of Trumpism is embedded and cannot merely be defeated by traditional election manoeuvres.

The second earthquake is on the left. For decades, the same political establishment marginalised egalitarian, democratic opposition to its policies and privileges, along with calls for climate action. The nature of its rule was to support finance and corporate capital, ameliorate the inequities and pollution where it felt it could – but always from above, to ensure its continued capacity to manipulate opinion and control outcomes.

Confronted by the audacity of Trump's far-right presidency, it crumbled. None of its usual mechanisms of control were able to contain him and his followers now that social media meant he could cultivate, organise and inflame opinion in the wide-open frontiers of cyberspace, while Rupert Murdoch provided a bully pulpit on *Fox News*. Only a popular mobilisation on the left, unwilling to demonstrate allegiance to the core power structures and determined to connect issues of the environment, race, gender, human rights and economic fairness, provided the necessary countervailing effort to frustrate Trumpism – for the moment.

Joe Biden said that he began to consider his run for the presidency in August 2017, when white-power fascists buoyed by Trump's success held a torchlight rally in Charlottesville, Virginia. At the time, he denounced the racists and emphatically excoriated President Trump for lending them his endorsement. In the week following Charlottesville, the far-right organised a 'free speech' rally in Boston. Tens of thousands of protestors, activists, feminists and anti-racists marched to oppose it. 'In Boston,' Biden wrote, 'we saw the truth of America: those with the courage to oppose hate far outnumber those who promote it.' For the first time in living memory, a successful presidential bid started out with a thank you to the progressive left.

It would not be the first time that such a campaign borrowed left-wing energy, only to abandon it outside the portico of the White House. Had Trump proved to be just a maverick who eventually embraced business as usual, then Biden too would probably have followed the usual course. But now everyone can see that any return to elite 'business as usual' opens the door for Trumpism to bounce back in. Without a popular counter-force, the far-right will have its way.

To succeed, the Biden administration needs to work with the progressive left – and, more importantly, it is aware of this fact. 'Progressives,' Biden's chief of staff recently acknowledged, are now a 'big part of our party.'

When Biden addressed the nation from the Rose Garden to present his signature $1.9 trillion American Rescue Plan, he acknowledged the progressive contribution of his fellow 2020 Democratic presidential hopeful Bernie Sanders, who in 'stepping up and making the case why this was so transformational made a big difference in how a lot of people voted'. The implications of this will be far-reaching. But, for now, everything depends on developments within the US – and, to understand their significance, we must start with how the Trump presidency came about.

*

The link between 6 January and 9/11 personified by Ashli Babbitt was more than a random echo.

America responded to the levelling of the Twin Towers by occupying Afghanistan and then launching a nationalist war on Iraq to demonstrate that its wounded hegemony was intact. To legitimate the aggression, the US – along with its close ally the UK – proclaimed, falsely, that Iraq had weapons of mass destruction, orchestrating a massive PR campaign to convince the public. Deceit and deception are normal in great power politics, but this was an obliteration of fundamental domestic norms.

It opened up a path that would lead to Trump's mendacity. It lent validity to his assertion that the media disseminated 'fake news' and that the political system was rigged. As he pointed out on the campaign trail in 2016, he was part of it and he knew.

More importantly, however, the rigged system failed. The scale and intensity of support for Trump is rooted in the cumulative frustration of the American middle and lower-middle classes, and their decades-long experience of income paralysis and increasing insecurity, accompanied by military stalemate.

The occupations of Afghanistan and Iraq were unmatched logistic and martial achievements, deploying a colossal use of firepower, that nonetheless turned into drawn-out strategic defeats. In 2008, the combination of dishonesty and failure opened the way for Obama, whose initial opposition to the Iraq invasion gave him the standing to seize the Democratic Party nomination from Hillary Clinton, who had supported it.

As president, Obama decided that his role was not to cut America's losses immediately, but to manage a withdrawal that preserved as much of Washington's international influence as possible. The result was eight years of global mortification and only partial domestic change, despite the symbolic milestone of America electing its first black president.

Obama's re-election in 2012 marked a turning point. Although he beat his Republican challenger Mitt Romney, the Tea Party was on the rise, while the Occupy movement had forced the issue of inequality into public consciousness.

A chilling *New Yorker* account of America's far-right elite by Evan Osnos provides a revealing cameo. A wealthy Republican backer, Lee Hanley, felt that there was a 'deep frustration with the status quo' and commissioned a pollster to investigate further. The results recorded that the 'level of discontent in this country was beyond anything measurable'.

Ashli Babbitt has now become a heroine of this unmeasurable discontent. Reportedly, one-fifth of those arrested for the Capitol Hill insurrection were military veterans of wars that were so misconceived as to be futile. Many more came from police forces around the US and other parts of the security apparatus that identify with the military and share in the frustration.

After her fourteen years of service, Babbitt started a business and went bust, ripped off by a loan company. The *Washington Post* reported that a high proportion of the individuals who took part in the assault have faced financial ruin: nearly 20% of those charged had previously gone bankrupt; a quarter 'had been sued for money'; while one in five had 'faced losing their home at one point'.

The mob that descended on Washington DC was no mobilisation of the poor, and many of them were down-the-line white supremacists. People flew or drove in from across the US, well equipped and clothed for the winter weather. They were drawn from an increasingly insecure middle class, who had seen their businesses go bust and the value of their modest wealth plunge while debts rose and health costs sky-rocketed. And that's before we consider the influence of the ranting, paranoid tentacles of social media that have become their key source of news.

In 2013, according to Osnos, Hanley 'huddled' with far-right ideologue and Trump's former campaign manager Steve Bannon and the billionaire Robert Mercer. They wanted to use the bubbling rage of millions of Babbitts to further increase their own advantage. Perhaps they were far-sighted enough to realise that if it crystallised around a left-wing challenger they might be done for. They agreed that they needed 'a populist challenger who could run as an outsider, exposing corruption and rapacity'. It seems that they thought Trump unsuitable at first, but he came through the Republican primaries in 2016 as the candidate who fitted requirements. This is the reality from which everything else follows.

Trump is not the cause of America's discontent – he became its voice and expression, backed by billionaires who investigated the strength of the discontent and then exploited it.

A crucial moment came in the Republican primaries when Jeb Bush, brother of George W. Bush, was still the favourite. In February 2016, Trump confronted a hostile audience of Bush supporters who booed him continuously. 'Obviously the war in Iraq was a big, fat mistake,' he told them defiantly. 'The war in Iraq, we spent $2 trillion, thousands of lives. We don't even have it. Iran has taken over Iraq with the second largest oil reserves in the world ... We should never have been in Iraq. We have destabilised the Middle East ... I want to tell you, they lied. They said there were weapons of mass destruction. There was none. And they knew there was none.' Trump then stated that the trillions should have been spent on rebuilding America.

Democrats and progressives were wrong to ignore or dismiss the quality of Trump's judgement. Tens of millions of families across America have members who are veterans or police and security officers. They are predominantly Republican. Trump was one of their own and when he spoke like this they lifted their heads, as did Ashli Babbitt. They knew he was right. He would put 'America first'.

Trump's opponents often ask how he 'had so much support among the public' when, with the exception of Murdoch's Fox News, the media and the establishment was so hostile to him. The answer usually turns on the financial crisis. But class issues are mobilised and resolved within national frameworks.

In a terrific, forensic interview by Zack Stanton, the veteran US pollster Stanley Greenberg says that he was impressed at the way Trump brought in 'all kinds of new voters' keen to protect themselves from immigration and diversity that they experienced as threats because the US was 'weak'. Their prime motivation remains to 'save the country'.

Trump had a message that addressed America's national reality and discontent. First and foremost, he spoke to the millions of patriots who, like him, believed in winning. He promised to be a tough, macho leader who would stop the waste, end the defeats, stand up to China economically, and withdraw the US from being a loser in the playground of globalists. Two million people had served, 6,500 had died and 50,000 had been wounded, in fifteen years of victory-less conflict. What pride could the Babbitts and their families and relatives take in the costs and anxieties they had been exposed to?

Trump provided the self-belief they craved and his pledge was the answer they needed. 'Make America Great Again' by ending wars overseen by the bipartisan elite responsible for the 'big, fat mistake'.

Then, of all the people to challenge this call for restitution,

the Democrats chose Hillary Clinton. She was the personifica-
tion of failed intervention, easily portrayed as someone who
acted as if she was entitled to lead, yet could not even show the
door to her lying, cheating husband.

Elected, Donald Trump delivered for his supporters. There
were no new wasteful, endless wars. Taxes for the rich were
cut, jobs boomed. Then the Coronavirus struck.

Despite his grotesque mismanagement, his denials and brag-
gadocio, plus a tanking economy and hundreds of thousands of
deaths, he fought back, campaigning with demonic energy.
Trump increased his overall vote tally in 2020 by a massive 10
million. How could this possibly mean that he had not won?

At the heart of his apparent success was the serpent that
would consume him. In the heady days of the 1960s, amid
opposition to the US intervention in Vietnam, the militant left
had a boastful slogan: 'Bring the War Home!' Ironically, it
describes what Trump did half a century later.

He sucked back into America the violence which had
been sent abroad. Trump did not start new wars overseas,
but he unleashed force against immigrants at home, hardened
the country's borders, pilloried the cultural 'elite' and permitted Russian intervention in domestic politics. He savaged
anyone who crossed him and unleashed militant antagonism
within the US. Ultimately, the President declared war on his
own country.

At a rally in Georgia on 6 December 2020, a month after the election, Trump told his supporters: 'We will not bend, we will not break, we will not yield, we will never give in, we will never give up, we will never back down, we will never, ever surrender.' When I first saw a clip of this speech, I didn't take any special notice as it seemed merely to continue the foul rhetoric he had spewed since he first ran for president. That was a mistake as this was a significant escalation.

Georgia's Republican governor had just overseen certification of the state's presidential election results, which delivered a narrow majority for Joe Biden. The votes had been counted twice. Trump had clearly lost there, as he had nationally, yet he proclaimed a militant defiance of the primary function of America's political system. True to his presidency, he brought the war home. The Babbitts rallied to the call.

But the whole point of elections is that losers concede. During the Second World War, at the height of the British Empire's confrontation with Nazism, William Beveridge – the economist who wrote the report that laid the basis for the UK's welfare state after 1945 – described the 'essence' of democracy as the 'effective means of changing the government without shooting'. It is a striking definition. Beveridge was an upper-class liberal and the democracy that his class developed on both sides of the Atlantic was not about self-determination or giving the majority its say. Its essence was to ensure the peaceful transfer of power, thus preventing dictatorship – an approach that David Runciman has described as 'the minimalist theory of democracy'.

Minimalist it may be, but the non-violent transition from one government to another, despite hard-pressed conflicts of interest, is the core achievement of representative systems. It preserves government from tyranny. Thanks to this, while the US may have been oppressive, imperialist, racist, corrupt and determined by corporate oligarchy, its government has none-theless always changed hands peacefully since the end of the Civil War in 1865.

Until now. When Trump made that declaration in Georgia, his wager was that, by mobilising his supporters, he could intimidate the Vice President, the Supreme Court, Republican politicians and state officials into overturning the 2020 election result. Instead, his wager culminated in the huge crowd of 'patriots', as Trump's daughter Ivanka called them, who came to the White House on 6 January and stormed Congress in his name.

If Donald Trump represented a threatening rupture from the norms of US democracy, it is because he had been met with an equally unprecedented response in the sheer number of voters who mobilised to defy him.

In 2020, he won 74 million votes – nearly 5 million more than any previous presidential candidate. But Biden won 81 mil-lion. When third-party candidates were included, 23 million more votes were cast in the US in 2020 than in 2016 – a stagger-ing increase.

From early on, Trump could see that he was unlikely to win the popular vote, that postal and early voting would favour his opponents – not least as ethnic minority voters felt intimi-dated going to polling stations – and that his re-election depended on the electoral college votes of swing states. The President therefore began a pre-emptive campaign against the legitimacy of the outcome, culminating in his wide-ranging and well-financed effort to declare himself the winner. Why did this fail?

First, the institutions and processes held. Votes were counted and re-counted accurately. Officials, even when they were Republicans, did their job, reported the data and refused to be intimidated. Courts threw out cases that had no merit in law, even when the judges had been appointed by Trump.

Second, influential Republican funders and supporters – not least Rupert Murdoch and his *Wall Street Journal* – whose businesses rely on a framework of law, did not feel threatened by Biden and refused to support illegal breaches of due process.

Third, a 'coalition of activist groups', as the *New York Times* described them, let officials know that they would be held accountable if they caved in to Trump's pressure. These groups avoided provocative celebrations immediately after the election, while also making it clear that the opposition would erupt in protest if the election really was stolen. Activists, according to a report by Molly Ball for *Time* magazine, had also spent more than a year working to strengthen the dilapidated voting systems of the fifty US states.

Finally, there was Joe Biden's stirring (if vacuous) opening proclamation in his inaugural address on 20 January: 'We celebrate the triumph not of a candidate, but of a cause . . . At this hour, my friends, democracy has prevailed.'

The real determining factor behind all four were tens of millions of votes. I'd like to say that it was feminism that defeated Trump, because of how much that would annoy him and his followers. In a way, it was the work of feminism, as Biden's victory was delivered both by a significant proportion of women voters who overall broke 57% for Biden and only 42% for Trump – while in many cases, it was the organising efforts of women, especially black women, who got out the vote. Stacey Abrams, who led the huge effort in Georgia to get citizens registered and to the polls, is the greatest such example.

The exemplary campaign to reverse voter suppression in Georgia proved critical in winning the state for Biden in November and then, even more importantly, in flipping its two Senate seats in January, depriving the Republicans of their majority in the upper chamber. It was part of a far wider and potentially much more important movement.

Molly Ball described how Michael Podhorzer, an advisor to the AFL-CIO trade union federation, began to build a progressive network in 2019. By 2020, according to her article, his weekly Zoom meetings 'became the galactic centre for a constellation of operatives across the left who shared overlapping goals but didn't usually work in concert'. It included 'the labour movement; the institutional left, like Planned Parenthood and Greenpeace; resistance groups like Indivisible and MoveOn; progressive data geeks and strategists, representatives of donors and foundations, state-level grassroots organisers, racial-justice activists and others'.

An observer on some of the calls told me that, while *Time*'s narrative of a central coordinating hub was 'misleading', the people mentioned in the piece, 'alongside thousands more, all played critical roles in defeating America's wannabe dictator'. He was most impressed by 'how bottom-up the whole process was'. In response to the 'flood of dark propaganda from the right wing', progressive US civil society 'developed increasingly effective network organising capabilities'. Groups on the left forged links with Silicon Valley technology experts and concerned businesspeople. By 2020, 'there were thousands of organisations and leaders involved in anti-Trump networks, operating mostly without any coordination with the Biden campaign – and they knew how to play well together'.

Some of these were alliances, such as Protect Democracy and the Voter Participation Center, or the Leadership Conference on Civil and Human Rights. One initiative arranged for 150 organisations to ask every member of Congress to back

$2 billion in election funding (they got $400 million). These networks also raised huge amounts from philanthropic foundations to shore up weak and underfunded state electoral systems.

This is a description of American civil society in action: groups that are notoriously competitive or work in silos collaborated. Trade unions, along with organisations and networks such as Planned Parenthood, Greenpeace and Black Lives Matter, worked together to secure the integrity of the voting system and increase turnout. The scale of cooperation between trade unionists, feminists, environmentalists and anti-racists is a historic breakthrough – one achieved partly through brilliant online campaigning, embodied by younger politicians such as the Democrats' Alexandria Ocasio-Cortez.

In my 2017 book, *The Lure of Greatness: England's Brexit and America's Trump*, I argued that such was the extent of gerrymandering, corporate funding and voter suppression in the US, that the country 'barely qualifies as a democracy'. Millions of people who qualified to vote stayed unregistered and millions more were effectively prevented from casting their ballots. At the low point of 1988, 91.5 million votes were cast in the US Presidential Election, a mere 50.3% of the voting-age population.

By contrast, in 2020 the total votes cast were 159.5 million, 66% of those actually eligible to vote. This is what brought Donald Trump down. Yes, the system withstood his pressures, his backers rejected blatant illegality, civil society made itself effective, and 'democracy' saved the day. But something else changed.

An unprecedented number of voters on both sides, across the country, decided that their vote mattered. If that huge increase in turnout lasts, it will transform the country into a genuine democracy and permanently alter the nature of the world's major power.

A full version of this essay was first published by *openDemocracy*.

'It's Coming from the Top': BBC Insiders' Concerns About Fear of Casting Boris Johnson in a Bad Light

Patrick Howse

31 MARCH 2021

Jennifer Arcuri's new revelations about her four-year affair with Boris Johnson have gone largely unreported by BBC News.

The American businesswoman admits to having an intimate relationship with Johnson while he was Mayor of

London, during which time she received public money from the mayor's office.

The story appears to have everything – sex, betrayal, abuse of power, lies told in high places. It is, however, completely consistent with the corporation's desperation to avoid a fight with the Government, and has roots going back far further. .

Part of the reason for this is that the BBC has always been desperate not to be thought of as prurient. I first came across it when I was working for the *Six O'Clock News* in 1994. Stephen Milligan, a Government minister, was found hanged in his flat. He had apparently strangled himself during an act of auto-erotic asphyxiation, and was wearing suspenders, had a plastic bag over his head and an orange in his mouth at the time of his death. The editorial gymnastics this news provoked in the TV newsroom was a wonder to behold. Could sex be mentioned? What about the suspenders?

This panicky, fearful process involved desperate phone calls between the top editorial figures in Television Centre and BBC Westminster, and culminated with a senior manager sprinting through the newsroom shortly before we went on air shouting 'don't mention the orange!' at the top of his voice. 'The BBC's never really done sex,' one seasoned older colleague told me, shaking his head as contradictory and ludicrous editorial instructions flowed unstoppably.

And so I can see why BBC News might be hesitant to wade through the weeds of the Prime Minister's complicated sex life. But that misses the whole point of the Arcuri story entirely – which is only really tangentially about sex. More important, by far, is what it reveals about the Prime Minister's character and his ability to tell clear and blatant lies and get away with them. It is also about concerns over the misuse of public money and what it tells us about standards in the UK's public life.

I think the BBC's senior managers must know this. So, what is really going on?

Former colleagues have told me that there is a deep-seated reluctance to cover this and other stories that cast Boris Johnson in a bad light, with one saying that such an approach is coming 'from the top'.

Some point the finger at Millbank, the offices of BBC Politics, while others believe that it comes from higher up. Whoever is behind it, it translates into a narrative which starts off with dismissal – 'oh, that's not a story'. It then moves on to 'well, that might be a story, but it's not for us to break it'. And then on to (a few days or weeks later) 'oh, that's an old story – we all know that already'.

I am told that some senior programme editors are extremely frustrated with this approach and have done what they can to challenge and get round it. But the BBC's big political hitters haven't wanted to touch this and other stories with a bargepole – presumably being too busy retweeting what Downing Street tells them about how marvellous everything is.

There are of course some Conservative appointees in the BBC's upper echelons – so it is possible that this is some sort of attempt to suppress anything damaging to the Government, at least to some extent. However, I think it is more likely that this all comes from fear: top BBC managers are absolutely terrified of the Government and are bending over backwards to appease it.

There are BBC journalists all over the world who do amazing and courageous things every day. As I write this, John Sudworth – a very brave and insightful correspondent who has done so much to expose the wrongdoings of the Chinese Government – is having to relocate from Beijing to Taiwan because of pressure put on him by the Chinese authorities. These are the standards for which the BBC is celebrated and admired internationally. But its domestic political coverage is cut from a different cloth – and courage isn't a commodity in huge supply in Millbank. The people who have made it up the career ladder didn't get where they are today by being brave. They got there by going to meetings and doing as they're told. And I'm afraid that has translated into a craven policy of appeasement. Far from feeling that their job is to hold power to account, they see themselves as a mere conduit through which the (Government-driven) political discourse of Britain should flow.

This approach has two main flaws. The first is that the people they are trying to appease will not hate the very idea of the BBC as a public-service broadcaster any less. These people are unappeasable and want the BBC dead. Until it's dead, they want it docile. The second problem is that the BBC is risking a disastrous loss in public trust by covering up for, and boosting, a government which has raised questions around corruption and incompetence unprecedented in modern times.

The BBC may soon find that, when it needs its friends the most, it doesn't have any left.

British History's Brutish Imperialism: Should Museums Hand Back Its Spoils?

John Lubbock

7 APRIL 2021

The publication of Professor Dan Hicks' *The Brutish Museums* on the British imperial looting of Benin City in 1897 has helped to accelerate a debate about the violent histories of the objects displayed in museums. It is also part of a wider reassessment of the role of history in the modern structure of racial discrimination, in which the voices of dispossessed groups need to be amplified.

Hicks' book describes how the expansion of Britain's milita-
rist colonialism in West Africa used the cover of humanitarian
intervention to overthrow local rulers such as the Oba of Benin,
killing thousands of people and destroying their cultural history.
African rulers were accused of preventing Britain's legitimate
commercial activities, as well as of slave-trading and cannibal-
ism. We now see these justifications for the crude excuses they
always were, perhaps prompted by more recent experience of
Western 'humanitarian intervention' in the Middle East.

The debate about cultural restitution of stolen items has
often centred on institutions such as the British Museum, even
though – as Hicks points out – it 'holds less than 10% of what
was taken in 1897' and, in his view, needs to be 'de-centred in
these conversations'.

But with the University of Aberdeen recently announcing
that it will return the Benin Bronze in its collection, and Germany's Foreign Minister continuing talks with Nigeria on the
full return of its looted Benin Bronzes, the spotlight is inevitably being thrown on the world-famous establishment to do
the same.

While the British Museum's website states that it has
around 900 objects from the historic Kingdom of Benin in its
collection, it also makes clear that 'His Royal Majesty Oba
Ewuare II repeated his request for Benin collections to be
returned . . . [but] no formal written request has been received
for the return of the Museum's Benin collections in their

entirety'. For Hicks, '"we haven't received a formal claim" is no longer an ethically acceptable reply'.

The Royal Collection at Windsor lists a Benin Bronze head on its catalogue website, with recent reports claiming that the police have been barred from searching the Queen's private estates for 'stolen or looted artefacts' and a spokesperson for the Queen dismissing 'any suggestion that stolen or looted artefacts were being held on the monarch's private estates'. Surely the monarch herself cannot be guilty of being in receipt of stolen goods? A Royal Collection Trust spokesperson told me that 'questions concerning the restitution of items from the Royal Collection are matters for discussion by the Trustees of The Royal Collection Trust . . . We have nothing further to add at present.'

The BBC meanwhile recently published an article about private collectors who continue to profit from the sale of Benin Bronzes. One said, 'Part of me will always feel guilty for not giving it to the Nigerians . . . It's a murky past, tied up with colonialism and exploitation. But that's in the past.' Another collector said that 'one bumbles along for 77 years and suddenly this has become a sensitive subject. It never was before.' The article states that one Benin Bronze was sold in 2016 for £10 million.

The Legacy Restitution Trust (LRT) is helping to create a new museum in Benin City to facilitate the return of stolen objects. Enotie Ogbebor, an artist and LRT board member, told me that the Government in Edo State created the independent trust to raise the funds and manage the museum so that it is protected from the whims of domestic politics and funding. The board of the LRT has a representative from the Royal Palace of Benin; the National Commission for Museums and Monuments; and the Edo State Government. It has commissioned Sir David Adjaye to design the museum, has acquired land near the palace and is collaborating with international partners to conduct archaeological activities. It is also constructing a pavilion, akin to a vault, which will be finished next year, where restituted items will be stored and kept until the museum is complete.

'Discussions are proceeding but it is clear to us also that, in the case of the British Museum, only an Act of Parliament will result in the restitution of objects in their possession,' Ogbebor said. 'Because, through an Act of Parliament, they have been prevented from giving out cultural artefacts from institutions. We try to be realistic here; the onus is on the British Government to do the right thing.'

Ogbebor also posed a question to the British people: 'Imagine if we had come into the museums in the UK 124 years ago and removed all the artefacts; removed all the works of Shakespeare, Mozart, Beethoven, Whistler, Homer, everybody; and locked it away for the past 124 years, and the British people had no access to any of these. Do you think Britain would be where it is today in terms of development?'

I contacted thirty-one of the institutions listed in Hicks'

book as holding at least one Benin Bronze, asking them about the status of any discussions they were having about the cultural restitution of looted objects. Eighteen replied.

Among the most forthcoming responses were from Washington DC's Smithsonian. Christine Kreamer, the Smithsonian's National Museum of African Art's deputy director, said that 'this issue of repatriation and return should be couched in a much broader conversation about restitution, which should address longstanding issues of equity, access, inclusion, diversity in museum practice, the ways collections are accessed, ownership'.

'These are issues that are fundamentally connected to ethical and moral concerns that we all should have as global citizens, to make a space for those who have been denied a place at the table,' she added. 'There's no reason to delay. Each institution will have its own processes which will include lawyers getting involved ... but there should be no impediment to going forward with a process of restitution that includes repatriation and being open to requests for return no matter where they might come from. The Smithsonian is aware of that moral imperative.'

The UK feels as if it is stuck in a rut. As Enotie Ogbebor pointed out, the National Heritage Act (1980) is an obstacle to returning the national heritage of cultures that Britain looted. But Ogbebor also said that private collectors have already come forward to discuss repatriation 'quietly and privately'.

'They want to do it anonymously and without fanfare,' he told me. 'This is what informed the addition of a pavilion before the museum is built, so that we do not have to wait for the museum to be built. The request for anonymity is not from our side. When someone requests anonymity, we have to respect that. A lot of people inherited these heirlooms without knowing the provenance, the stories leading to it. Now that information is out there exposing the fact that the invasion was premeditated for economic reasons, the moral burden that goes with the fact that you are in possession of a looted artefact, that your relative took part in an act that is considered despicable, some people might not want the publicity that goes with it.'

As for the museums that are keen to show that they understand their ethical imperatives in response to the violent histories of their collections, the test will be whether their new rhetoric leads to action or not.

The Government's Race Commission Couldn't Find Something It Wasn't Looking For

Jonathan Portes

9 APRIL 2021

The politicisation of research relating to racism in the UK – and attempts to distort or minimise it – is nothing new.

A lot of ink has been spilled over the Commission on Race and Ethnic Disparities report, in particular its supposed conclusion that the UK is not institutionally racist. In fact, not only did the report itself not say that, it is not even clear what such a claim would even mean: a country is not an institution.

The major problems with the report relate to its argument on the crucial issue it was set up to address: what causes 'racial disparities' – or differences in outcomes – in terms of health, education, employment and more between people of different ethnicities?

The Commission's approach in dealing with this was profoundly flawed, conceptually and methodologically, because it divided observed disparities into two categories: 'explained' and 'unexplained'. So disparities are either explained by factors other than racism – or there is no evidence so they are unexplained. Thus, apparently, while racism does exist, there is no way, within the Commission's framework, to demonstrate, through the use of evidence or analysis, that racism or discrimination, indirect or direct, is actually causing the observed disparities in outcomes.

Therefore, it is not that the Commission did not find any evidence that disparities are the result of race or racism – it excluded the possibility *ex ante*. It is hard to find something if it is not being looked for. And it's even harder to do so if a methodology is used which excludes, by definition, even the possibility of finding it.

'The evidence shows that geography, family influence, socio-economic background, culture and religion have more significant impact on life chances than the existence of racism,' the Commission concluded. But this is not scientific and makes a very basic statistical error. The impact of someone's race on their health cannot be dismissed by saying 'well, actually, poverty is the "real" cause', if poverty and race are inextricably linked.

Structural inequality is a complex interplay of causes and outcomes – and one variable can be both at once. The disparities the Commission was trying to 'explain' – education, employment, etc. – are complex and multi-dimensional economic and social outcomes. Of course, they are not directly 'caused' by the colour of someone's skin, but by other, intermediate channels and drivers, themselves mostly social and economic. Showing the influence of those channels is not about explaining away the impact of race, but about explaining how race (and other factors) relate to outcomes. This does not mean that race or racism drives everything – that would be equally reductive. What it does mean is that, if racial (or other) disparities are to be understood, they have to be unpicked and what is driving what needs to be thought about. But 'explaining them away' – and hence giving up on doing any serious or credible analysis – is precisely what the Commission has sought to do.

It is almost impossible to find a topic on which someone with acknowledged expertise has not demolished the report's analysis or complained about the distortion or misrepresentation of their own research, including the globally respected public health expert Sir Michael Marmot. In thirty-five years of both producing and consuming Government reports, I don't think I have ever seen one where the evidence and analysis have been so comprehensively discredited so quickly and completely.

Some people were quick to accuse the Commission of 'policy-based evidence making' (instead of 'evidence-based policy making'). I believe that the report is better viewed as 'rhetoric-based evidence making': the point was not to distort the evidence to provide a basis for specific policies, but to justify the Government's rhetoric. Does this mean that the facts, data and evidence – and their misuse – don't really matter? No, quite the contrary.

By commissioning and endorsing such an egregiously and obviously flawed report, those who would like to take us backwards have overplayed their hand.

The Empty Rhetoric of 'We Did Everything We Could'

Sam Bright

21 APRIL 2021

'The Government said it did everything it could to get the right equipment.' This was the official response to reports that the Prime Minister was lobbied by billionaire Sir James Dyson to give his firm a tax break, so its staff could build ventilators in the UK at the outset of the Coronavirus pandemic.

This mantra – 'we did everything we could' – has been repeated by the Government regularly during the past year. But, on many levels, aside from its general mismanagement of the disease through delayed lockdowns and epidemiologically illiterate relaxations, the Government has failed Britain at a time of desperate need.

Ministers have fallen back on a system of favours and inside deals, in turn clamping down on competition and unleashing rampant cronyism. Given that ministers themselves appear to have been appointed due to their unwavering loyalty to Boris Johnson and Brexit, this 'jobs for the boys' mentality is perhaps unsurprising.

The net effect of lobbying scandals involving former prime

ministers, Johnson's reliance on a few masters of high finance for his political funding, and the Conservative Party's general lack of concern for the sources of its donations has been an unparalleled national calamity – one that has real-life consequences and is far from the Government's assertion that it did everything it could to tackle the Coronavirus crisis.

Last March, officials and ministers still believed that the existing procurement system would be able to cope with surging demand for personal protective equipment (PPE). They were quickly proven wrong. And so began the scramble to purchase masks, gowns and visors from private-sector firms in a bidding war with countries across Europe and Asia.

The Government vastly overpaid for the equipment, according to the National Audit Office (NAO) – the independent spending watchdog. In normal times, the PPE procured by the Government before November would have cost £2.5 billion. In the chaos of 2020, it cost £15 billion.

Despite this outpouring of public money, the goods did not arrive in time for many frontline health workers. Thousands of NHS and social-care staff contracted the Coronavirus during this period and hundreds died. While NHS trusts received 80% of their estimated PPE need from the Government, social-care providers were supplied with only 10%.

Shirking established suppliers, the Government implemented a procurement process that entrusted a number of unusual firms with delivering and shipping PPE. Examples included a hotel carpeting company, a naval design firm, a Florida fashion designer, a four-month-old DNA analysis firm, a one-year-old 'micro' firm, a small 'luxury packaging' company, a one-month-old firm owned by offshore finance specialists, a dormant firm, a company owned by an individual listed in the Panama Papers, a fast-fashion supplier, and a lifestyle company with no employees or trading history.

This process also featured a high-priority 'VIP' lane that benefited firms with links to ministers, officials and MPs, which were ten times more likely to win a contract than their competitors, according to the NAO. It said that there was 'a lack of documentation recording the process for choosing the supplier, the justification for using emergency procurement, or any considerations around potential conflicts of interest'.

Yet, by November, the majority of the 32 billion items of PPE procured by the Government still hadn't arrived. Even when they did, the Government often didn't have anywhere to store them – leaving the PPE in storage containers at ports, with eye-watering daily costs attached. With PPE scattered across the country, the NAO's auditor general Gareth Davies has said that the Government does not know where all of the equipment is stored and has drafted in consultants to find it. 'It certainly isn't all sitting neatly in an NHS store somewhere,' he told a parliamentary committee.

*

Meanwhile, the 'Test and Trace' system has often been elevated to a heroic status which, in reality, is mythic.

Baroness Dido Harding was appointed to run the programme at the outset of the pandemic, doing so on a voluntary basis. She was ennobled by David Cameron in 2014 and her husband, John Penrose, is a Conservative MP. He also works as the Government's 'anti-corruption champion'.

The system immediately ran into problems.

While testing and contact-tracing was being used to suppress the Coronavirus in Asia and parts of Europe, the UK's scheme lagged far behind. This was the case throughout the first wave, ultimately forcing Health and Social Care Secretary Matt Hancock to pledge that, by the end of May 2020, the UK would be conducting 100,000 tests a day. This figure was only met after his department changed the way in which tests were recorded.

The system has also been repeatedly overwhelmed by high case rates. Only 41% of people, for example, received their test results within twenty-four hours between the end of last May and early November – despite Boris Johnson's pledge in June that all Coronavirus test results would be turned around in twenty-four hours by the end of that month. While the system's performance did improve in June, the proportion of tests turned around in twenty-four hours deteriorated to a low of 14% in mid-October, before rising to 38% in early November.

Mounting pressure on the system during the second wave also stalled the efforts of contact-tracers. By last October, the proportion of contacts – people who had been in close proximity to a positive case of COVID-19 – reached by tracers within forty-eight hours had fallen to 64%.

The Government's scientific advisors have also suggested that less than 20% of people are fully self-isolating when they are asked to. Part of the reason for this, it has been suggested, is a lack of financial support provided to do so – currently a £500 payment.

Epitomising the Government's approach to the pandemic, the Test and Trace system has also relied heavily on the private sector. In December, the NAO noted that the Government spent an initial £720 million on contracts for 18,000 contact-tracing call handlers – awarded to the outsourcing giants Serco and Sitel. However, it reported that, by June, call-handler staff had only been occupied for 1% of their contracted, paid hours. Recent reports have revealed that more than 2,000 private-sector consultants have been employed by the Test and Trace operation, at an average cost of £1,000 a day. Baroness Harding has budgeted for just short of £500 million to be spent on this army of consultants, while the overall budget for Test and Trace has recently soared to £37 billion – more than the GDP of Latvia. The system has only recently handed more responsibility to local, established public health teams.

Billions of pounds have also been spent on rapid, lateral

flow tests – the central element of the Government's 'Moonshot' testing plan, which involves the mass and regular testing of the entire population. However, it has recently been reported that rapid Coronavirus testing may be scaled back in some parts of the country due to concerns that a high proportion of positive results are inaccurate.

The Nightingale hospitals were launched to much fanfare, with the idea that, if hospital wards became overwhelmed with patients, people could be transferred to them for treatment.

In March, however, the Government announced that the Nightingale facilities would be imminently closed. Ultimately, they treated very few patients, despite a combined price tag of £532 million. The £66 million Nightingale facility in Birmingham, for instance, had not admitted a single patient in eight months. This is partly down to the fact that pre-existing hospitals have never become overwhelmed with patients – a fact that should be celebrated. But poor planning from the Government is also a reasonable criticism.

'I am the first lord of the treasury and you can take it that we are backing you to do what you need,' Boris Johnson reassured Sir James Dyson last March, whose firm is headquartered in Singapore.

The irony of the messages is that, just forty-one days after the final exchange between the pair, his firm was removed from the ventilator challenge scheme by the Cabinet Office, with the Government having originally said it intended to order 10,000 machines from it.

The Government made a number of commitments that it hoped would incentivise companies to produce ventilators. This included 'protecting their private-sector partners from financial risk; making early commitments to contracts; paying cash up-front for ventilators before they could be inspected; showing a willingness to accept that prices were higher than the normal market rate', according to the NAO.

As it turned out, the supply of ventilators in the UK far outstripped demand and the Government spent a total of £569 million on machines that have largely been kept in storage. Once again, established companies were shirked in favour of niche innovators.

These four crucial areas of Government policy in response to the Coronavirus pandemic have been marked by inconsistency. There has been a haphazard blend of overcompensation, negligence, overspending, secrecy and cronyism.

The Government's 'we did everything we could' argument seems to be premised on the notion that ministers and officials may have occasionally spent too much, acted too hastily or disregarded competition procedures – but they only did so to protect the nation at a time of crisis. Ultimately, however, the nation – and the 150,000 people who died from the

Coronavirus in the UK – were not protected adequately enough. And, with tens of billions of pounds now saddled on the public purse, neither were our wallets.

Britain's Political Media Corruption: A Coalition of the Guilty

Peter Jukes

26 APRIL 2021

During the recent furore over leaks from Number 10, and the apparent internecine warfare between Boris Johnson and his former senior advisor Dominic Cummings, one piece of information emerged which, if true, does a lot to explain the current febrile state of British politics.

According to *The Sunday Times*, Cummings has feared arrest for the past three years 'since details emerged of irregular spending during the Brexit referendum'. If so, he will not have been alone in this fear of the rule of law and potential criminal consequences. Most of the media establishment around him have feared the same for a decade.

With a prime minister on the ropes and a complicit media not sure if its fate will be bound up with his, these days are like waiting for a storm to break. But break it will. And the cycle of corruption, the mutual blackmail and private co-dependencies, can be broken at a sweep by one man: a former advisor who has gone from 'on the run' to loose cannon.

It is nearly ten years since the phone-hacking scandal around Rupert Murdoch's News International erupted into global consciousness with the revelation that the murdered school-girl Milly Dowler had been one of the thousands of victims of the *News of the World*'s industrial voicemail interception. The then Prime Minister David Cameron's former chief press spokesperson Andy Coulson was arrested. Then his friend and the chief executive of News International Rebekah Brooks.

The ensuing public inquiry, chaired by Lord Justice Brian Leveson, revealed the proximity of Britain's press barons to the political elite, and the unaccountable power that they had exerted on prime ministers – through a combination of cajole-ment and coercion, offers of gainful employment and threats of privacy intrusion.

During that inquiry, two up-and-coming Conservative leaders emerged as mouthpieces for the cartel, which effec-tively ran much of our media: Michael Gove – with his affinity and friendship with Rupert Murdoch; and Boris Johnson (who initially dismissed phone-hacking as 'left-wing codswallop') who was paid handsomely as a columnist for the *Telegraph* by the Barclay brothers, who also owned the *Spectator* magazine, which he used to edit. Flash forward a decade, the media moguls' gambles seem to have paid off and their pals are in power.

The first half of the Leveson Inquiry was always designed to be followed by a second part (investigating the relationship between journalists and the police) once the numerous trials of journalists accused of phone-hacking and bribing public officials were over. Only then could the criminality of the newspapers be investigated without threatening to prejudice the trials. But consistent lobbying and pressure from the mainstream newspapers managed to get the second part of the Leveson Inquiry half-delayed and then eventually cancelled. A second Leveson would have been a bloodbath, with potential criminal sanctions for perjury during a public inquiry. Not only would past criminality have been shown to be much worse than expected, but various senior figures had also made statements that even Lord Leveson himself considered to be lies.

But cancelling Leveson Two was not just a priority because of embarrassment or bad publicity: it was, for many in the media, a get-out-of-jail-free card.

What did Boris Johnson and Michael Gove get out of supporting the cancellation of Leveson Two? In retrospect, it is pretty clear.

David Cameron, though supported by Rebekah Brooks,

was never a favourite of Murdoch's. The fury from other quarters, especially Paul Dacre's *Daily Mail*, at Cameron for allowing the Leveson Inquiry to go ahead in the first place was hectoring and incessant. One of their key ways of punishing the then prime minister was to back the Brexit campaigns during the 2016 EU Referendum, with the official Vote Leave campaign led by Johnson and Gove. The *Sun* actually became a registered campaigner and used the slogan 'BeLeave' as a front-page headline just as a youth offshoot of the Vote Leave campaign, BeLeave, splashed out £625,000 in an overspend which was later found to be unlawful.

Whether this coalition of politicians and Leveson-averse media proprietors actually expected to win the referendum is another matter – but they wanted to draw enough blood to make the positions of Cameron and his Chancellor George Osborne untenable. They did that, and a lot more.

By the time Johnson and Gove eventually joined forces to oust Theresa May in 2019, they both owed (apart from a large slug of their salaries) everything to the newspaper bosses. Their new Government paid off the favours rapidly, promoting friendly journalists to cushy Government sinecures, removing VAT from digital news services, and keeping the newspapers afloat during the Coronavirus crisis with millions of pounds of public subsidies for information campaigns. The fix was in.

None of the journalists and editors who lied to Leveson

would ever face the legal consequences of what they had done, even though civil cases revealing the use of private detectives and various forms of privacy intrusion at the *Sun* and Mirror Group continue in the High Court a decade on.

For most people watching the unfolding drama of the Leveson Inquiry, this was a warning about how powerful forces in the media could use a mixture of bribes and *kompromat* to get their way. But, for others, it was an instruction manual.

At the same time as the phone-hacking trial involving Rebekah Brooks, Andy Coulson and other senior *News of the World* journalists and executives was underway at the Old Bailey in the autumn of 2013, *Breitbart* impresario and far-right ideologue Steve Bannon and hedge-fund billionaire Robert Mercer were setting up Cambridge Analytica, the now-defunct data analytics firm which would hack up to 75 million Facebook users (including their direct messages) to psychometrically profile voters for their digital election campaigns.

Apart from being Donald Trump's election engine, Cambridge Analytica worked directly for Nigel Farage's Leave EU campaign during the 2016 referendum. Cambridge Analytica's offshoot firm, AIQ, was also the main recipient of election spending from the official Vote Leave campaign. When Carole Cadwalladr exposed this in the *Observer* and the *New York Times*, Cambridge Analytica – like the *News of the World* before it – was shut down because of the scandal. Billions were knocked off Facebook's share value; congressional inquiries were called in the US and Canada; and the UK Parliament's Digital Culture, Media and Sport (DCMS) Committee, chaired by Conservative MP Damian Collins, produced one of the most comprehensive reports of its time on election interference through dark money and dirty data. But Dominic Cummings, director of the Vote Leave campaign, refused to attend the DCMS Committee to answer its questions, as part of its inquiry into disinformation and fake news, and was held in contempt of Parliament.

Many in the media dismissed the allegations as 'conspiracist' or minimised the unlawful activities as 'rule-breaking' and, in the past three years, have mounted a concerted push-back to discredit both the Cambridge Analytica and Vote Leave stories. The fact that Cummings has reportedly feared arrest for all of this time not only emphasises how credible Cadwalladr's investigations always were, it also explains the culture of aggression coming from Johnson and his entourage.

These are not normal politicians with just votes or reputations to lose, but public figures fearing fine or imprisonment. Like the newspaper proprietors who feared the consequences of Leveson, they have doubled down and sought to undermine any agency or voice who could expose the original wrongdoing.

Together, the two hacking scandals explain much of the psychological force of the past decade: a politics of prevention, intimidation and cover-up, which – rather than give voice to any clear-cut policy agenda or vision of the future – is neurotically obsessed with silencing the past.

Facts are facts, and though the Metropolitan Police tried to ignore the stash of documents that proved the extent of phone-hacking for five years, the persistence of journalists such as Nick Davies, politicians like Tom Watson, and the slow process of legal civil disclosures eventually caused the then Director of Public Prosecutions Keir Starmer to reopen the criminal investigations which led to the phone-hacking scandal a decade ago.

Also important in this process were whistleblowers who came forward to document what had really happened in the tabloid newsrooms (two of whom now lead *Byline Times*' sister organisation, *Byline Investigates*). I had the honour of getting to know and help the whistleblowers over the Cambridge Analytica and Vote Leave scandals – Chris Wylie and Shahmir Sanni.

But, when it comes to the misfeasance or malfeasance of Johnson's Vote Leave administration, where are the whistleblowers to be found?

I may now shock some by naming the key whistleblower who could unravel all of the corruption and negligence that vitiates us: Dominic Cummings.

Cummings is clearly compromised. But the truth is that

most whistleblowers are compromised and are often able to divulge historic malfeasance only because they have been engaged in it. There is no moral simplicity or sanctimony about informing on your past bad behaviours or those of former colleagues. But it is a social and political necessity and the only way to rescue institutions from continuing corruption.

For all of his many flaws, and no doubt an element of vengeance, I believe that Cummings can be a legitimate whistleblower, especially when he soon attends Parliament to reveal what happened during the disastrously late second Coronavirus lockdown last winter.

I and others have previously said that blame for the original otiose 'herd immunity' approach towards the virus – which the Government and many of its advisors were promoting in the early days of the pandemic – lay at the door of Johnson's former chief advisor. Cummings attended SAGE and COBRA meetings in Johnson's absence last spring, and was reported (though he denies this) to have originally supported the idea of shielding the vulnerable and letting the virus run 'hot'. But the same reports emphasise a 'Damascene conversion' to the need for a rapid lockdown in late March. And he has been pretty consistently fighting the COVID minimisers and denialists ever since.

Cummings is one of the few in Johnson's circle who was scientifically literate enough to see that the original plans for mitigation – letting the virus spread among the young and healthy while protecting the vulnerable – was modelled on the flu virus, and that – once the realities of this novel Coronavirus became clearer – it would have led to a soaring death rate last spring as critical care services were overwhelmed.

Cummings also has a young and vulnerable family and, though his excuses for breaking lockdown by driving around Durham are laughably implausible, the underlying panic is not. More importantly, as all the reports consistently attest, by last autumn Cummings was well aware of the rising levels of Coronavirus infections as schools returned after the holidays, and SAGE, supported by the Labour leadership, was urging a quick 'circuit-breaker'. Johnson's failure to do so, after meeting with Chancellor Rishi Sunak and a group of largely discredited anti-lockdown sceptics, led to a much worse second wave in the UK compared to other European countries. More British citizens died in that second wave than the first. The recently reported comments that the Prime Minister would allegedly let 'bodies pile high in their thousands' before committing to another lockdown came tragically true.

Given the stakes of this decision, the scale of the outcome, and the breach of a government's first duty – to protect the lives of its citizens – I (for one) would rapidly forgive Cummings for his role in Vote Leave or his iconoclastic attitudes towards data, governance and the Civil Service, if he could come clean about this: one of the most deadly and disastrous episodes in modern British history which, through needless incompetence and venality, will have cost more lives than any single event since the last world war.

A Smokescreen for Tragedy: The Human Cost of Populism

Hardeep Matharu

5 MAY 2021

When my mum left India for Britain – homeland for mother-land – in 1975, it was the beginning of a lonely journey.

She was twenty-six, a master's graduate and teacher from a town on the outskirts of Delhi who gave up everything about the life she knew to come to London and marry my father.

Despite making her life 4,000 miles away, as the eldest of four siblings, she was – and still is – considered the wise and respected one by her family in India. As her parents passed, this became more so. Her three brothers, looking to her for counsel, would send air-mail letters, have phone calls and then more recently WhatsApp conversations about developments in their lives.

Her brothers had done exactly what their mother had

wanted for them: to all live together in one house, as one family. When I visited them in 2018, that's just what I found – each brother had a floor in the modest but bustling house for their family. There were now three generations living side by side; all so close that the three brothers were known as everyone's fathers.

Within five days over the past week, my mum found out that two of her brothers are now dead. They went suddenly and their bodies were cremated within hours.

They were victims of what has been called India's 'humanitarian crisis' and 'a crime against humanity'. A crisis which has laid bare, in all its ugly glory, the disregard for human life by nationalist-populist politicians seeking to divide, and the institutional corruption and poverty running through the country on multiple levels.

My uncles' lives were not insignificant. But, to the Government of Narendra Modi, they absolutely were.

As with any aggressive populism, despite its name, it cares nothing for its people. And too many in India are now finding out its cost in the second wave of the Coronavirus devastating the country.

While India has officially recorded more than 20 million cases of COVID-19 and the official death count stands at 226,000 people, many of us hearing the horror stories emerging first-hand from India know that these are gross underestimates. They do not take into account all those dying in their homes, on the streets or awaiting intensive-care treatment.

Despite the claims of senior ministers, hospitals in the capital and elsewhere have made desperate pleas after running out of oxygen. The sons of my uncles spent the last weeks of their fathers' lives rushing around a COVID-engulfed Delhi, queuing for hours for oxygen cylinders. Quackery, corruption and the black market is thriving in this chaos.

Meanwhile, the Hindu nationalist BJP Government of Modi continues its steady march to fascism. A complacency that India would not be hit with a second wave and warnings ignored about the lack of preparedness of the country have ushered in no new lockdown. There continues to be a lack of social distancing or mask-wearing and large public events are continuing to go ahead – including the famous Kumbh Mela on the banks of the river Ganges and elections in West Bengal.

In Varanasi, where Modi is the local MP, a furious restaurant owner told the media that the 'Prime Minister and the Chief Minister have gone into hiding, abandoning Varanasi and its people to their own fate'.

'The local BJP leaders are in hiding too,' he said. 'They have switched off their phones. This is the time people need them to help with a hospital bed or an oxygen cylinder but it's total anarchy here.'

In New Delhi, construction workers are being moved in to start on a new, post-imperial Parliament building in Modi's image. As the Government prepares to erase the remnants of the British Empire, it is already executing the same approach towards minorities, in a bid to recast India's civilisational history as that of an exclusively Hindu nation.

Millions of Muslims have been stripped of their Indian citizenship under draconian new laws and detention camps have been erected in the state of Assam and elsewhere. Ethnically motivated violence, often sanctioned by police, is a regular occurrence. Conspiracies and misinformation around the Coronavirus are also widespread, with Muslims being condemned for being carriers of the disease.

Many concerned about India's precarious state believe that widespread bloodshed and genocide will follow in the years ahead. It seems that the Coronavirus crisis may be harnessed to accelerate this end.

Modi's Government has been keen to emphasise that the public health system – virtually non-existent for decades – has failed the country, rather than its governance and structures.

'Last time, the situation was different,' Modi told the nation as the second wave hit. 'We didn't have health infrastructure for fighting the pandemic. We didn't have test labs, PPE kits, or knowledge about the treatment. But in very little time, we improved ourselves. Doctors have gained expertise and are saving more lives than ever.'

To me, such words have an echo closer to home, voiced by

another shameless populist degrading democracy who has presided over the deaths of 150,000 people in the UK.

Would collective international pressure on Modi help? Perhaps. But is it there?

Until weeks ago, Boris Johnson was getting ready to fly to Delhi for his post-Brexit wooing of his Indian counterpart. Today, the UK Government has announced a new deal with India to fight people-smuggling – part of the Home Secretary's clampdown on immigration. For Priti Patel, Modi is 'our dear friend' – a term of endearment she used after his 2019 election win.

In this age of British authoritarian populism, 'historic ties' mean nothing, exerting no sense of accountability or duty, just shared interests to exploit. Among debates about Empire, railways and Churchill in Britain's confected 'culture war', no one asks why India, a country shaped so significantly by colonial rule, has ended up so corrupt. In the UK, we still feel it taboo to refer to the many investigations currently underway into the Prime Minister's conflicts of interests as corruption. Corruption, outwardly, is not the British way.

Yet, the corrosive effect of corruption can be seen in the human cost of populism. Up close, I have seen its trauma and indignity in the past week.

Nothing has made me wake up more to the dangers of a disillusioned and disengaged democracy propped up by demagogues than the Coronavirus pandemic. In the face of a deadly virus, populists – with their symbols and fake history; hope and false promise; their ignorance and incompetence – inevitably require others to pay the price of their power.

This ultimate cost is always there, waiting to be brought home. It was for me on Sunday when I heard my mum's anguished cries and the shocked, traumatised voices of my cousins down the line from Delhi – boys who stepped up as men to watch their fathers burn.

The next day, I visited the National COVID Memorial Wall, across the river from Parliament, in central London. 150,000 hearts for the 150,000 dead. And there I saw them – no truer words . . .

. . . *my heart is broken.*

Index

Unbound is the world's first crowdfunding publisher, established in 2011.

We believe that wonderful things can happen when you clear a path for people who share a passion. That's why we've built a platform that brings together readers and authors to crowdfund books they believe in – and give fresh ideas that don't fit the traditional mould the chance they deserve.

This book is in your hands because readers made it possible. Everyone who pledged their support is listed below. Join them by visiting unbound.com and supporting a book today.

Stuart Bailey

Elizabeth Bain

Valerie Bainbridge

Colin Baines

Paul Baker

Richard Baker

Robert Baker

Francesca Ball

Jason Ballinger

Emily Bamford

Kenneth Band

Chris Barclay

Jamie Barker-Starr

Damon Barkley

Anthony Barnett

Dee Barnfield

Elizabeth Barrett

Paul Barrett

Gosia Bartram

John Bavington

Gail Beach

David Beckett

Laura Beckingham

Chris Beddoes

Stefan Bednarczyk

Jayne Bellenie

David Benjamin

Julie Benson

Ryan Bestford

Stuart Betts

Nikki Bi

Brad Biglin

Chris Billing

Patrick Binks

Andrew Bishop

Bill Bishop

David Black

Chris Bligh

Arthur Blue

Richard Boardman

Chris Bolt

Becky Bolton

Su Bonfanti

Etienne Paul Botes

Audrey Boucher

David Boughton

James Bourke

Stuart Bowdler

Suzanne Bowen

Emma Bowles

William Boyce

Owen Braithwaite

Mark Braund

Richard W H Bray

William Breaden Madden

Mark Brenchley

Siobhan Brennan

Julian Brewer

Norman Brewerton

Neil Brewitt

Britannia Communication

Brad Brooks

Alison Brown

Julie Brown

Brian Browne

Karen Browne

Jonathan Bruce

Lesley Bruce

Tess Brunskill

Kathryn Buchanan

John Burgess

John Burns

Mike Butcher

Jake Butt

Guy Butterworth

Alan Byron

Colin Campbell

Xander Cansell

Matthew Carpenter

Doug Carr

Philip Carr

Jackie Carroll

Áine Carson

Andrew Carter

Damon Carter

Sean Carter

Jordan Cartmell

Sean Casely

Nigel Cates

Katharine Cawsey

Kara Ceriello

Matt Challinor

Alex Charlton

Hannah Charlton

Anne Cheng

Lucy Childs

Sue Childs

Robert Chilton

Neil Clappison

Ben Clarke

Caroline Clarke

Debbie Cleaveley

Sue Cochrane

Mordechai Cohen

Lou Collins

Melusine Colwell

Iain Common

Karl Connor

Sarah Conyers

Michael Cooper

Russell Cooper

William Cooper

Bernie Corbett

Tina Cordon

Anita Coulson

Lesley Coumans

Ed Coupe

Lesley Coutts

Imogen Cowan

Kim Cowie

Catherine Cox

Rohan Cragg

Mike Craig

SJ Crampton

John Crawford

Carol Croft

Mark Cronfield

Rob Crowley

Elise Cummings

Neil Curr

John Curran

Jethro Curtis

Paul Cutler

Dylan D'Arch

Emma Dally

Samantha Dare

Steve Dargon

Mark Davess

Nigel Davies

Alice Davis

Christopher Davis

Elaine Davis

Martyn Day

Will de Silva

Amy Deas

Justin Deegan

Lauren Denney

Aiden Devine

Sukhpreet Kaur Dhindsa

Bradley Dodd

James Doleman

Martin Domin

Aceedo Domingo

Kevin Donnellon

Jennie Donnelly

Thomas Doran

Hazel Douglas

Janet Dowling

Simon Dowling

Brenda Downes

Paul Dredge

Jessica Duchen

Keith Dudleston

Michael Dunn

Timothy Dunn

Rachael Dunstan

Riccardo Durante

Peter Durbin

Paul Duxbury

Thomas Eagle

Michael Eastwood

Kate Edmonds

Calum Edser

Kathryn Edwards

John Egan

Mark Einon

David Elliott

Grace Elliott

Gill Ellis

James Erskine

Neil Erskine

C.J. Esplin

Chris Essen

David Evans

Dominic Evans

Julie Evans

Simon Evans

David Fairbrother

HJ Fantaskis

Charlotte Farish

Nathan Farquhar

Laine Farrell

Ric Featherstone

Peter Feenan

Tony Fenn

Patric ffrench Devitt

Sally Field

John Firth

Stuart Fisher

Barry Fitzgerald

Mark Flagg

Molly Fletcher

Alison Flood

Matt Fortune

Luke Foster

Andrew Foxcroft

Lena Frain-Atallah

Pauline France

Lyndsey Fraser

Neil Fraser

Roger French

Bridget Frost

James Fulker

Lewis Fuller

Jan Fuscoe

Helen Gale

Jacqui Gale

Mark Gamble

Julia Gammon

Carol Gardiner

Trevor Gardiner

Ed Garland

Peter Gavagan

Amro Gebreel

Kris Gibson

Julie Giles

Jim Gill

GingerCharlie

Salena Godden

Thomas Going

Christopher Gooch

Tim Gopsill

Una Gordon

Brian Gorman

Mark Gradwell

Stephen Grant

Dan Greatorex

Giles Greenway

Keith Gregory

Michael Gregory

James Gregory-Monk

David Grierson

Kay Groom

Carole H

Rudy H

John Habershon

Sue Haddleton

Daniel Hahn

Andy Haigh

Aimée Hall

Mike Hall

Niklas Hall

Patrick Hall

Richard Hall

Angela Hallatt

Evelyn Halliday

Kate Hames

Claire Hanley-Öpik

Judith Hannam

Wendy Hannon

SUPPORTERS

Elizabeth Hanson

Gary Hardwick-Bishop

Andrea Harman

Charles G Harper

Stephen Harris

Lucy Haskell

Barry Hasler

Colin Havard

Patrick Haveron

Jonathan Heawood

Davina Hemmings

Ian Henderson

Jimmy Heritage

Jeremy Hill

Caroline Hilton

Sian Hingston

Marian Hobson

Neil Hoggarth

Jinx-Jae Hood

Ellen Horton

Delphine Houlton

Simon Howard

George Hughes

Richard Hull

Theleedsunitedcollection.
co.uk Hunt

Martin Hunwicks

Lee Hurley

Sumayyah Ibrahim

Jawad Iginla

Michael J Ingham

Michael J Ingham

Emma Innes

Ian Irvine

Johari Ismail

Yvonne Jackson

Brian Jacobs

Nacho Jammers

Rhys Jeffs

Dai Jenkins

Robert Jenkins

David Jennings

Paul Jeorrett

Paul Jepson

Chris Jessenberger

Christopher John

Marjorie Johns

Graeme Johnson

Ian Johnson

Boris Johnson Climate
Criminal

Brian Johnston

Gina Jolliffe

David Jones

Ian Jones

Nicola Jones

Simon Jones

Velvet Jones

Robert Joseph

Jack Joslin

Indra Joyce

Roderick Joyce

Peter Jukes

Samreena Kamran

Kiron Kang

Mo Kanjilal

Helen Karamallakis

Lesley Kazan-Pinfield

Stephen Keeler

Daniel Kelly

Shane Kelly

Jamie Kelsey

Gill Kemp

Anthony Keough

Jacqueline Kerr

Katherine Kerr

Linda Kerr

Chris Keulemans

Sean Keyes

Fozia Khanam

Piya Khanna

Ifat Khawaja

Dan Kieran

Tom Killick

Megan Kimbell

Stephen Kinsella

Mike Kiriakakis

Jackie Kirkham

Victoria Kitchiner

Martin Kitt

Simon Kittle

Alexander Klein

Peter Kolodziej

Jane Lake

Ruth Lamb

Rupert Lang

John Lange

Susan Lansdell

Kevin Lansdown

Justin Lawler

Stephen Laws

David Lawton

Kate Laya

Brian Lee

Stephen Lee

Rik Leedale

Stella Leighton

Russell Lemon

David Leonard

Hsinjui Lin

Michelle Lincoln

Barbara Lindsay

C S Lindsay Smith

Jerry Lindsey

Liz Linell

Mark Linnett

Jonathan Lloyd

Mari Lloyd

Dunc Lockwood

Charlotte Logan

Dan Lougher

Shiela Lumsden

Jose Miguel Vicente Luna

Brian Lunn

Michelle Lyden

Andy Lyons

Alasdair MacArthur

Andy Macdonald

Sarah Macdonald

Janet Mackay

Jen Mackay

Ross Mackenzie

Kevin Mackintosh

Russell Mackintosh

Fiona Macleod

Jim Madden

Yvonne Maddox

Duncan Maguire

Anton Maigre

Katharine Malcolm

Marianne Malonne

Jonathan Marsh

Alex Marshall

Denise Marshall

Angela Marston

Malcolm Martin

Catherine Matthews

Michael Matthews

David Maxwell-Lyte

Neil Maybin

Nicholas McAnulty

David McClelland

Janice McCombie

Paul McCormack

Michael McDowall

Angela McEvoy

Siobhán McGrath

Josephine McGuire

Janet McHugh

Neil Mchugh

Roy Mchugh

Jeff Mcinery

Susan McKendrick

Bob Mclean

Brian Mcleish

Hugo McNestry

David McPhillips

Simon Meacher

John Meacock

Alasdair Melrose

Mark Mendoza

Annalisa Merrilees

Charles Metcalfe

Christopher Michael

Nicole Mickey

Terry Miles

Fiona Millar

Aaron Miller

Ian Millington

Joan Millington

Carole Mills

Andrew Milne

John Mitchinson

David Moat

Jo Molyneux

Frank Monaghan

Simon Moore

Anna Morgan

Jackie Morgan

Cari Morningstar

Pen Morris

Jan Muhammad

Billy Muir

Simon Muller

Judy Munday

Rachel Mundy

Jenny Murley

Colm Murphy

Jane Murphy

Siobhan Murphy

Caroline Mutch

Vikiy Myers

Carlo Navato

David Newbould

Lynne Newman

Penny Newman

Chris Newsom and Jasmine
        Milton

Jack Newton

Isabel Nicholson

Jenny Nicholson

Gary Nicol

Sue Nieland

Ezi Nnochiri

Gillian Noble

Patrick O Donnell

Deaglan O Dubhda

Adrian O'Donoghue

Jenny O'Gorman

Derek O'Hagan

Tim O'Hara

Liam O'Hare

Rose O'Reilly

Maria Oakley

Michael Ohl

Angela Oldershaw

Samantha Oliver

Tomasz Ondrusz

Laura Ovenden

Sharon Owen

David Palmer

Amit Pansuria

Mark Papp

Jim Parker

Philip Parker

Leonard Parkin

Selina Parmar

Andy Parrott

Stephen Parsons

Shockat Patel

Vijay Patel

Audrey Paterson

Lindsey Paton

Helen Pattison

Eifion Paul

Simon Paul

Dave Payne

Lawrence Peachey

John Peake

Melanie Peake

Anita Pearce

John Peek

Mike Pennell

Andrew Perry

Ian Perry

Paul Perryment

Julian Petley

John Petrie

Anthony Phillips

David Phillips

Josephine Phillips

Monica Piccinini

Kenny Pieper

Sean Pillot de Chenecey

Robert Pinchen

Alicia Pivaro

Justin Pollard

Barbara Potter

Graham Potts

John Powell

Ian Power

Matt Power

Dev Prakash

Leon Prescod

Harry Price

Antony Pritchard

Fi Pugh

Jumina Qureshi

Sarrah Qureshi

Owen Ramsay

Edward Randall

Maggie Rawlings

Martin Read

Colette Reap

Recluse52

Addison Redley

Alison Rees

Lisa Reichenbach

Alan Reid

David Reid

James Reid

Christopher Reilly

Daniel Reilly

Marina Remington

Janet Revesz

Marion Reynolds

Scott Reynolds

Amy Richards

Mary Angela Richards

Matthew Richardson

John Ricketts

Mark Ridgway

Liam Riley

Mark Riminton

Susan Rios

Lesley Ritchie

Nick Roberts

Tony Roberts

Martin Robertson

Bob Robinson

Paula Robinson

Sean Robinson

Zach Robinson

John Roden

Alan Rodgers

Roland Rodgers

Matt Rodrigues

Lisa Rogan

Charles Rolfe

Paul Rollason

Andrew Rose

Rosie Ross

Peter Rouch

Carol Rowley

Nicole Rugman

Andrew Russell

Valery Ryan

Andrew S

Saba Salman

Christoph Sander

Shrikant Sawant

Gary Sawyer

Clare Scanlan

Lesley Scarles

Thomas Schiestl

Rosslyn Scott

Paul Seabridge

Matthew Searle

Akhil Sebastian

Rebecca Seibel

Roland Serjeant

Daniel Sewell

David Sharp

Patrick Shaw

Chris Sheehan

Graham Shirling

Adrian Short

Ronnie Sievewright

Anthea Simmons

Alan Sims

Jonathan Sindall

Kieran Singh

Anne Skulicz

Michael Smeeth

Anneliese Smith

Jim Smith

Joshua Smith

Karen Smith

Owen Smith

Vanessa Smith

Victoria Smith

Tina Speed

Anna Spiteri

Wendy Staden

Sue Stainer

Ann Stapleton

Justin Steele

David Stelling

Alastair Stevenson

Norrie Stewart

Rosalind Stewart

Katy Stickland

Andrew Stimpson

Carmen Stone

Ian Stone

Christine Stones

Mark Stott

Evelyn Strasburger

Alexander Stuart

Julie Stuart

Bella Sturt

Geraldine Sutcliffe

Fiona Sutherland

Jimmy Sutherland

Oliver Swingler

David Symes

Diane Tams

Jordan Tandy

David Taylor

Michael Taylor

Mike Taylor

Pam Taylor

Paul Taylor

Dan Tea

Matt Terry

Marcella Thérèse Johnstone
McIlroy

Mike Thirlwell

Lisa Thomas

Gordon Thompson

Tim Thornton

Phil Tidy

Chris Todd

Michael Toes

Malcolm Toms

Andrew Tooke

James Topham

Andrew Towler

Louisa Tratalos

Lucy Traves

Paul Tredwell

Jane Trobridge

Voula Tsoflias

Grant Turner

Jae Turner

Mike Turner

Alice Twaite

Sophia Ufton

Sandra Umney

Clive Upton

Christopher Uren

Phil Vajánszky

Wayne VanDeveer

Mark Vent

Leonor Vital

Wil Voitus van Hamme

Jo W

Chris Wade-Evans

Andrew Walker

Karen Walker

Phil Wall

Amanda Wallace

Andrew Walsh

Carole-Ann Warburton

Mitch Ward

Tom Ware

Erik Warfield

Andrew Waring

Georgina Wathan

Lisa Watt

Richard Watt

Diarmid Weir

L J Wellens

Brian Weller

Gary Weller

Lynn Wells

Steve Westlake

Jane Weston

Cecilia Wheeler

George Whiles

Clare Whistler

Peter White

Rob White

Terry White

Terry White

David Whitehill

Tecwen Whittock

Carol Whitton

Marcus Wilkinson

Chris Williams

Colin Williams

David Williams

Gen Williams

Gwyn Williams

Jen Williams

Lisa Williams

Mike Williams

Shaun Williams